THE SOCIAL
SUPERPOWER

KATHLEEN WYATT

THE SOCIAL SUPERPOWER

THE BIG TRUTH ABOUT LITTLE LIES

Biteback Publishing

First published in Great Britain in 2022 by
Biteback Publishing Ltd, London
Copyright © Kathleen Wyatt 2022

Kathleen Wyatt has asserted her right under the Copyright, Designs and Patents Act 1988
to be identified as the author of this work.

ISBN 978-1-78590-705-0

10 9 8 7 6 5 4 3 2 1

A CIP catalogue record for this book is available from the British Library.

Set in Minion Pro

Printed and bound in Great Britain by
CPI Group (UK) Ltd, Croydon CR0 4YY

MIX
Paper from
responsible sources
FSC
www.fsc.org
FSC® C171272

This book is dedicated to my father, who combined supreme honesty with a supreme talent for imagining and reimagining.
We miss you and love you.

'I can't believe that!' said Alice.

'Can't you?' the Queen said in a pitying tone.
'Try again: draw a long breath, and shut your eyes.'

Alice laughed. 'There's no use trying,' she said:
'one can't believe impossible things.'

'I daresay you haven't had much practice,' said the Queen.
'When I was your age, I always did it for half-an-hour a day.
Why, sometimes I've believed as many as six impossible things
before breakfast.'

LEWIS CARROLL, *THROUGH THE LOOKING-GLASS*

CONTENTS

CHAPTER 1

THE FIRST LIE | *AMNESIA*

I know where it started, this fascination with lies. I know when: 9 January 1995. But if I know those two things, the events themselves are faint.

I was walking to a bus stop. I was well, happy, possibly care-free. Then suddenly, I collapsed.

A few decades later, I can guess at the long seconds, the confusion, the panic.

Why was I on the ground? What was happening? It made no sense.

My scarf. It was my scarf. I thought my scarf was strangling me.

I clutched at it. But the harder I fought, the tighter it got. I could not breathe.

My head, my body, my senses... they were all failing.

Why.

Was.

I...?

There was no...

Air.

The report said I kept fighting. But there was nothing I could do. There had been no warning and now my chest was shutting down.

I was a healthy, fit twenty-year-old. No pre-existing medical condition. No clue. Just sudden and complete failure.

My heart had stopped.

But somehow, they restarted it.

'Off-duty 999 hero saves girl.' It was the front-page headline in the *Cambridge Evening News*. Below, it read: 'An off-duty ambulance-man has been hailed a hero for saving the life of a student who was having a fit at the side of the road.' The collapse happened so quickly that my first reaction was to rip at the tight piece of fabric around my neck. I remember none of this, but my family's recollections and a black-and-white photocopy of the front page stand as a record.

The paramedic, Tony Collings, said: 'I couldn't leave her.' My father was quoted too. 'The debt we owe this man is beyond description.' My father later kept in touch with Tony. I did not. And only now do I understand that I was afraid to see him. What had happened? Why did I collapse? Was it all my fault?

It was the end of the Christmas holidays after my first term at university. I was at my parents' house, studying for exams. I planned to catch the bus into town to return some library books but then, it happened.

We had only recently moved house, from one side of Cambridge to the other. The move put us within five minutes' drive of the largest hospital in the area, Addenbrooke's. Tony was driving home after his shift but made an unplanned detour to pick up a birthday card.

He was pulling into the shops when he saw me. I had collapsed metres from the bus stop. Just round the corner was a doctor's surgery. Nearby, a payphone. As Tony told the newspaper, he realised I was 'in difficulties'. He ran to my aid, got someone to fetch an airway from the surgery and someone else to use the payphone to alert the hospital. Few people had mobiles in those days, and payphones often did not work. This one did. Those casual facts and Tony's quick action saved my life. 'If anyone had luck on her side,' he said, 'she did.' It was not a fit, as the reporter had written: it was a cardiac arrest.

Cambridge Evening News, 11 January 1995
Published with kind permission of Reach plc

The ambulance crew tried twice to restart my heart, but it was not until they tried the more powerful defibrillator in the hospital that it started beating again. Tony's guess was that my heart had stopped for about ten minutes. I was in a coma for thirty-six hours, and when I came to, I had lost my memory.

I responded to my name and recognised friends and family, but if someone had asked me their names or why they were there, I would have been blank. In the subsequent months and without any sense of it, I started learning how to be 'me' again.

The first few weeks were uncertain. My brain had swelled and the specialists were unsure if there would be any long-term effects. The amnesia lingered. Doctors, nurses, loved ones came in and out of the different rooms I was in, but I could make no sense of it. Why was I there?

I stayed in hospital for six weeks until the medical team operated on me and fitted a heart device. It was an implantable cardioverter defibrillator and it would intervene if ever my heart went into another irregular rhythm. The main box with the battery sat just below my left rib cage, its wires passing through my veins and into my heart. It meant I no longer needed constant medical supervision. If my heart stopped again, I would have back-up power. Not long after Valentine's Day, I left hospital with what felt like a new heart.

I have had three other heart devices since, as the technology improved and older models needed replacing. None of them has ever gone off – and I have never since had a problem with my heart. Despite numerous tests over many years, my case remains medically unexplained. In 2010, I had the last defibrillator removed. The surgeries had started to take a greater toll on my health than the benefits I got from this highly sophisticated back-up plan. I had been lucky, lucky beyond belief – but now my body was protesting.

What caused the cardiac arrest? The specialists could never find a clear explanation, but back then, the name they gave it was Sudden Death Syndrome. The adult version of cot death.

I returned to university and slowly resumed my studies – and my life. Five years later, I wrote a piece about it in *The Times*. I had just started at the newspaper, first doing work experience, then on the arts desk, and it was my first lead feature. It was a big moment. But although I told the story as carefully as I could, I left something out. Something significant. Fear lurked behind my tidy, journalistic words.

I lied then, as I had before. Guilt and shame silenced me. Because on New Year's Eve 1994, ten days before my 'sudden death', I had taken class-A drugs at a party. Could that have been the cause? I did not write about it.

When I was rushed to hospital, my friends had a difficult choice to make. Should they tell my horrified parents about the drugs? Would that knowledge give my parents comfort, or hurt them even more? Tests revealed nothing in my blood and the only damage to my heart was likely to have been caused by the collapse. The medical team chalked it up as an unknown.

My friends had summoned their courage and told the doctors about the drugs but decided not to tell my parents. And because I was over eighteen, they could also ask the doctors not to tell them. The lie was brave and kind, and it was decided by a group of friends. When the doctors were asked to keep the truth quiet, it became an institutional lie. A silence that heals. Soon it would become my lie too.

As I woke, and began to recover, parts of my personality seemed to return. But it took time. Those close to me had to put up with the wearing routine of telling me what had happened, seeing some kind of understanding dawn over my face, only for me to then look puzzled and greet them again with unfeigned pleasure.

'How lovely to see you!'

Silence in the room.

'But… why are you here?' And so it went on.

When I finally did stop looping the same goldfish bowl and started to remember, I was horrified to realise that I was the one who had caused them so much pain. It was me they were visiting, me who had sucked up so much of their love and resilience. It was devastating. A simple story, with a beginning, a middle and an end, was starting to make sense to me. But remembering what might have caused it was beyond my reach.

As for lies… they were too complex for me to grasp at that stage – too abstract. I could understand one version of a story only. But lies would come back to me. And it was just a few weeks later that I would feel their poisoned little teeth for the first time.

It was after the operation, when I was still recovering. A doctor came to see my parents and me, to talk us through possible explanations and what it meant for the future. I had a morphine drip, and was in a pleasant haze, loosely following what he was telling them.

What my parents really wanted to know was: what could have caused a cardiac arrest in such a healthy young woman? What was his medical opinion?

'Well,' he said. 'There is, of course, the drugs incident to think about.'

'What incident?' they asked in unison.

The discussion came to a screeching halt. I snapped out of my haze as the horror hit me that the doctor was about to tell them something deeply unpleasant. Something my friends had tried to tell me about for weeks, without it ever sinking in. Something about New Year's Eve.

The gentle tone of the discussion was gone. Everything came into focus. I remembered the party, the recreational drugs, the smiles. My wide-eyed parents took turns looking at the medic, then back at me. The shame was acute. My poor, courageous, exhausted parents. This talented doctor had unwittingly broken the doctor's oath – the promise of confidentiality.

But something else was happening. Something confusing and unsettling. My brain was still healing, but I was having to wrestle with two versions of 'the truth'. In one version, I was responsible for everything that had happened. In another, I was in a mysterious cocoon, the injured party being looked after by others. How could there be two versions? What did it mean? Who was I? Perhaps it was all a mistake?

The lie bit me hard – the memory of drugs I had taken covertly, mischievously, a frivolous choice I had made. Was it my own actions that had unstitched so many things? The lie was a snake, returned to me, but it came from my friends' kind intentions.

The facts are that there were no residual drugs in my system, they could find no link to unexplained substances and I was fit and well for eight days after the party. The alternative facts are that I took something unknown and illegal, and my healthy heart stopped soon afterwards. Those two versions of the truth comfort and torment me still, because there is no way to know.

Later, years later, I asked my mother what she remembered about the moment the doctor said the words 'drugs incident'. How did she feel when he said it?

'I was relieved.' I did not expect such a brief, clear-cut answer. And did she talk about it with my father?

'Of course! We both felt exactly the same way. We thought... at least there is a reason. Now, we know.'

'And... have you ever blamed my friends for hiding the truth?'

'Not at all.' She spoke without hesitation. 'We totally understood that. Your friends were brilliant. They were so supportive. We never, ever thought they should have told us.' She paused. 'It was just so nice to have them around.'

I felt a strange combination of relief and panic mounting as we spoke. It was a tough subject. I braced myself and asked my next question.

'And do you still think that drugs were the reason for my collapse?'

'Now, I don't think so. There were no traces of anything in your body. And we have heard of similar situations with young people. We just think that there was... a coincidence.' Another pause. 'Maybe helped a little bit by the drugs?'

I remember her voice fading off. When was the last time we sat down and talked about any of this? She continued, a little shaken.

'But when I saw you that first day in intensive care, the nurse kept saying: "Our hope is she's healthy." I just could not take it in. She was saying they hoped you would survive.'

I could see that she was imagining herself in that ward again. We quickly changed the subject. I would never learn the true cause of what happened by poking around in painful memories, but over time, I have learnt something astonishing. Grave, life-stopping moments demand lies as much as they do truths. They are when stories meet. And if my friends and the doctors had kept something from my parents, I later found out that my parents had kept something from me.

I knew that they had not told my grandmother about my cardiac arrest. What I did not know was that she had had a heart attack that same month. My father's daughter and mother were in different cardiac wards, in different hospitals, and neither knew about the other. My family kept the doubled pain for themselves.

And it is with all of those lies together that I start this book.

Lies. Why is that word so difficult? Why is it hard to tell my story without remembering them? What is it about mistruths that leave such a stamp on what happens to us and what we do?

Growing up, every source of information told me that lies were bad. I should always, always avoid them. At home, at school, at play. Don't fib. Don't cheat. Don't make things up. But the lies that surrounded my collapse were of a different order altogether. And they were vital to all of us at that time. They were neither harmful nor destructive. They may have come from fear, they may have caused pain, but they were kind, they were careful and they were proof of love.

I wonder now if our lies bound us together in a way that would never have happened if we had just stayed silent. Back then, we needed our lies as much as we needed our truths. Could it be that what we choose to tell each other is what counts? The details of the cardiac arrest are on that black-and-white photocopy, but what lives on is the story we tell.

I am now more than twice the age I would have been, if it were not for Tony Collings. I think differently about a lot of things (like wrinkles and hangovers and pop music). I think differently about my life and how to live it. But now, I realise that I think differently about lies too.

Especially today, with fake news, alternative truths and leaked secrets making constant headlines. We are telling stories about ourselves all the time and we are telling them in so many different ways. From vlogs and blogs to tweets and posts, from photos to gifs and live streams. From instant updates that disappear, to rash words that last for ever and data trails that chart every step we take. Even if I had wanted to, I could not stop thinking about lies, misleading, pretence, fibs and fabulation.

And while all the saner people around me shake their heads and mutter bad things about the new levels of day-to-day deceit, I am busy marvelling at how society manages it. How do we do this extra-ordinary thing – often under the most ordinary of circumstances? How do we convince each other to suspend disbelief? How old are we when we start lying? And why do we do it?

Could it be that lies hold us together as much as they push us apart? Are they vital in a healthy society?

I thought of my own daily, social mini-fibs. The white lies I tell my young nieces about the world they are discovering. Information management at work. Family secrets. The lie I told (or tried to tell) my father about the doctor's assessment of his condition, in a cancer ward, when my father knew it was bad. I was adjusting the truth every day. I still do.

I have told two big lies that have frightened, shamed and changed me. But is it possible that they have been good for me too? One is about the drugs. The other is about identity. And if lies were less tricky, I would also write about that one now, but I am not ready. Not just yet. What on earth makes lies so powerful? I had to find out.

But why would a reader take my word for anything? To see if lies should be celebrated or shut down, I set out to find those who could tell me more. From scientists to investigators, from professors to practitioners, from toddler specialists to a fallen titan of industry.

But to begin to understand lies better, I had to start at the extreme.

I had to find a group of unfindable people. Professional liars. Spies.

CHAPTER 2

SPIES, LIES AND MEN | *FOXTROT*

There were three of them. A shadow triumvirate, all deeply different, all flitting in and out of sight. One I would meet in person, one I would speak to on a bad telephone line and one would ultimately evade me.

I braced myself as I entered the shadows. I knew the lies I had experienced in my life were trifles compared with what I would find in here. But it was no use being safe and warm at home if I really wanted to understand what it takes to live a life of lies.

The spy I met in person took so much finding that the search itself was a lesson in subterfuge. The deeper I went into the shadows, the more I had to promise to keep identities and connections secret and the more I dreaded who or what it was I would eventually track down. And just like the best kept secrets or most effective lies, the meeting, when it did happen, seemed entirely unremarkable from the outside. I remember trying tensely to look relaxed as I approached the agreed rendezvous.

He rises to greet me and smiles disarmingly. He is not what I expected. There is a bustle of people around us. In the rituals of coming and going, arriving and leaving, I sense that no one notices us. It is daytime, in an ordinary place, but we are inside the shadows.

We chat a little. There is a polite preamble while I order the coffee that I will forget to drink. Then, he suddenly blurts something out that proves incredibly alarming.

'I'm a terrible liar!'

In a flash, I forget all the cloaks and all the daggers. Have I been set up with a civil servant? I wonder if our interview is going to work at all. But just as suddenly, his smile disappears, he starts rattling off his stories and I know that I am talking to the right person.

Here is someone who has lived a secret life, in darkness, obscured, but always watching. I'll call him a friend, or F, Foxtrot in the NATO phonetic alphabet. Foxtrot is patient, deeply calm and talks at length about his life of extreme measures.

Foxtrot has worked at the very top of intelligence operations and analysis, both at home and abroad: he is a highly trained agent specialised in fighting terrorism and the narcotics trade, 'containing belligerent activity' and working in post-conflict scenarios. Foxtrot also tells awful fibs in his daily life, likes extreme sports and has been caught in the shower singing Blondie songs loudly – and badly.

If I said he had spent time in America (Virginia) and in Britain (Gloucestershire and London, north and south of the river) it would be true, even if it were not the whole story. Foxtrot has military decorations and decades of experience yet he wears his service lightly. The interviews are conducted in English and I meet him several times face to face. Where, I cannot say. I find answers but not hard facts as I look deep into a life defined by truth and lies.

None of Foxtrot's answers are black and white. About his career, he says: 'My role is to ensure that information is as truthful as it can be.'

He seems candid under the veil of anonymity. Too candid for me to write many of the sensitive details discussed, but he gives enough material for me to describe a twilight world – and one that shows me how much I assume about my own day-to-day interactions. I begin to see that there is a set of tacit rules that mean I expect most people I encounter to be honest most of the time. And it is not just me. Society's default is to assume that someone is who they say they are and this unspoken social contract is what allows a person like Foxtrot to hide in the open. I scribble a quick note in the margin of my pad that this might also be why people get away with telling fibs. We expect truth.

For Foxtrot, though, it is not about being honest; it is about presenting the truth of a situation as events are unfolding. The gist of my discussions with him is the deceits that are justified in the pursuit of this kind of truth.

So how does someone take the first step on a path like his, one that leads deep into obscurity, illusion and danger? He smiles at my question as he thinks back.

'I was very fresh-faced.' He says that it was a few years before he felt ready for his first challenge, which was to be what he calls 'a runner'.

'I'd meet people, pick up things, move things around. All within the community.'

The community being the intelligence community. During that time, he was 'talent-spotted' and given a sleeper role.

'It was great. I was paid to take a year out and have a good time with other young people. "Enjoy yourselves," they said, "but if you hear anything, you know what to do."

Foxtrot says that in that time, his only lie was his name, because everyone had an alias. He was a 'clean skin', he had nothing else to pretend about.

He was partnered with a woman, whose real name he would only find out years later.

'We were like any other young couple – except that we slept with pistols under our pillows.'

As well as a gun each, loaded and ready ('at any one time, one of us was ready in case someone came through the door'), they had a phone hidden in a shoebox under the bed. This was a time when almost no one had a mobile phone. It was so big that it filled the box. Foxtrot is matter-of-fact and brisk when recounting the dangers, almost talking fondly about those old days, recalling visits to 'all the hotspots. The notorious areas. It was all about the flight mechanism. If there was any risk, we knew we had to get out as quickly as possible.'

Were the young operators a couple: two aliases, but one real relationship?

'I've been asked how close we got. We were physically close, but not emotionally. We would go to events as boyfriend and girlfriend, and you know, do what girlfriends and boyfriends did. Did we lie? We behaved as something that we weren't.' Foxtrot is wistful about this. He pauses. 'It was a professional relationship. You only need to know what you need for the job.'

They were told not to put themselves in danger, but otherwise they were free.

'We could go anywhere, mingle with whoever we wanted, but we were looking for people who would tell us what we wanted to know.' They were there for nine months. 'I would say that 98 per cent of the time, nothing happened. But for the 2 per cent, it was high-octane, life-threatening stuff. There were two situations when I thought: "Really lucky to get away with my life on that occasion."'

His amiable cool is unnerving; he could be any other middle-aged man, remembering high jinks on the playing field or in a bar. But he is not. He has steel inside him that shows only because of the little fuss he makes about these incidents.

Needless to say, Foxtrot is not impressed when I use the word 'spy'.

'Please don't call me that.'

I assure him that I will not use that word. I want to kick myself. I have just told an astute and now trusted contact what I am sure is a fib. But in my defence, what else would a member of the public call someone involved in so many covert enterprises?

'People think it's cloak and dagger, James Bond stuff. It's not. You're part of a team, a well-oiled machine, not an individual. It's all about information. Intel is information with value added.'

I promise him not to use the term too liberally.

His work has led to some moments of supreme irony. He smiles as he recalls how many times he has filled out the forms needed to enter America. The I-94W visa form has yes/no tick boxes with references to engaging in 'espionage or sabotage'. The boxes make him pause every time. 'It says something like, "Have you ever participated in subterfuge or the overthrow of a regime?"' He continues, shrugging, 'I always tick "no".'

He says that it was down to accident and luck that he went through the recruiting process to become an officer:

My attitude was: it's just another day. I had no long-term plan to make a career of it. But I do think that people who want to go into this line of work have a certain resilience. It's part of their psyche and their make-up. They have characteristics that are slightly different to other people. Resilience is a key element of what makes us the sort of people we are.

In his next move, he joined a specialist unit tasked with surveillance: 'a variety of tactics and techniques, with a view to being able to interdict if necessary'.

Whenever doubts about what he is telling me cross my mind, Foxtrot's words give me a jolt. 'Interdict' is not a word a civilian would use. The unit's focus was on narcotics, and he worked both domestically and internationally with a variety of teams, focusing on disrupting 'distribution networks, home-grown agricultural developments'. If a target was 'sponsored and surveillance-aware', for instance, his team could be called in to 'outmatch' them.

Foxtrot's next steps took him deeper into surveillance, and away from the 'human interface' at which he had proved a natural. He entered the world of remote sensing, 'air-breathing imagery, multi-spectral radar, thermal imagery', where an opponent can be given away by anything from movement to size, density or heat distribution. It is a world where, for example, a lie about munitions deployed for conflict is exposed by heavy freight moved suddenly, cross-country, by train. Is it steel for construction projects, or could it be new tanks, fresh off the conveyor belt and ready for war? It is intelligence gleaned at speed from elements that do not add up. It is a robust, much magnified version of the sort of lie detection we all use in daily life. Like a fake smile that jars when you see it in action.

Foxtrot did not know it then, but he says he was being 'groomed' for his return to a capital city as a liaison officer.

His next move was into the tinderbox of the Balkans in the bloody period after the break-up of Yugoslavia. He headed up an intelligence unit and was back in the thick of it:

> Once again, I had interface with targets. But this time these guys were open. They thought they were justified in the actions they had taken. They had a rough idea about what my role was but they didn't know who I was passing information onto. I even used my own name. Just my first name, though. I went to have tea at their houses, I talked to these people in their gardens.

Foxtrot even kept a few signed, translated autobiographies by these men, as he grappled to understand them better.

They were 'predominantly Tier 2 military commanders', men who had ordered the execution of families or whole villages, explains Foxtrot, reeling off the numbers of slaughter without pause. Many of the commanders would have been one tier down only from Slobodan Milošević, Ratko Mladić and Radovan Karadžić – the lead figures who were brought before the International Criminal Court in The Hague on charges of genocide, and whose names ring so loudly in the twisted metal of this region's history. How could Foxtrot decipher these men, understand them, thickly camouflaged as they were by the changing events in their native lands?

Foxtrot did use an interpreter, but he says that it was not their words that gave them away. And this is how my first formal lessons in lie detection start, over a coffee with Foxtrot.

'You could tell when someone was not telling the whole truth. Communicating directly was much less important than seeing their body language. How accurate was I in judging that? Well,' he laughs, 'I had a lot of information behind me. They'd break from a pattern of conversation. They'd fidget. It depends on the person. Is there a standard format for spotting a liar? No, there isn't. But the key is that you have to know your target.'

I look up at Foxtrot and wonder briefly if I should trust what he is telling me. I certainly do not 'know my target' but I do know that ever since I entered the shadows, I have been prone to unhelpful bursts of sub-journalistic paranoia.

Foxtrot does not let me record him. Later, when I look back through all my furiously scribbled notes, his words come alive in my mind, his mannerisms, his abrupt changes of subject, his constant flipping between amiable and courteous, hard and formal. It makes me think of the disconnect between the things we choose to show when we communicate and the things we hide.

Unprompted, Foxtrot carries on: 'Does what I do produce the truth?'

Perhaps he is telepathic too? Or perhaps he is simply very well versed in assessing his targets. I wonder who else he has been talking to that day.

'... Does it produce the truth?'

He peppers our discussions with his own questions, seeming to search himself now, as much as he has searched the world in the past. He tells me that I am the first journalist he has spoken to, and perhaps that is because he has come to a point when his own story has begun to matter to him.

'When you're questioning someone...' I sense he is back in the Balkans.

You have to try to be as objective as you can be, you have to remember the three different viewpoints. Remember your perspective, their perspective and the third perspective in the room, the invisible eye. And in my report, post-event, I try to take the view of the third eye.

The more I listen to Foxtrot – and watch him (I am learning) – the more I think about the awkward splits in the tales we tell. Different stories of the same event rarely match. I see it one way, you see it another and most of the time, those gaps do not matter. Up the stakes, however, and that dispassionate third eye is crucial.

Foxtrot says that he learnt a lot about human nature back then, especially when the different intelligence communities were forced to work together in the same conflict.

'I was really thrown into it, and it was the first time I worked with other agencies, from other countries.'

He built good relationships with his counterparts and had a good 'portfolio'. Sometimes he speaks in a remarkably corporate way about the wilderness that is his field of expertise. I ask him carefully about another of the shadow triumvirate, aware that I might compromise two of my spy interviews in one go. Was I being paranoid again?

Foxtrot's extensive CV and his contacts mean that after the terrorist attacks of 11 September 2001, he became part of the international effort to find Osama bin Laden. I ask him if he has ever come across my second spy. I give him two names that, at this point, have been made public.

There is a deathly silence. Have I crossed a line?

'I cannot confirm or deny that. I'm not at liberty to do so.'

I realise I have been holding my breath, waiting for his answer. I look down, hoping my prepared questions will save me. I move on hastily to how the agencies worked alongside each other. His one-word answer is 'cautiously'.

'Back then, I was a liaison officer, a gatekeeper, if you will, with multiple roles to fulfil. Those I worked with never told me anything that they didn't want to tell me. I drip-fed elements of our intelligence, and they drip-fed elements of theirs back to us.'

In his career, he has made some judgements crucial to national security:

If you take a pause, you give the adversary an advantage, you lose the momentum. Think of it like this. In the heat of battle, a commander has this choice: do you follow your moral compass, your instincts, or do you wait and allow activity to happen, then live with the consequences?

No information was ever safely delineated and much has hung on his assessments.

'Far more devastating than dropping a bomb is mishandling information.'

'The pen is mightier than the sword,' he says. Coming from him, the cliché suddenly resonates. The consequences of incorrect information can be profound.

Foxtrot recalls being in a 'very sophisticated playing field' in Africa and the Middle East.

'I became exposed to intelligence departments not being honest with each other. It got to the stage where you needed three independent verifications for a piece of info before it would be accepted. And agencies would present intel as their own.'

It is unnerving to think of the informed disinforming each other with borrowed or 'dubious' information, but it is not surprising when competing interests battle over scraps of truth.

'Why do they do it?' he asks, once again interviewing himself. His answer is: funds ('we're all bidding for money from the same pot'), kudos and power ('precedence in the pecking order'). He had to be more practical than ever and accept that almost all the information would arrive part-lie, part-truth.

I ask him if the ambiguity weighs on him:

I never have twinges of conscience about what I've done, the number of things I've been involved in. But then, when you're involved in what we do, you often reflect on how you've gone about your work. So, do I lie? Have we lied? The best deception is based on truth anyway. Why lie if you don't have to? Instead, you took a different point of view, you omitted relevant information.

And would he say that what he does is 'good'? Perhaps I am trying to reassure myself with this question. In my world, I need clear lines between the goodies and the baddies. Foxtrot talks about one of his most complex missions. As he puts it, the mission was to deconstruct a country.

I try to seem unfazed as I look briefly at my now-cold coffee.

'We were mindful of what might come next. What might fill the vacuum. Did we do a good job? We did the best job at the time with the information we had.'

Foxtrot is detached from the emotional impact of his stories. He looks at me clear-eyed, impassive.

When I ask him if it ever gets personal, he pauses for a long time. I look up and wonder if it is a CCTV camera I see behind him. Is it watching us? I wait for his answer.

'When I ask myself if I have ever gone too far, I weigh my actions and activities against if they had been in 1930s or 1940s Germany. If I had been an officer then, would I have been justified in my activities working for the state?' His stern stare falls on me again.

'I have socially engineered situations, manipulated circumstances, used tactics and schemes.' He has been part of the 'deconstructing and reconstructing' of countries, but, he says, 'my social conscience is based on a belief of what is moral and defensible. I believe in democracy.'

Considering everything he has said so far and the way he has talked about it, it is surprising when he then suddenly illustrates his point by talking about his own fear. However, it is not his own peril that scares him, but the extremes an organisation can go to in order to maintain its grip on information.

'I remember being scared witless in Berlin, when I went to visit

the Stasi Museum, when it hit me that I had worked near an institution that was torturing its own people.'

It seems that for him, fear is when every single alarm in his conscience has been set off – and the former headquarters of the East
German secret police did just that. If the listening devices and chilling techniques of the Stasi are now safely consigned to a museum,
what about the effect of modern technology – the sort that everyone
has at their fingertips?

Today, intel will be reported before I can brief my bosses. Everyone has a mobile phone. It's instant comms and that has changed
things. We have sometimes banned TVs from the analysis centres
because we didn't want to be influenced by what an unverified
third party was reporting. We have to make sure that the analysts
are not tainted. Remove the distractors.

Just think, he says, of how fast social media has reported on the
deaths of prominent international fugitives in the past ten years.
How long it then takes for official confirmation. This puts the average person in a position where if they are in the right place at the
right time, they could affect world events with one tweet.

Foxtrot uses social media, hiding in plain sight, pretending like most
people do on their digital résumés that they are something slightly
different. If the digital world has changed how we see each other, and
even how we watch each other, it has redrawn the rules of intelligence
gathering. Does this mean that intelligence is more vital than ever, or
that it is more prone to failure? I ask him what the future holds.

'It is a question of the fear factor in society. The data is there, it is just a question of retrieving it. Every call and text. But the question is do we have the technology to identify the right question at the right time?'

It seems a daunting challenge and Foxtrot does a good line in devil's advocacy:

What is the purpose of intelligence in a liberal society? Does it protect or incriminate? How many of us can put hands on hearts and say that we don't have a secret that we don't want exposed? The UK, for instance, is the most surveillance-oriented society in the world for its size. If you have your mobile on you, you cannot go potentially five minutes without being found. And if I can find you, I can drop a bomb on you.

This makes me sit up. Now I really grasp the concept of The Fear Factor. I do not like to be reminded that my phone emits something like a silent whistle that brings all nearby bombs calling. But then I am a lily-livered civilian. Foxtrot carries on without pause:

What lengths do you have to go to today to become invisible? It is a balance between incursion of liberty on the one hand and risk on the other. Some people say why worry if you've got nothing to hide? But something innocuous to me isn't to someone else. Just think of the Balkans, where atrocities were committed in part because of the secrets people kept – or tried to – about their religion or ethnicity.

Everything he says has been weighed and measured, and that is what a modern democracy needs from its gatherers and builders of information, its safety engineers: balance. That balance is what can transform big lies into even bigger truths – but who judges that truth and how much it should be shared is another matter.

Foxtrot is pragmatic about following orders. Even when he 'controls activity' and leads an 'influencing' team on the ground, his directions still come from 'strategic thinkers' in his home country.

'We are, for the most part, conservative, non-political and we work for the long-term good of whatever hue or colour rules the country at that time.'

He talks about the role he played bringing about 'attitudinal change' post-conflict, and how both government and public mindsets can change.

'The Taliban were our friends once.' He smiles a little ruefully. 'The state will demonise or elevate particular organisations to suit its own purposes. I have no particular qualms about working for the state. I just hope that the policy-makers have got it right.'

And what about the policy-makers in his personal life? How much do his friends and family know about his career?

'They know what I've been involved with up to a point. That's part and parcel of who I am.'

And what about low-level fibs – does he tell those? His face breaks into an enormous grin that somehow alternates with a grimace. The demeanour that has remained tranquil talking through so many tumultuous events becomes animated the moment we turn to his private world. He is searching himself. He goes back to the first thing he said to me.

'When I heard about your book, my partner said: "But you're such a bad liar!"' He is smiling broadly now:

And the thing is that *I am* very bad at telling fibs. I'm a real risk-taker outside work. I like to push the boundaries. See what I can get away with. But I am a terrible liar! I get caught out every time. If I thought I could get away with something, I would do it.

Is it because he spends so much of his professional life chasing truth?

'Yes.' He pauses, still smiling. 'It's like a friend of mine who runs a big budget but is terrible with his home finances.' He laughs again, but I do wonder how he manages the low-level travails of day-to-day life.

In a strange way, it's a relief to get caught outside of my work. In my professional life, the consequences of getting it wrong are so great and you have to make sure that everything is wholly verified within legal constructs. So it's critically important, and you are not unilateral, you are part of a team. You are not believed until it has been verified.

When he puts it like that, it is easy to see the temptation of being naughty, not thinking about it and breaking those unspoken, ordinary rules.

'Do I lie privately? Everyone does. The question is to what extent.' This from a man who has spent his life measuring truth.

How does he manage the different personas, and make sure that it is not the naughty side of him that suddenly jumps out, while deep in an undercover mission?

I think that personality is like a Venn diagram. Your true personality is in the middle, where each part of you overlaps. In the rest
of it, you adopt and adapt to the environment. The people who
are most successful in life are true to themselves, and they are a
chameleon.

What is arresting about Foxtrot's Venn diagram is how dangerous it
would be if the wrong person could link two of those personas, bring
together the family man on social media and the agent behind so
many manoeuvres. I shudder when I realise just how thin a thread
of 'intel' could change everything. It would take one small piece of
information to see the whole in a vastly different way. Unless, of
course, Foxtrot is lying to me.

I steady myself again and tell him I am surprised he is so phil-
osophical about what he has done in his career. I had expected a
more rigid view on his part, for without that, how does someone
avoid being swallowed by the shadows? In Foxtrot's case, the answer
is to keep checking every step he takes and remembering that third
eye.

Part of the training we receive is about understanding what the
truth is in the information you've handled and the consequences
of mishandling it. When you get to a certain level within the organisation, it becomes a huge part of your thinking.

So, do I lie? I have socially engineered things. The info I provide is declassified and repackaged, but does that distort the
truth? I would suggest not. I am divulging only what is absolutely

necessary. So it makes me laugh when my partner says I'm not a very good liar! You don't need it. It's about levels of truth. It is all about shading, scales of grey.

I wonder about that grey zone, and where day-to-day lies would sit next to the spy lies – the macro lies compared with the mini lies.

I think about the times I have been caught in a lie and that moment before the fall, that terrible feeling of weightlessness when the trapdoor has suddenly opened beneath you. Has Foxtrot ever been caught out in the middle of an operation? He said he had been lucky to get away with his life: was that because someone caught him out or saw through him?

He has had a couple of 'close calls', where he was seen in the wrong place at the wrong time – more importantly, wearing the wrong or 'unconventional' kit. Both times it was digital media that got him. As the 45th President of the United States knows only too well, 280 characters and an image or video can damage even the most sophisticated of communication strategies.

Foxtrot has many personal photographs from his decades of work, but one stands out. It is an arresting shot taken by a photojournalist – and it had to be removed from every possible public platform. The powerful image was used in the wrong context and contained clues to Foxtrot's 'purpose and identity at a particularly sensitive time'. He has the only remaining copy framed and hanging in his study as a reminder. 'However careful you might think you are, someone else is always looking at you – or for you.'

It is hard to meet Foxtrot and not wonder if there will ever come a time when he can step out of the darkness and show his face, tell

his story in full – so that on his bookshelf, next to the sullied autobiographies by the Balkan warlords, his own might stand proud.

Back to the present day, and Foxtrot has vanished – or at least our
dialogue has. He tells me that he is 'currently on loan' to someone
and something else and I realise that my time with him is up. In today's world, where everything leaves a digital trace, the committed
hiders and misleaders do not leave their channels of communication open long enough for the wrong person to follow the clues and
come looking for them.

Whenever I have spent time in the shadows, I have found it
deeply unsettling. There is always a moment when something feels
'off' and certainty slips away. Still, I think Foxtrot gave me a good
sense of his own character.

In his deceptions and subterfuge, Foxtrot said he had always
acted on behalf of the state. He may have spoken for hours on the
blurred distinction between truth and lies, he may have spent his
early years with a false name and a loaded gun under his pillow, but
as far as I could tell, he had a single set of loyalties. This is what must
make him so clear on how to proceed as an intelligence gatherer,
a concealer, a narrator of the stories that will determine national
security. His lies seek to produce the official truth – the truth of a
country at a given time.

The second spy (apologies to Foxtrot) in my shadow triumvirate
would not be as easy to fathom.

CHAPTER 3

DEEPER INTO THE SHADOWS | *THE DOUBLE AGENT*

'I thank God every day that I did not end up spilling innocent blood. There is no innocent blood on my hands. That is the truth that I live for.'

Aimen Dean must count as one of the best liars of modern times, having survived deep undercover at the heart of al-Qaeda for eight years. His story comes second because it is so much more complex than Foxtrot's, but I came across him first and almost by accident. It was as I started to put this book together and, at the time, I had absolutely no sense of just how deep in the shadows I was when I spoke to him. This man had lived more than one lie, had more than one loyalty and served more than one power.

When I interviewed him in 2015, he had only spoken publicly a handful of times, he was still difficult to get hold of and hard to pin down.

He was certainly one of the most perplexing people I had ever encountered. Was he lying when he spoke to me? He gave me permission to record our conversation and I was glad I did. The sound of his voice is still clear in my mind, but his words fly, they swoop and they dive. When I was listening to him, I sometimes found it hard to be sure if I had caught them properly.

Since those interviews in 2015, Dean has gradually become more and more public – to the point where now I can find him everywhere. From social media to television, newspaper, radio and podcasts, to his own autobiographical book.

This man from the shadows now has the brightest of spotlights shining on him. When it came to the twentieth anniversary of the 11 September attacks, he seemed to embark on an odyssey of telling. However, the more he talks, the more small contradictions appear, confusions of time, place and certainty. The main story is always the same, but little details collide with each other.

I am, of course, deeply grateful for this. If complex lies were easy to tell, this would be an entirely different book – and even at this early stage, I can say with confidence that society would be very different too. The more Dean tells his story, the more I marvel at the psychological, intellectual and emotional resources required to sustain such deception. I had, unwittingly, started at the very extreme end of lying.

To try to present his story in a coherent way, I will use the different versions to explain the one he told me, on a crackly line from the Middle East. It comes in many jigsaw pieces. It was 30 July 2015.

We had arranged a time, but it feels like long minutes before the foreign dial tone stops and a voice answers. Who is this bubbly man, whose name is an alias and whose light tone belies words of warfare and terrorism?

Dean sounds as if he is moving, through shops and crowded

places, then empty streets with vehicles rushing past. He says he is in Dubai but I have no way of knowing. I feel a chill speaking to him, even though I can hear only warm sounds down the line. A strange anxiety creeps up my neck. Should I be talking to him? Will he ensnare me? I fight off my discomfort. If his story is unbelievable, it is at least matched by his towering self-belief.

He is unnervingly talkative. Everything he says cascades from one story to the next, making it hard to be sure of the chronology.

'And er yes, at the same time, er yes… the only reason why this story is rather lacking in richer detail is only because it went on for too long, you know, it was a twelve-year journey from October '94 all the way until December 2006.'

This is a man who is more than happy to talk about the truth and lies of what he has done but is he a fabulist, an idealist who stopped an atrocity or a traitor who hedged his bets and survived to tell his tale?

As I would find out in the following years, I actually knew very little about him when I spoke to him. This is what I had: Dean was a young jihadi, recruited by al-Qaeda in 1997. He was 'turned' by the secret services in 1998 and then spied for MI5 and MI6 until 2006. When a journalist published details that could point only to him, he was finally too close to exposure and had to be pulled out. I also knew from an excellent interview by Ben Macintyre, a colleague at *The Times*, that Dean would be talkative and colourful in his descriptions.[1]

---

1   'A brilliant MI6 spy in the midst of al-Qaeda … That was me', Ben Macintyre, *The Times* (7 March 2015).

Back then, it seemed his main task for al-Qaeda was as a preacher and fundraiser – a religious recruiter to the cause.

Sure enough, in our phone interview, he proves to be calm, rational, almost charming – and he remains courteous throughout. He is never once distracted and rarely stumbles. If he were an actor, I would tell him to try to be more natural, stop reeling off facts, lose track. But he never does. No wonder al-Qaeda used him to pass on their ideology to aspiring jihadists.

I had seen him referred to as a founder member of al-Qaeda, but this did not seem to fit with what he had said up until our call. I ask him about it.

'Basically, it was *quite* a puzzle to me when I saw that! I was thinking: no, I didn't say that… I didn't like it at all.'

It is interesting to see how much he dislikes the mistelling of his story. He has many talents, but if he is an accomplished theologian and philosopher, it seemed to me, in 2015 when I had scant information, that he might also have a very dangerous mind.

As we talk, I realise that like the best liars, he proposes seductively simple solutions to complex problems. In a war of ideas, his words are persuasive and resonant. For instance, he can sum up the many complicated steps of his journey in just one phrase: 'I do my work against al-Qaeda as a service to my faith.'

That he passed on invaluable information is unquestionable, that he saved many lives too must be true but when someone has lived such disparate identities, espoused such different views, it is difficult to trust what they say. He laughs when I ask him if he is genuine. He says that 'senior ex-MI6 officials' could confirm his identity.

'No one would touch me with a bargepole without that.'

With great difficulty, I found the best source I could – someone who knew someone who knew someone – and they confirmed that he was who he said he was. They were mightily unimpressed when I asked if they were 'sure'. This is the 'wilderness of mirrors'[2] that I had read about when looking at double agents. I knew I had to take what glimpses of the truth I could find and piece them together myself.

'Basically, I joined in 1997, in September 1997, which is, you know, post-Sudan.' I did not know. It turns out that Dean had just summed up the five crucial years al-Qaeda spent in Sudan, growing, training, learning. 'I joined the jihadi movement as a whole before, but if we're talking specifically al-Qaeda, it was September.'

Our conversation is full of similarly oblique references and chronological jumps. I soon realise that the basic facts I had jotted down in preparation would not be enough to test him. He knew his own lines too well. Immediately after we spoke, I put a timeline together, found every interview and clue that was in the public domain and gradually, the outline of a story started to appear. At least that is what I thought at the time.

Dean had given a limited number of interviews when he identified himself in March 2015. The first was with the BBC journalist Peter Marshall, and some of the adolescent glee with which Dean recounts his early days suggests a gratitude at being able to tell his tale at last. I recognise a little of that relief – it is the loosening of a lie.

Dean recalls being a teenager when he first arrived in the jihadi movement, stepping suddenly not just into a warzone but into history. It was October 1994:

---

2   *Gerontion*, T. S. Eliot (1920); *A Spy Among Friends*, Ben Macintyre (2014).

I was a bookish nerd from Saudi Arabia just weeks ago and then suddenly I find myself prancing up on the mountains of Bosnia holding an AK-47 feeling a sense of immense empowerment – and the feeling that I was participating in writing history rather than just watching history on the side.[3]

I look back now and this sense of jaunty japes on jagged peaks is very much at odds with the story he tells in his autobiography three years later.

The kaleidoscope of tales is difficult to put together. Dean's book *Nine Lives: My Time As MI6's Top Spy Inside Al-Qaeda* was published in 2018. In an opening note, the co-authors, two CNN journalists, Paul Cruickshank and Tim Lister, spell out the considerable time they spent verifying and stitching together all the different stories. They even include a cast list at the end of the book to help keep track of the many characters.

One event stands out from Dean's first year in Bosnia. It is when Dean's group had captured about 250 Serbian prisoners. To put it in historical terms, this moment refers to the mujahideen brigade who executed prisoners after the Battle of Vozuća in the northeast of Bosnia and Herzegovina. Dean writes that he was asked to take part in the executions but could not bring himself to do it.

During the course of several days, our brigade put to death more than one hundred prisoners. They were paraded, told to admit to crimes and executed in batches, while several of our fighters

3 'The Spy Who Came In from al-Qaeda', Peter Marshall interview for BBC Radio 4 (3 March 2015).

recorded the scene with camcorders. There was nothing surgical about the executions: axes, knives and even chainsaws were used. Some prisoners were crudely beheaded, their heads kicked across the dust.[4]

Again, there is a chilling jollity that occasionally creeps into Dean's narration. He writes of a prisoner who was 'foolish enough' to pretend he was a magician and said he could not be put to death. 'His head was placed on a concrete block, and another block was dropped on it.' About the magician, he says nothing else. It is staggering.

It took one killing in particular to make Dean finally walk away. It was when he watched his childhood friend Khalid take his turn to execute a prisoner. This was the boy he met when he was nine and joined the Islamic Awareness Circle, the one with whom he had entered poetry competitions in Saudi Arabia, the one he had followed to Bosnia, and now, the one who stood before him with glazed eyes and a 'demented' expression.

'He dragged a prisoner onto the bloodied earth, forced him to the ground and, crouching over him, began sawing at his neck with a serrated hunting knife.'

After he had severed the head, he kicked it away in contempt, Dean adds. This is the moment Dean left. He went back to his tent, where he could hear the executions continuing all around him. He was, he writes, 'sickened by the spectacle'.

Dean's recall of detail is quite remarkable, even if it can be hard to stomach. This could be explained by what the book calls Dean's

---

4   *Nine Lives: My Time As MI6's Top Spy Inside Al-Qaeda*, Aimen Dean, Paul Cruickshank and Tim Lister (Oneworld, 2018).

photographic memory – indeed, it tells us that by the age of twelve, he had memorised the Koran. It would certainly account for vivid recollections that test credulity and almost sound like someone looking at photographs and describing them.

So where does Dean's story start? He was born Ali al-Durrani on 17 September 1978. Remember that first name. It is very common but also very key to Dean's story. His family is of Arab, Afghan and Turkish heritage. They were Bahraini citizens living in Saudi Arabia. Tellingly, he writes: 'It was enough to confuse anyone's loyalties,' as if places were the source of confusion, not the person who grew from them. His father died in an accident when he was four and his mother of a brain aneurysm when he was twelve. When his mother died, he writes that he lost his teacher, mentor and companion. He found solace in the pages of the Koran and, as those around him became more involved in the Islamic resistance, in 1994, he followed his friend Khalid to Bosnia – the same friend who would decapitate a prisoner a year later.

Today, he looks very much like the 'bookish nerd' he described. Dark hair and eyes, rimless glasses, a trimmed beard and a polite manner. There is something about his face that conveys a Mona Lisa almost-smile. A hint of complexity that gives something and seems to take it away at the same time. Could that thing be honesty? It is also a face that could pass by unnoticed; the perfect spy's face.

His prodigious memory is what made Dean such a valuable intelligence asset, someone who could spend months at a time undercover and still emerge to unload mental filing cabinets full of accurate details of dates, locations, logistics, names, bank accounts, code names, chemical formulae and quote after quote after quote. His mind is wired differently.

In one of his most recent interviews, he says: 'I didn't wake up one day and say to myself, "I'm going to be a spy," just as I didn't wake up one day four years earlier and [tell] myself, "I'm going to become a terrorist."'[5]

He said he was a religious student with a rebellious nature.

'I decided, and I have no idea what took over me, to go and fight in Bosnia.' It was the idea of defending the defenceless that seemed honourable to him.

Dean says that Bosnia schooled many of the top talents in al-Qaeda. Khalid Sheikh Mohammed, who Dean refers to as the mastermind of the 11 September attacks, visited Bosnia towards the end of the war. Dean says he met Mohammed, or KSM as he calls him, at the wedding of one of the fighters in the city of Zenica, north of Sarajevo. KSM was 'looking for talent' among the veterans of the conflict, to recruit and train militarily in Afghanistan. He says KSM told him it was better for him to go to Afghanistan. 'And so I did.'

After Bosnia, Dean says that the jihadi thinking started to shift, moving away from the notion of being warriors defending the innocent, to terrorists who would strike first. His doubts began to take root, but his path was set and it led to Kandahar, Afghanistan, in September 1997. There, he would kneel with Osama bin Laden, make a personal pledge of allegiance and join al-Qaeda.

In later accounts, Dean is more explicit and says he first met bin Laden in the summer of 1996, when bin Laden had fled from Sudan

---

5 'Life As A Spy Inside Al-Qaeda', LADbible TV (14 February 2021), www.youtube.com/watch?v=Pxij_nd3BAA

to Afghanistan. The light of information shifts, the shadows shift, but the essential story is the same – Dean was now at the heart of al-Qaeda.

In later interviews, he will also go on to detail exactly what he did for bin Laden and al-Qaeda. In each retelling the emphasis is different, tiny details change and my impression of the man behind the words alters. This man is such an extraordinary liar that even something provable, that has been tested by the world's top intelligence agencies and verified by acclaimed journalists becomes unbelievable. I had a sense of this when I spoke to him in 2015. What I did not realise was that I was talking to a bombmaker.

On the twentieth anniversary of 11 September, Dean featured in a Channel 4 series that looked at the life of bin Laden. Early on in the first episode, he says in a matter-of-fact way: 'When I became an al-Qaeda bombmaker...'[6]

This throw-away introduction chilled me to my core. It is that same melodic voice, that untroubling face I have come to recognise over the years and again he is referring quite pleasantly to working on projects that will destroy lives.

In the second episode, he says: '[Al-Qaeda] sent me to a specialist camp that was for bombmaking, chemical warfare and poison.'[7]

Dean talks about the 'beautiful' area in the mountains around Darūnṭa, in the east of Afghanistan, near Jalalabad. He says, 'Tobogganing was one of the favourite pastimes for the jihadists who were there.' He makes it sound like a high-end holiday package.

In another interview in 2021, he said his move to Darūnṭa was

---

6 *Bin Laden: The Road to 9/11*, Episode 1, Channel 4 (6 September 2021).
7 Ibid., Episode 2 (13 September 2021).

bin Laden's personal decision.[8] It is discombobulating – but the discombobulation does not stop there. He goes on to describe working there from dawn until mid-afternoon.

'And that is where we are learning – and sometimes either experimenting in blowing up new kinds of explosives we are trying to perfect, or… ah… *unfortunately* testing, you know, the latest batch of poisons or chemical weapons on *poor* rabbits.'

For a millisecond, he sounds genuinely distressed. His written words show no such similar distress at the memory. In his autobiography, he writes about going through more than eighty rabbits as they tested a nicotine poison and testing a nerve gas on rabbits in cages, set at different distances from the source so that the poison team could test its effectiveness. Could he be acting out expected emotional responses? For me, his deceptions are too well layered to be able to unpeel the layers all the way back to the truth of him. He does also write that for years, he had nightmares about being chased by rabbits. This almost comic vision, like a dystopian Disney production, sits very oddly alongside the words of someone who was perfecting the art of mass poisoning.

In 2015, when I thought I was talking to a misguided preacher, Dean told me that it did not take long for his world view to change. He said then that he began to see the group in a very different light. This part of the story never changes. It centres on what Dean calls 'al-Qaeda's first terrorist attack'. There had been al-Qaeda attacks before, but for Dean, this one was different and merited the moniker of terrorism.

---

8   'Life As A Spy Inside Al-Qaeda', LADbible TV.

On 7 August 1998, two lorries carrying explosives approached the American embassies in Nairobi, Kenya, and Dar es Salaam, Tanzania. At about 10.30 a.m. local time, and within minutes of each other, the drivers detonated their cargo. The two attacks killed 224 people, including twelve Americans, and injured more than 4,500. Almost all the dead were civilians.[9] This was the moment that al-Qaeda entered the wider public consciousness, and it was the moment Dean says that his belief in their cause curdled. The horror sank in. That November, bin Laden was charged by America for all 224 murders.

When Dean had to leave soon afterwards to seek medical treatment in 'a small Gulf state' – Qatar, I would learn later – he decided to leave for good. He was recruited by Qatari intelligence, then passed on to the British over an eleven-day period. Once his belief in the cause was gone, he says there was no looking back.

On 16 December 1998, he landed in London. His life as a spy began with training, debriefing and intelligence sharing. The medical treatment he needed explained his absence to al-Qaeda. After seven months, he 'missed the action' and was ready to return to Afghanistan. He went back ostensibly the same man but with a changed heart.

Al-Qaeda believed it was them sending him back and forth to Britain as both a preacher and a messenger. In reality, it was the cover Dean needed to pass information back to his handlers. He used the paranoia rife in the group to his own advantage, mirroring his targets' fears, extracting information and successfully hiding himself for years.

---

9 'Hunting Bin Laden', *Frontline* (18 November 1998), www.pbs.org/wgbh/pages/frontline/shows/binladen/bombings/summary.html

During our call, I ask him how he did this. How did he cope with his double life? Even the best strategist must tire and weaken when putting on a persona at all times.

'Well, basically by immersing yourself into the other identity and believing it with passion, you know.' He is on a roll now. 'You cannot survive eight years with people who are exceptionally paranoid without having immersed yourself into their mentality. And you know, it was easy for me because I had that mentality before.'

The image he uses for this other 'mujahid' identity is as telling as it is banal.

'It was like an old pair of shoes I was able to slip into comfortably whenever I wanted.'

I am staggered. For Dean, a successful double life is about knowing your lies, wearing them, moulding them around you – and choosing when to 'slip' them on, or take them off. This was how an al-Qaeda agent spied on al-Qaeda.

The worn shoes served him well, and not only did he hand over significant details and data, he managed to pass on information about plans for 'something big', about jihadis told to hurry back to Afghanistan by the end of August 2001. Eleven days later, the Twin Towers would fall. The information he passed on was accurate, but it was not enough to stop the attack. There were also details about the chemical devices that al-Qaeda was testing and preparing to use, and about the activities and schemes of senior figures in London. He even attended the same meeting as three of the men who went on to commit the 7 July bombings in London in 2005.[10]

---

10 'Spy inside al-Qaeda goes public "to confront jihadists"', Gordon Corera, BBC News (3 March 2015).

I wonder how someone so devout could go through with being 'commissioned by bin Laden to educate recruits', fire up would-be jihadis with tales of the Afghan camps and plant the poison seeds that would grow into someone else's evil actions.

Dean is so loquacious that his answers come in many forms. The core of what he says is that he had to recruit in the short term if he was to help stop al-Qaeda in the long term. In the past he has said: 'If you want to catch rats, you have to go into the sewage system basically and get dirty yourself.'[11]

It is hard not to think of those he might have persuaded towards violence on his path towards the truth. He admits feeling guilty, but, he argues, how else could someone gain access to the highest levels of a network such as al-Qaeda? How else could someone remain in a position to retrieve invaluable intelligence and potentially prevent numerous terrorist plots?

I ask him how he lives with the scale of his lies over such a sustained period.

'Basically [it was] the rational, logical me, the one who always existed… and thinking in a more humanist way, let's put it this way, you know, rather than absolutist.' The streets of Dubai – if it is Dubai – now sound a little emptier.

Dean believes that it was American sources who gave him away, and indeed it was a book by an American journalist that dealt the blow. On 26 June 2006, these were the words printed on the cover of *Time* magazine: 'Al-Qaeda's Plot to Attack the NYC Subway'. The articles inside were based on excerpts from a book on the USA's

---

11 'The Spy Who Came In from al-Qaeda', Marshall.

'War on Terror' by Pulitzer Prize-winning journalist Ron Suskind. In it, a figure Suskind calls 'Ali' appears, bearing chilling information about a plan to use poison gas in New York in 2003. These were details only a chosen few would know, identifying details.

Mubtakkar is an Arabic word that translates as 'innovative' or 'ingenious'. As a noun, it can mean 'inventor' or 'creator'. It is also one of the war words used by al-Qaeda, a lexicon of death, and in that context, it referred to something known to only a secret few.

Dean, of course, knew the secret intimately. In his book, he calls it by its full name: 'the unique invention' or '*al-mubtakkar al-farid*'.

It was a chemical weapon – the very one he had tested on 'poor rabbits' – all five of them in one go. It was not just its name that was a cynical lie. It would have come in a rucksack that looked carelessly left behind in a carriage, but instead, contained carefully planned murder. The device had two chambers joined by a seal that, when broken, would disperse hydrogen cyanide – the colourless gas also known as Zyklon B. This was the gas used by the Nazis in the concentration camps. The target was the New York subway system and the device could be activated remotely.

As Suskind put it: 'In the world of terrorist weaponry, this was the equivalent of splitting the atom. Obtain a few widely available chemicals, and you could construct it with a trip to Home Depot – and then kill everyone in the store.'[12]

What shook the intelligence officers, though, was that the plot had been in its advanced stages, little more than a month from execution, but it had been called off. 'Ali did not know the precise

---

12 *The One Percent Doctrine: Deep Inside America's Pursuit of Its Enemies Since 9/11*, Ron Suskind (2006).

explanation why,' writes Suskind. However, Dean later claimed that it was a direct instruction from bin Laden's deputy, Ayman al-Zawahiri, because of fears of the retaliation such an attack would incur.[13]

When the *Time* magazine issue was published, the news that Dean had always dreaded came to him in the form of a text message: 'Brother go into hiding because someone among us is a spy.' His time had run out. His handlers told him to get out. Another chapter in his life was about to begin, and with it came a new name: Aimen Dean.

But was this true? How could he be 'Ali', and plausibly be talking to me as he moved freely from street to street, phone in hand, possibly distracted and discussing al-Qaeda loudly in public? I ask him. For a moment, I succeed in confusing even this man of multiple identities. His words come to a halt. I can clearly hear a vehicle whooshing past in the background. I repeat the question.

'Are you Ali?'

'Ah. You mean the intelligence source? Ah… er… yes.'

In later versions of his story he does not hesitate. He is Ali. He was born Ali, he was Suskind's Ali and he must still be Ali to his core. Dean's version differs in detail from Suskind's, but the substance is the same. Dean puts this down to factual errors by Suskind's sources. In his book, he confirms that he was consulted about the attack by one of the al-Qaeda cells because he was an explosives expert and that in return for helping them, he got more information about the attack.

---

13 'The Spy Who Came In from al-Qaeda', Marshall.

When the terror cell made contact with him, they said they needed his help in deciphering his own handwritten notes about *mubtakkar*. If his scrawled notes were the answer to what they were looking for, then I can only conclude that Dean's acquaintance with terror is itself terrifying.

Does he ever consider himself a traitor to his own faith? Is he ever haunted by the thought that he betrayed the jihadi 'brothers' he fought with in Bosnia?

> Al-Qaeda never represented the faith anyway to begin with… so I always enjoy it when I see someone being angry with what I did [working with the British agencies] and then I realise that either they are a) extremists, b) vulnerable to extremism or c) they bought the whole propaganda.

He recalls being asked the same question in recent years by a young Muslim woman who worked for a think tank in London. She studied international politics, 'if you can believe that', and left a strong impression on Dean.

'She basically found what I did repulsive. She called me a traitor to my face. And I looked at her and I said: "Well, you can't be a traitor to a bunch of traitors. You know. They are the traitors. They betrayed their faith, they betrayed their countries."' He says that those who find his actions repulsive are the ones to watch.

'I'm not being narcissistic here,' he says, 'but I decided to set myself up as a barometer. Basically, if [someone] finds what I did repulsive then, why? You know. You have to ask this question, why?'

And how do people react to him at home? Has he been able to return to his 'usual self', as he puts it?

'What is so amazing about Dubai is that you can be invisible. You just walk around – hardly anyone recognises me at all – it's amazing because it's an international city, it's a tourist city, it's a transient city.'

I ask him if he fears reprisal.

'I know their capabilities and targeting mentality and mindset. They do not chase people who got away, they do not have a pursue policy. I'm not a target of pursuit, I'm a target of opportunity.'

His tone borders on flippancy. I have to keep reminding myself that he is referring to the organisation that destroyed twin towers in the heart of one of the world's most powerful cities, a group whose ideology is stained in blood.

'If I happen to stumble into their areas, then they are definitely likely to have a go, but they wouldn't spend tens of thousands of dollars trying to chase me.'

Did his family know what he was doing at the time?

'They had no idea.' He says that he 'came clean' to them in 2010. 'They are exceptionally supportive, blood's thicker than water and thicker than any other consideration.'

Family support and understanding aside, I still find it difficult to match the devout family man with the teller of so many powerful lies. I push him.

'But isn't lying as an act, a dishonourable act?'

'Of course!'

Once again, he wrongfoots me with his reply. But, he adds, there is a 'very beautiful' proverb written by the fourth caliph of Islam,

Imam Ali. He stops, another of his rare pauses. He starts to enunci-
ate his words as, I realise, he turns preacher.

'Being faithful to treacherous people is treachery. And betraying treacherous people is an act of faithfulness. So being faithful
to people who are murderers – mass murderers to begin with and
perpetrators of atrocities – is lying to them dishonest? No! It is the
epitome – the summit! – of honesty and loyalty.'

He makes it sound so simple, but did he, in turn, ever have doubts
about working for MI5 and MI6? Did he ever suffer an identity
crisis?

'The biggest crisis was really the Iraq war. I was completely against
it. I thought it was a *monumental* mistake: strategically, politically.'
Back then, he was still active, infiltrating al-Qaeda from 2003 to
2004 'in Saudi Arabia and elsewhere in the Gulf'. He is fired up now
as he thinks back. 'I was *exceptionally* angry about that and I was
questioning *everything* I was doing.'

What did it take to stop that inner turmoil?

'If I have to thank anyone for restoring that sense of calm and
belief in the mission, it was al-Qaeda. With their atrocities in Iraq,
the public beheadings... you know, the wanton destruction of
mosques and shrines. Yes. It restored my faith in my mission.'

The story he is telling now, however, his truth-telling, is happen-
stance, not the final act of a crusade. When I ask him how it feels
to have finally come out of hiding, he says: 'It was a relief. But the
whole thing was accidental.'

After he was extracted in 2006, he worked in the banking sector in
the Middle East for more than seven years. He investigated 'cases of
terrorism finance', in a supreme case of poacher turned gamekeeper.

He gave a talk on the finances of ISIL (otherwise known as ISIS, Islamic State or Daesh) at the Royal Air Force Club in London in 2014, under the Chatham House rule. The information he disclosed could be used by those in the room but neither his affiliation nor his identity should be revealed. This meant his host could be 'generous in his introduction' and, he laughs, 'definitely, definitely there was an ambush after that' by a journalist.

His first interview was with the BBC, when he was interviewed as an expert on the financing of terrorism. It made no reference to his al-Qaeda past. He says that after it was aired, interview requests 'snowballed' and that pressure, combined with the deaths in 2013 of a nephew and cousin fighting in Syria, led him to tell his own story, in full, two months later in March 2015.

Dean is now on Facebook and LinkedIn. It is another implausible detail that makes me pause, gives me cause for concern. Search for him and he appears. Where most people put in generic job titles and industry jargon on LinkedIn, he describes himself as: 'Highly experienced in the fields of counter terrorism finance, Islamic theology, history and modern Islamic political and militant movements. 21 years of exposure to Islamic related terrorism, political Islam and violent extremism/counter-violent extremism.'

It is a summary that invites attention and certainly not one written by someone who is afraid of the fatwa placed on them in 2008. Such an astonishingly successful liar manages to be astonishing still.

On Facebook, one of his photos shows what could be a hideout, yet there are fresh flowers on the table, and one could guess that the person allowed into this intimate scene and taking the photograph is the same one who has added a softening touch to the wooden bolthole, where daintily stacked eggcups sit under a shelf crammed full of books. This is what happens when you look so deeply into someone else's lies – you begin to question every visible detail of their lives.

How does he make himself traceable enough to earn a living and live his life, yet hidden enough to escape discovery and retaliation?

'I don't have any death wish, I can assure you!'

He laughs, as if he were talking about having stolen a pen from the stationery cupboard. Dean is an extremely unusual man – perhaps unique, or at least, uniquely placed in history. The fervent belief that underlies everything he does surfaces again. After all, what can men do when God is on your side?

'I travel all the time. I have an office but I never show up there.' He laughs again. 'I did take some measures to ensure that anyone trying to find me would have a very difficult time.'

In 2015, he laughs off my question. In 2021, asked if he had made al-Qaeda angry, his answer is different.

'Yes, they are angry. Enough to try to kill me twice. Once in 2009 and once in 2016. It's a badge of honour as far as I am concerned.'[14]

When I try to contact him again in 2017, the door that was opened is now firmly shut. Did he think I could not be trusted or was driven by ulterior motives? Could the curse of a committed liar be losing the ability to trust?

This very extreme end of lying may have made for a chilling encounter, but it gave me deep insight into how anyone manages to sustain multiple lies over a period of time. Dean never loses himself

---

14 'Life As A Spy Inside Al-Qaeda', LADbible TV.

('his usual self') because he believes in the truth of what he has done. He believes in his own stories. He believes himself.

Back in 2015, on that phone line, my final question is: what is truth to him, on a personal level?

Dean does not hesitate.

'I believe that there is a supreme being in this universe, for sure, I mean... I believe that our lives were given to us as a debt, you know, and I think there is a moral compass in every individual, what is right and what is wrong.'

He says again that there is no innocent blood on his hands.

'That is the truth that I live for, and live up to, the fact that I did not take lives, I saved lives. That is the ultimate truth.'

Even then I could sense that no matter whether Dean carried on telling shifting versions of the same story, no matter who he served or which pair of worn shoes he wore, his faith in the righteousness of his actions would remain unshakeable. That is how he believes what he has done is ultimately good and also quite separate from the bombs he helped to make, the young minds he shaped and the promises he would break.

Ali-Aimen's story is out in the open, Foxtrot hides in plain sight but my third spy is someone who remained hidden in the deepest, darkest of all the shadows.

CHAPTER 4

SPIES, LIES AND
WOMEN | *ROSE*

It started with a niggle. My two spies had revealed a lot, but the
more I looked, the more male the art of spycraft seemed to be.
Granted, it may have been the limits of my contacts but I wondered
why I had yet to come across a female intelligence officer. Could I
find a woman who operated in this world – and was willing to talk
to me? Was it specious to wonder if there might be differences between the deceptive abilities of men and women? Or was it simply,
as Foxtrot said, that just as every individual has a different moral
compass, so we each tell lies differently?

This niggling question did not come from a quest for equality; it
was prompted by a very unusual encounter. So unusual that I knew
I had no hope – and certainly no way – of reaching her. Instead, I
began to look for female spies in the back catalogues of espionage.
When it comes to women, the books seem almost bare. This, however, can only be an advantage. The sheer lack of famous female spies
makes them more unlikely. When spies are expected to be male,
a woman's most lethal weapon becomes not her ability to deceive
but the social, cultural and historical assumptions that do the job
for her. I marvelled at evidence that a woman's gender was one of

her best disguises. I was not the only one. An unlikely combination of Winston Churchill and the North Korean regime both benefited from recruiting female agents when others hesitated.

Sure enough, the more I searched for the elusive creatures, the fewer I found. The well-known ones stuck out like bookmarks in the history of spying. Whether it was the elusive Agent 355 (thought to be code for 'the lady'), who was part of George Washington's Culper Ring during the American Revolution and was (perhaps) arrested in 1780, or Mata Hari, portrayed as a glamorous and defiant traitor until the moment of her execution by firing squad in 1917. Or Kim Hyon-hui, the North Korean actress who trained as a spy and became a notorious state assassin in 1987 when she planted a bomb on Korean Air Flight 858, killing all 115 people on board.[1] She escaped not by biting down on her poison pill as planned but by defecting to South Korea. There, in a final twist, she was deemed to have been 'brainwashed', pardoned in 1989 and now lives in hiding, for fear of assassination herself.

Meanwhile, when it came to wider attitudes towards female recruiters and orchestrators, there was certainly an extraordinary fanfare in December 1991 surrounding the appointment of the first female head of MI5. The former director general has described it rather laconically since.

'The media got this fantastic announcement about this woman in this spooky, spooky job that they'd never known anything about.'[2]

---

1 'Female of the spy is deadlier than the male', Ben Macintyre, *The Times* (17 February 2017).
2 'American Intelligence: Technology, Espionage and Alliances', Chautauqua Institution, New York State (July 2011).

Dame Stella Rimington was quickly identified by the tabloid newspapers.

'So who was I? I was a woman. And where did I belong? I belonged in the kitchen. So we had [headlines like] "Housewife, superspy". The outing was brutal.

'Imagine what it's like to be suddenly thrust into the limelight after a career in a secret intelligence organisation. Like everybody else, I'd created a carapace... a shell of anonymity.' She stood down in 1996 and seized back the initiative five years later by publishing her autobiography, *Open Secret*.

She intrigued me. I thought of Foxtrot and his 'Venn diagram', Aimen Dean and his 'worn shoes'. She described the life she let others see, her other life, as a hard, protective layer enclosed around her secrets. Once she was stripped of that, she fought to be the one to tell her story. How would this particular woman characterise the difference between the men and women who worked in the security service?

She has said that when she joined MI5 in the 1960s, women were 'second-class citizens' who were not allowed to recruit targets, but that female skills were precisely what was needed:

> It's about persuasion, it's about sympathy, it's about listening, it's about giving an air of confidence, a calm confidence. All these, I think, are female skills, and there's also a need for a degree of ruthlessness which I think is also a female skill, although perhaps, it's not necessarily always wise to say that.[3]

---

3   The *Sunday Times* Festival of Education, Wellington College, Berkshire (June 2015).

I had to speak to Dame Stella, to press her on how she marshalled the nation's secrets, dealt with the media intrusion, then took back control of the narrative.

Eventually, I found a go-between, who said they would pass on a message. I waited tensely. Then it happened. She agreed to speak to me, very cautiously and with the most confusing of caveats. She told me that I must not 'air her views in print'. I was baffled. I would happily have kept her anonymous but how could I discard what she told me? Still, I fell over myself like a fawning fan – of course I would talk to her in confidence and treat whatever she told me in whichever way she asked. But it was no good. Days later, just as mysteriously as a character in one of the ten spy thrillers she has now written, she 'declined the offer after further consideration'. I shuddered. Had she been watching me? Her owl-like face turned away, and in a puff, she was gone. The spymistress who evaded me. Perhaps the female of the species is smarter after all – or the subject of lying is simply too taboo, even for a pioneer in the world of spying.

How would I find my quarry? The sisterhood of spies was proving very difficult to identify, let alone interview. I would have abandoned this distant sorority if it had not been for that one very unexpected encounter, years before I started this book. My 'niggle'. In fact, my strange meeting with this lady was one of the nudges I needed to start writing about the power of lies. This particular spy was a stubborn, magnificent, courageous woman.

We were brought together by chance. Our stories crossed. Her giant one, my tiny one. It was another moment when my mind was boggled by the power of lies, big and small. It was the telling of our secrets, the ending of our lies, that meant we shared a day together on the same front page. But I would never meet her.

The day *The Times* published her photograph in glorious black and white, the day her striking face finally emerged from the shadows, was, by coincidence, the day I wrote about my second lie. I will explain this later – after all, how can I find it difficult to write about it again? It should get easier to tell after the first time of telling, shouldn't it? That day in 2010, my small strip of a photograph sat above hers. Her face, her spirit, her story had stayed with me for years. Of all the unfindable female spies, this one found me.

Her tale started with the creation of Churchill's 'Secret Army'. The Special Operations Executive (SOE) was formed in 1940 to 'set Europe ablaze', as Churchill put it. They were to combat the Axis powers by covert means, fair or foul. Despite another of the group's soubriquets, 'The Ministry of Ungentlemanly Warfare', it was ahead of its time in the training and deployment of female agents.

The SOE's ambitions for women may have been modest at first, but gradually female would-be agents were introduced to guerrilla tactics, learning how to 'creep silently … live off the land … tail people and avoid being tailed'. Significantly, they were also told 'how to kill silently',[4] and among their arsenal was an L-pill. L stood for lethal – it was a cyanide capsule for use if ever they were left with no escape.

The role of these wartime women began to emerge as time passed and books, films and newly released archive material brought them back to life. In 2009, when a bronze memorial was erected in

---

4   *The Heroines of SOE: F Section – Britain's Secret Women in France*, Squadron Leader Beryl E. Escott (2010).

memory of the organisation, it was crowned by a bust of Violette Szabo, who, the plaque said, 'was among the 117 SOE agents who did not survive their missions to France'. However, if the list of these secret female agents had kept on growing, one of their company was missing. Rose.

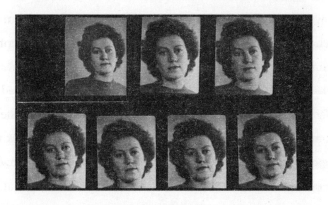

Source: National Archives

To her neighbour, she was Eileen the Cat Lady. She let few people approach her flat in Torquay and she died alone, aged eighty-nine. Her body was found on 2 September 2010.

To the council officials who searched the flat to identify her after her death, she was a lost cause. Until they found her medals: an MBE and a Croix de Guerre.

To her niece, she was Didi, an inspiration, a strong character and a deeply private woman. Didi had been involved in the war but would not talk about it.

To the inmates of Ravensbrück concentration camp, she was one of the few who got away.

She had many identities, but her codename was Agent Rose.

In her later years, Rose did give a few interviews, in disguise or under a pseudonym, but she hid her past from the people she met day to day. When the author Susan Ottaway interviewed her as part of her book on the much celebrated Szabo, Rose said she would talk to her but that she did not want to be identified until after her own death. Ottaway honoured her wish.

It was not that Rose was ever forgotten, or cast aside, but that she chose obscurity. And she chose it to escape from her horrific wartime experiences.[5]

Eileen 'Didi' Nearne – or Rose – would have been buried unknown and unrecognised but for the artefacts she kept, the last remnants of her lifetime of secrets. Along with her medals were some letters written in French and some French currency, which were enough to point towards her real identity. The lonely cat lady had a most unexpected place in the story of a terrible war.

Rose had an English father and a half-French, half-Spanish mother and was one of four siblings who were educated in France.[6] As the German army rampaged across Europe, both she and her elder sister Jacqueline fled to Britain in 1940 and joined the First Aid Nursing Yeomanry. Their fluent French brought them to the attention of the wartime agencies, and soon they were being vetted and recruited.

Jacqueline flew into France first. What she did not know was that her little sister would follow soon afterwards. Rose dropped near

---

5   *Violette Szabo: The Life That I Have*, Susan Ottaway (2002). Ottaway kept her promise and only published her book *Sisters, Secrets and Sacrifice: The True Story of WWII Special Agents Eileen and Jacqueline Nearne* (2013) after Eileen's death.

6   'My aunts, the unlikely spies', Joanna Moorhead, *The Guardian* (30 March 2013).

Châteauroux[7] in central France, on one of the moonlit nights on which so many operations were flown.

In her only television interview many decades later, she appeared named only as Rose, wearing a wig and speaking French.[8] She recounted one of her many near-misses. Her resolve, bravery and nous were tested early on when she was stopped on a train by a German soldier. Her suitcase looked heavy. What was in it, he asked? Rose was carrying her 18-kilogram portable transmitter – the device she used to send messages and information back to the British.

'What? In my case?' she replied. 'It's a gramophone.'

That seemed to satisfy him. He moved on. But something was bothering him and he kept looking back at her. Was he about to change his mind? She got off at the next station and continued her journey on foot. As the train pulled away, she could still see him debating with his colleagues. Debating her. But he had left it too late. She was safe.

Her luck would not last. While her sister returned unharmed after her missions, Rose took one risk too many. She returned to an apartment in Paris that she knew was unsafe for one last, urgent transmission.

On 25 July 1944, the Gestapo finally caught her. She was taken in chains to their notorious headquarters at 11 Rue des Saussaies. Her recollection is chilling.

'They took me into a room where there was a bath.' Rose knew this was bad. She knew what she faced: water torture. 'And they held me under the water.' But she knew what to do.

---

7   *The Heroines of SOE*, Escott.
8   'Secret Memories', *Timewatch*, BBC2 (11 March 1997).

'You suffocate under the water but you must stick to your story. I remembered what we'd been taught. Never to be afraid, never let them dominate you.'[9]

When the Gestapo could get nothing from her, they sent her to Ravensbrück concentration camp on 15 August 1944. Seven months later, she escaped on foot at night-time and in the snow as she was being transferred, just days before the Allies swept in.

Files released from the National Archives at Kew in late October 2010 reveal that early on, Rose's talent for deception fooled even the most practised of operatives. Labelled as 'lacking in shrewdness and cunning', she was deemed to have a poor memory and was 'inaccurate and scatter-brained … very feminine and immature'.

It was the head of the French section of the SOE, Colonel Maurice Buckmaster, who overruled this verdict. He had detected in her a skilled liar. Indeed, this same 'scatter-brain' would score a powerful coup when her demeanour fooled the Gestapo even as they interrogated and tortured her. Their verdict? She was 'a silly little girl who had wasted their time'.[10]

Sadly for her, this same talent prolonged her misery when she was finally in the hands of the Americans. They did not believe her because she told them the truth but refused to divulge details about the SOE. Her interrogator wrote that she created 'a very unbalanced impression'.

'Her account of what happened to her … is held to be invented.'[11]

Her liberators ended up putting her in a camp with Nazi women

---

9 Ibid.
10 *The Heroines of SOE*, Escott.
11 'Eileen Nearne's role as SOE agent revealed only after her death', *Today*, BBC Radio 4 (October 2010).

and it would be at least a month before Rose was returned to England. When she finally made it home, she was hospitalised and suffered the nervous breakdown that would make her remove herself so successfully from the story of her own life.

It was her sister who nursed her, her sister who went on to pursue a career at the United Nations and was even part of a film about the SOE, but Rose herself never recovered.

Eileen and Jacqueline Nearne's names are now carved alongside the seventy-three other women listed on a memorial in Tempsford, Bedfordshire. The village sits near the site of the most important secret airfield of the war, set up in 1940 and known as Gibraltar Farm.[12] It was here that SOE missions began and ended. These seventy-five are the known female agents who parachuted in behind enemy lines, and whose life-changing deceits influenced the course of a war.

Rose's deceptions came from serving her country; her truths, she rarely told. Was her silence habit, or was her lie so deep-rooted that it excluded her from the easy, everyday connections most people make with others?

'When I returned after the war,' she said in her television interview, 'I, along with lots of others, missed that kind of life. Everything seemed so ordinary.' Perhaps she could not trust in the safety of the civilian life she had spent so many years fighting to protect? Still, it was she who kept those mementos: the medals that spoke of her facts, her motivation. It was this testament that meant her own story could be reclaimed, published and told.

---

12 'Tempsford Memorial Trust', www.tempsfordmemorial.co.uk/history.html

She told the perfect lie – and her story etched in sharp detail the effort and strain it takes to do this. But now, being able to see her whole story, I feel an incredible admiration for her. Her lies were how she lived her truth. All those years, she kept it safe, hidden away in a dusty drawer, waiting to be found. Perhaps.

Revealed at last: wartime heroism
of Torquay pensioner Eileen Nearne

The Times, page 1, 14 September 2010
Published with kind permission of *The Times*; photograph of Eileen Nearne © SWNS

On the day of her funeral, a week after her story was published, crowds lined the streets, the Royal British Legion paid tribute to her and her coffin was draped in a flag. In death, she was finally recognised for every single role she had played.

When her medals revealed her story, those truths were so resonant that her image adorned newspapers and screens across the world, almost a hundred years after she was born. Rose was the perfect third agent to give me an insight into the world of high-stakes lies, but her deception was so good that I encountered her only by chance and got to know her only through other people's accounts and after her death.

My three spies (apologies again to Foxtrot) were proof that those who live a lie – or even live several lies – find meaning beyond the push and pull of daily life. But their stories show that the comfort of day-to-day interactions is what they lose. Those big lies are heavy to bear and leave even someone as composed as Foxtrot searching himself still. I learnt a lot about agents, intelligence gatherers and concealers; those who narrate the stories that determine national security. I had a sense of how they might choose between what they allowed to be said and what they hid, and even how and when they decided to plant their own snake in a viper's nest.

I had started big, and where bigger than the crossroads between state secrets and personal lies? I now had a clear idea of the three things that are necessary to sustain a complex lie.

The first is belief. An agent has to believe in what they are doing. If they do not believe in themselves, how could anyone else? The second is commitment. They need to tell a persuasive, plausible and malleable story – again and again... and again. The third is that there is an extraordinarily fine line between truth and lies. The most successful lies are daringly close to the truth. Belief, commitment and truth: the three unexpected ingredients of successful subterfuge.

I also saw, up close and personal, examples of how expectation can make people fall for the simplest lies; how the most basic mis-truths can become a labyrinth and how, if a liar wants to find their way back through the maze, they need their own strict rules: a golden thread to pull them through.

But setting aside the chill of talking to committed liars, the frustrations of hunting for female spies and the twists and turns of those three lives, what really stayed with me was the remarkable effort needed to create even the smallest illusion. To shift perception, bend time and change facts. To get off that train, with an armed enemy soldier still staring at you, and make sure you get to safety with your transmitter intact.

CHAPTER 5

WHAT IS A LIE? | *THREE PARTS*

‘ Trust and integrity are precious resources, easily squandered, hard to regain. They can thrive only on a foundation of respect for veracity.’

Respect for veracity. I eyed this quote from the celebrated philosopher and ethicist Sissela Bok with some trepidation. Later in the same book on the moral implications of lying, she writes:

> The function of the principle of veracity as a foundation is evident when we think of trust. I can have different kinds of trust: that you will treat me fairly, that you will have my interests at heart, that you will do me no harm. But if I do not trust your word, can I have genuine trust in the first three? If there is no confidence in the truthfulness of others, is there any way to assess their fairness, their intentions to help or to harm? How, then, can they be trusted? Whatever matters to human beings, trust is the atmosphere in which it thrives.[1]

Bok's book was published in 1978 and is referred to without hesitation

---

1   *Lying: Moral Choice in Public and Private Life*, Sissela Bok (1978).

and numerous times as *the* book on lying. (Sample review quotes: 'ground-breaking', 'influential', 'seminal'.) It also won the Orwell Prize that year for its 'Distinguished Contribution to Honesty and Clarity in Public Language'. It is hard to argue with an honest book that champions the truth.

This eminent philosopher was raised in Sweden and Switzerland, studied at the Sorbonne and Harvard, is married to a former president of Harvard and is the daughter of not one but two Nobel Prize winners. I am an ex-journalist with a chequered cardiac history who thinks lies are fascinating. Surely, I should just take her word for it that lies are bad and stop poking around? Her considered, nuanced work made me hesitate. Was I on a fool's errand?

As I persisted in my quest, this small, 87-year-old lady with very blue eyes kept popping up in my head, gently telling me to stop typing, switch off my computer and study truth instead. But it was too late, I was hooked. I had an idea about lies and I could not let go just because it risked being ill-conceived, unwise and even immoral.

For a start, I suspected that by vilifying lies as a whole, we were missing something very important – the power of lies to do good. And my hunch was that little lies had a particular power to do good.

The spies had taught me a lot – and not just to keep watch on my phone as it keeps watch on me. But what Foxtrot, Dean and Rose had not done was help me to get to grips with the complex world of day-to-day lies, the lies almost all of us are capable of telling. If the biggest of lies are incredibly hard to spot, I had a sense that little lies would be devilishly difficult to pin down. I realised that before I could go any further, I had to answer one rather daunting question: what is a lie?

I typed 'tell a lie' into Google and it took less than half a second to spit out 4.34 billion results.

That is more than 4 billion potential lies found in less time than it takes to blink. 'Thou shalt not bear false witness' is an unequivocal instruction, millennia old, but it seems that we do and we do it all the time.

So, what do I know, simply from being a human, living side by side with other humans? I know that lies are subjective: one person's sweet thought could be a sly manoeuvre to someone else. I know that no matter how much I prepare myself with a mental matrix to identify and sort lies instantly, I still fall prey to them and they rarely lose their power to bewilder. I also know that the smallest, flimsiest, most apparently insignificant lie can be the one that holds you hostage for years, decades even.

The questions started to multiply the more closely I looked. Why do we change things? Why do we tell stories a certain way? Art and folk songs, cave paintings and scripture – they all show humans finding ways to tell and retell their stories. We learn that our physical lives are finite, we perceive a past, present and future, we have the power to ask 'why' and our answers come in a narrative. A subjective one. My story is not necessarily your story, history may resemble neither and then there is always Foxtrot's 'third eye' to remember – the dispassionate view of events on the ground at a certain time.

And what of religion? What role does it play in the stories we tell? Christianity, Judaism and Islam all have commandments against falsehoods, instructions on following the straight path, a truth that existed before humankind. One of the eight practices of Buddhism is 'the right speech': its goal is that we should abstain from 'lying, divisive or abusive speech and idle chatter'.[2] In Hinduism, honesty is one of the eternal duties, or Dharma. In one of the oldest living religions, Zoroastrianism, Asha (truth) is a divine entity through which the Creator acts against Druj (deceit).[3] If it is a question of faith and belief, the concept of truth is paramount – how else could religion set about enlightening, improving and instructing us? A book about truth would be a beautifully pure thing, but it is precisely the complicated accommodations of daily life that fascinate me.

So what about me? Can I be trusted? Do my own experiences make me more honest? Or do they simply make me more careful about the tricks of telling? I kept Bok's book in mind as I decided to follow this thread wherever it led me. No matter how honest I try to be, I know I tweak versions of myself, I tailor my tales. Which tribe do I belong to? Why did I do that? Who am I? When I think about my answers, I realise it is hard not to stray from the truth – not to embroider, edit the facts or fabricate by degrees depending who I am speaking to.

Finally, what about a lie's power to do good? Some lies had forced my nearest and dearest apart, but others bound families, communities, society together. I thought about my parents' lie about my grandmother's heart attack when my memory was just beginning to return and I had asked how she was. Seen like this, certain lies are a vital social glue, but how could I prove this?

As I finally stopped playing hunt-the-spy – and managed to avoid

---

2   'Maha-cattarisaka Sutta: The Great Forty', accesstoinsight.org/tipitaka/mn/mn.117.than.html
3   'Zoroastrianism', www.iranicaonline.org/articles/zoroastrianism-i-historical-review

ending up with the spies hunting me (I think) – I turned instead to white lies.

Where do white lies sit in all those dramatic deceits I had discovered? What about ordinary untruths, the ones that are never detected, do not shake the world nor change history? Do they count? Do they matter? It was time to find my answers. I knew that Foxtrot was 'terrible' at fibbing, but I had an inkling that many people, myself included, were pretty damn good at it.

'You look wonderful.'

'This is great.'

'We'll be fine. Trust me.'

I started to talk to friends, family, strangers about this quietly amazing, often unnoticed thing we do. What I found again and again was that when I asked about lies, people recoiled. But when I called them 'fibs', suddenly everyone was happy to talk. They discussed them as if discussing necessary foibles. Tweaking the truth, it seems, is just another everyday event. As long as you do not call it a lie.

Of all those I spoke to, it was the parents of toddlers and tweens who helped me begin to answer the question of what is a lie. They led me to a trio of fibs. There they were, hiding in plain sight, just waiting to be discovered: Father Christmas, the Easter Bunny and the Tooth Fairy, skipping with delight.

This is an unusual but mighty alliance that has done battle with many a sceptical parent over the centuries. The gang has fought off modern technology and online exposés, and they persist to this day, hogging the chimney, laying eggs and patrolling children's pillows without ever being caught. How have they done it?

Apart from the allure of presents, chocolates and money, there seem to be bigger things at play. Religion, culture and tradition have helped them to take root but so too has the basic need to explain complex things with one bright image. In their different ways, they all begin to tell a child how they relate to the outside world. They are like a socialising mechanism with a big beard, a fluffy tail or a pretty tutu.

These white lies are safe, recognised by society and in certain parts of the world, they are expected. So why call them lies, with all the distaste that invokes? Is this a hint of the power they possess – the power to transform?

I was beginning to see that if I wanted to understand our contro-versial talent for truth-fiddling, then a) even the gentlest examples needed to qualify and b) I had to get a handle on the words people use when talking about white-lie-fibs. When it came to words and their types, function and meaning, there was only one person I could turn to.

Ian Watson could be a librarian. He could be a rocket scientist or even a superhero – he is difficult to decipher. His clothes are un-assuming and his youthful face has no giveaway lines. The biggest clue about what he does is his intense eyes that let no detail go un-noticed. Dr Watson is a consumer of information – and this Watson would certainly not play second fiddle to Sherlock Holmes. He is a professor of modern languages at Christ Church, Oxford, and taught me linguistics when I was an undergraduate at Brasenose College. I thought if anyone could help me to crack the white-lie-fibs code, he could.

It was almost two decades since he had tutored me, but nothing had changed. Christ Church was still a daunting set of gates and quads and stone pathways. It still took me several attempts to find his staircase. And when I did find it, I forgot again about the two sets of doors to go through to get to his study. I knocked on the first door and waited.

Silence.

I remembered, opened the first and knocked on the second one. ('Heh. It's an intelligence test.') I found him at his desk, consuming a mountain of papers and books and unfinished essays. Nothing seemed to have changed in his world. But I had. And I came with a lot of questions.

This was my thinking. If I was going to explore the many forms of deceit – minor to major – I had to decide on one term. And so, a little ruthlessly (thank you Dame Stella), I ended up with this definition: anything that has been changed or transformed in the telling is a lie. Yes, even the Easter Bunny. What matters is the kind of lie we tell, and I would have to find a simple way to assess and identify lies.

Old habits die hard and before my meeting with Dr Watson, I had done some frantic, last-minute studying. I started with my first obvious challenge: finding the words.

Evolved language has to be one of humanity's great gifts, but definitions can be slippery: our words reflect us as much as they reflect our society, and they change. Across languages, it turns out that lying is the wriggliest of all subjects. Is it confection, protection or deception? Is a mendacious man the same as a father who makes up fairy tales? We 'tell' lies, but does that make them stories? Lies come in many forms, including silence, but words, as one of our main units of communication, gave me a useful gauge of the importance society attributes to lies.

It turns out – just as I had found when I started surveying those around me – that in all languages, the word 'liar' carries a stigma; in Parliaments and assemblies across the world, it is a banned term and lies and liars even muscle their way into the most ancient languages and cuneiform script. Enter 'to lie' in the Pennsylvania Sumerian Dictionary, which has managed to digitise this part of the Bronze Age,[4] and you get three symbols that look like spiders' webs. They translate as: *eme* 'tongue' + *sig* 'weak' + *gu* 'eat'. The dictionary equates this with the phrase 'to speak falsely'.

The idea of swallowing a weak tongue is a vivid image of what might happen to someone who lies too much. Even in this glimpse into the Sumerian symbols of the 3rd millennium BC, lies are singled out as a negative activity. These results cannot be compared to an exhaustive list of terms in a modern dictionary, but if you are looking for nuance, 'imagine', 'pretend' and 'tale' do not return any results. Enter 'liar' and there are four results ranging from 'a liar?' to 'extreme liar'.

The word itself is so resonant yet so loosely defined that it is no wonder people become wary whenever I start talking about lies. In contemporary British English, an army of words attempts to define the quality and character of a lie. The verbs queue up to be included. In fact, over the years, I have built up quite a collection.

---

4 'ePSD', http://psd.museum.upenn.edu/nepsd-frame.html (2006). The ePSD is an online lexicon of Sumerian as it occurs in cuneiform texts from ancient Iraq, dating from about 2700 to 1600 BC. It allows a search of the basic definitions of words in English and is linked to a corpus of 90,000 texts. The project was carried out in the Babylonian Section of the University of Pennsylvania Museum of Anthropology and Archaeology, working with projects including the University of California, Los Angeles, the University of Oxford and the Max Planck Institute for the History of Science, Berlin.

From airbrush to bamboozle, bluff, bullshit, calumniate, cheat, con, conceal, concoct, confabulate, confect, contrive, counterfeit, deceive, defame, defraud, delude, disguise, dissemble, dissimulate, doctor and dupe (running total = twenty-two), to embellish, equivocate, evade, fabricate, fabulise, fake, falsify, feign, fib, flatter, forge, hide, hoax and gaslight (thirty-six), on to: inveigle, invent, kid, libel, make up, manoeuvre, manufacture, mask, masquerade, misdirect, mislead, misrepresent, obfuscate, perjure, pretend, prevaricate, scam, sham, slander, sophisticate, swindle, trick and whitewash (fifty-nine), and that's not even thinking about diddling, skanking, selling a pup, yanking a chain or telling a porky (sixty-four).

I rattle off my research to Dr Watson. Then I try out my theory.

While a splendid array of verbs articulates lying, there is none for 'truthing' – and the same applies to other languages. The way humans communicate seems to be hardwired to make truth a concept, not an act. It becomes an absolute, in relation to which we have at least sixty-four ways of 'doing' things.

He nods. Dr Watson keeps nodding as I babble on, encouraging me with raised eyebrows, chin resting on hands and the odd spate of frowning.

'Yes…' I wait. 'Yes,' he says. He is thinking. He laughs and adds 'whopper' to my slang list.

'We have all these terms for things that are to some extent not being completely truthful,' he says. 'Whether you want to call them lying is a different matter. Yes? And sometimes it is extremely difficult to judge when you cross the border.'

I am fascinated. Even this 10th-dan blackbelt of words is not comfortable using 'lie' to cover every instance of truth-tweakery.

But then he begins reeling off a complex set of propositions tied to the act of lying, and he does, quite quickly, start bracketing it under the same term: lies. Whether he likes it or not, for the purposes of our discussion, we need one universal term for adjusting the truth – and this is it.

'When you said you were interested in this, I think my first response was that people lie for two sorts of reasons which are perhaps connected.' He says that the first is to gain some personal benefit. That is the minority case. And the rest of the time, people lie to spare themselves difficulty.

'Probably a difficulty they hoped would be fairly minor, and yet it would be unpleasant if they had to face it. And I come face to face with that professionally… when students lie to me about why they haven't done their work.'

There is a long emphasis on that last word. Is he thinking back to my time as a student?

'Generally speaking… it's just that they don't want to admit that they were lazy… or they just didn't get round to it.'

Seriously, is he talking about me? I must have lied to him once, at least, if I am getting these thoughts, sitting in this chair, listening to him as I used to twenty years ago.

'That, in a sense, is just a variant on what we all accept are forms of politeness.' I feel politely relieved.

He discusses 'politeness phenomena' in different languages, how different cultures 'systematise the value of saying something unpleasant to somebody'. How politeness 'softens reality'. He compares his own experience of the forthright Dutch with the squeamish

British. 'We [Brits] are probably far more adept at social lies than other countries,' he says.

And is there a common linguistic trait, across languages, when people lie?

'No,' he says, swatting that theory in mid-air. In terms of formulating lies, he says, in all languages people seek to lie as 'naturalistically' as possible. 'And I'm not sure that there is a linguistic clue to the fact that you're doing it.'

And what about all those 'lie' words? Why is there no 'truthing'? He quickly comes up with two reasons for the lack of a verb.

'One is that we take it as the default case that someone is telling the truth, and how would society work if that were not so? Secondly, there is the notion of "one truth", "one state of the universe is so about any particular phenomenon" and human beings are not capable of "creating" this truth, whereas they can create the lies they tell.

'So you can see why you would have verbs for lying,' he says. 'I don't create the truth, it is there. So I can only allude to it. Whereas a lie is something that a human being creates.'

I have what I came for. We talk a while longer, until he politely reminds me of the time. As I leave, shutting the two doors behind me, I realise one of the things I find so fascinating about lies. Truth and lies are bound together and define each other, but the manner in which a person tells a lie, even in the smallest ways, is what reveals so much about them. People show themselves by how they hide themselves.

I might fib with words or without words, I might use sixty-four different ways of describing it but when I am doing it, it is not just a bad thing, black and white, full stop. Lies are shaded, complex and varied. The number of words used to describe a type of lie suggests that it is a significant social activity and the politeness factor shows how lies can contribute to social harmony.

So to measure everyday lies and their significance, I began to use words. They were my 'How'. To try to be Watsonian about it: words identify, categorise and communicate the many different degrees of a lie.

To get the measure of different lies, I had to find a way to sit them all together. I went from higher reaches of professorial thought and got as low-tech and basic as I could. Primary-school basic: I borrowed a whiteboard and marker pen and started scribbling.

By then, I had been talking about white-lie-fibs for so long that I had amassed a wide range of anecdotes that I could not retell but that I could use to fathom the different degrees of lying. From small childhood lies that still bothered adults, to lies about infidelity, petty theft, domestic violence and self-harm.

There was the GP who admitted to occasionally 'editing' death certificates so that the cause of their patient's death would be less upsetting for the family. There was the woman who found out she was adopted in her sixties. She only discovered the lie her parents had told her when she was forced to get a copy of her birth certificate so she could travel. She then hid the truth from her own child for another twenty years, before suddenly blurting it out at his birthday meal. And finally, there was the friend of a friend who quietly spent everything the family had and everything they did not have shopping online in secret until the bailiffs came.

Some lies were sweet and kind, some were frivolous, a couple were shocking. And these were just the ones that people remembered or mentioned when the subject of my book came up.

I also applied my lessons from Dr Watson. No 'truthing', just establishing a lie's relationship to the truth – the different lies we 'create'. I drew a plain box for truth and started adding the pile of mismatched lies next to it. Then I moved them around. How much did they distort the truth? What effect did they have? Where should they sit? What kinds of lies ought to be in the grey zone between white and black?

It was 11 a.m. on a balmy August morning in England. It was such a subjective enterprise that at another time, in another setting, the lies might have sat in different places. On that day, this was where they sat.

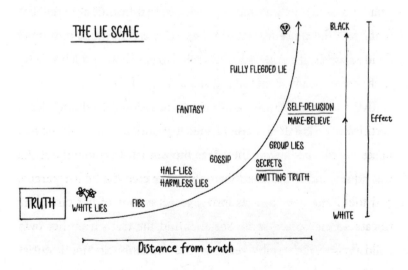

At the lower end are the *white lies*, the halcyon days in which the nitty-gritty of a story does not matter, just the happy ending. These are hotly followed by *fibs*, the dodges of childhood that carry quite easily into adulthood. *Harmless lies* are a step up because they take harm into consideration, but even if they are slightly less white, they are still made of good fabric. They are *half-lies*.

Omitting the truth, the lie that comes cloaked in silence, still has one foot in the 'white zone'. *Keeping secrets* is an act of deception, but because it can be one of protection too it is one small step up only. *Gossip* involves knowingly spreading something sensationalised, something likely to have at least a measure of untruth to it. A small amount can be entertainment; a large amount can be toxic. In the days of social-media shaming, these lies seem a little darker.

Group lies, the ones that are told in packs, sit firmly in the grey zone. When a lie is suspected but never questioned because it is part of the status quo, it has the power to weigh heavily on a conscience. I thought of the institutions embroiled in the Jimmy Savile scandal in 2012, or the abuse scandals in the Catholic Church, or the global financial crisis of 2008. 'Why didn't they do something?' It was such a common refrain at the time, but was it a fair one? If a group behaves in a certain way, it takes a mighty individual to stand apart. The grey zone is a difficult place, and appropriately it got greyer as I found myself erasing one inky lie to replace it with another. Collective silence and wilful blindness were other contenders.

Some of the words still darted around, even though I thought I had found their place on the scale.

Is *fantasy* an acceptable sideline, outside reality, or does it undermine the truths of someone's life? The boundaries started to blur. Where should propaganda sit, when the effect it has is multiplied by the mass of people who fell prey to it? And what about *make-believe*, with the forceful verb 'make', and its wayward partner *self-delusion*?

I put them higher up because of their potential to distort and corrupt, but still, make-believe could just amount to a fairy tale.

My semantic scale started tilting alarmingly as it hit the *fully fledged lie*, the conscious act, and reached critical mass in the world of sadistic deception.

Here, I could not forget the despicably innocent eyes of British murderer Ian Huntley as he made an appeal in 2002 to find Jessica Chapman and Holly Wells, the young victims of a crime he had committed. Why had the eyes of a child killer suddenly appeared in my mind?

If I wanted to find out about the lies we are all capable of telling, I had to explore as much of the grey zone as I could, but what I found chilling was how easily it bordered a very dark territory. In the grey zone, lies can still be good – and this is what I wanted to explore. In the black zone, all bets are off. This is where Huntley sits, adopting the gaze of a little boy who could never, ever do anything wrong.

As I stood in front of the whiteboard, those clear eyes came back to me, translucent with deception. Decades later and thanks to the criminal justice system, I knew what really lay behind that gaze – and I knew that his kind of lies were not the ones I was after.

I put down the marker pen. By then, I had ink on my fingers. The more I looked at the different types of lies in the grey zone, the more I moved them around and looked at them in relation to each other, the more I could see the potential for beauty as well as ugliness. There, before me, was the majority of deceptive behaviour, neither evil nor saintly, but most people on most days. There was good and bad, there was conscious, subconscious and unconscious.

But if I had a better handle on how we lie – at least sixty-four

'Hows', in fact – it was not enough. The manner in which we lie was one thing, but motive and context were crucial too. My 'How' needed a couple of partners if I was really going to pin down what a lie was. The second element was easy to identify but hard to capture. It was my reason for digging up painful and delightful memories, for following one form of human behaviour like a lunatic for years and years. It was the 'Why'.

But how could I capture motive? I sought out a senior lawyer. The legal profession does, after all, work on the cliff face of other people's lies day in, day out. The lawyer I quizzed was duly unimpressed. She pointed out that a straightforward distinction already existed: a legal one. Knowledge of wrongdoing, aka a guilty mind or *mens rea*. I looked it up: 'The act does not make a person guilty unless the mind is also guilty.'

I had gone back to square one. If I wanted to explore the grey world of lies, it was not right and wrong nor the red lines of criminality that would help me. It was the blue lines I had already drawn. If I had picked out and scribbled on the board a set of lies, without realising it, I had arranged them according to assumed motive – and that was what fluctuated so much with each different type of lie.

For my spies, their motives were entwined in the ethics of state, religion and individual action. For myself, it would take years to unpick certain motives. For others, I would come across many motives as I worked on the book, from the funny (toddlers), to the horrifying (a convicted criminal), to the inspiring (a Nobel Peace Prize-winning journalist).

In 2017, I wondered what the internet would have to say about who were the top liars in the world – and why they had lied. Those were the days when search engines were less refined in finding results to suit the searcher and it was still possible to come up with more left-field, unexpected results. There was not much science to my approach but I did find lists from across the world and even old web pages in bad formatting that had long been abandoned. I became a little hypnotised by the endeavour and I ended up with forty lists in total, which added up to 213 different liars as nominated by everyone from experts and authors to passionate amateurs and single-issue bloggers. Some lists copied each other, some were niche and some were utterly over-the-top; what they all shared was a fascination for motive.

The three people who featured most were Bill Clinton (whose affair with Monica Lewinsky became an internet juggernaut in 1998; he appeared in twenty of the lists), Richard Nixon (the Watergate scandal, 1972, nineteen lists) and Bernie Madoff (arrested in 2008 for a whopping $65 billion fraud, sixteen lists). And just like the female spies, far fewer women made the lists of top liars. I counted them: there were 173 men (including two who pretended to be women) and thirty-one women. The others were groups of people listed as a single entry, like suspect Olympic teams or car giants accused of manipulating emissions data, and two rather old creatures: one, a wooden horse from Troy, the other, the Garden of Eden's resident snake. The lists were too mismatched to aggregate, occasionally libellous, dubious and inaccurate, but they did give me what felt like a democratic sample of opinion.

The woman who got the most mentions (eight) has the motive that is hardest to pin down. She is the imposter most picked by people for their lists.

Her Wikipedia entry is quite something and it allows me to give her a proper introduction. She was the Grand Duchess Anastasia Nikolaevna of Russia, from the House of Romanov, the youngest of the four daughters of Tsar Nicholas II, the last Emperor of Russia. Or so she claimed. That name would have made her the lost daughter of the royal family executed in 1918 during the Bolshevik Revolution.[5]

Her history of names began in 1920 when she was first known to have appeared, without papers, in a German asylum and was called *Fräulein Unbekannt* (Miss Unknown). Gradually, according to the whispers of her fellow patients, her identity ascended into the exalted ranks of Russian royalty, first as Tatiana, the second daughter; then Anastasia. By the time she became Anna Tschaikovsky, she had been released and was being alternatively hosted and questioned by a series of people connected to the royal family.

Those who fervently denied her were countered by those who passionately believed in Anastasia/Anna. She became Anna Anderson when she ran into trouble in New York, but continued the merry-go-round of belief and disbelief, rising and falling in the high echelons of society. Was she the troubled and potentially amnesiac Polish factory worker Franziska Schanzkowska, who an investigator had unearthed, or was she the real thing? She and her supporters continued to insist that she was Anastasia until her death in 1984. However, almost twenty-five years later, DNA evidence would prove

---

5 'Anna Anderson', Wikipedia, https://en.wikipedia.org/wiki/Anna_Anderson

otherwise. She was a fake – and one that could be genetically linked to the great-nephew of the Polish factory worker in question. Incontrovertible evidence aside, her story is so compelling and confounding that it has been explored in several books and plays, a silent film, an Oscar-winning one starring Ingrid Bergman, two ballets, a mini-series nominated for a Golden Globe and even an animated musical drama.[6] Motive can be the most haunting aspect of deceit. For me, this is the second part of what makes a lie, the 'Why'.

The third part was less obvious but was essentially about practicalities. In what context did someone tell their lie? I would see a vivid example of this when I interviewed a leading industry figure whose deceit nearly cost him everything. A white lie told many times over many years to many colleagues has a very different effect when it is told once in court papers. Context is capital.

The third defining feature I returned to repeatedly was the circumstance in which a lie is told – the 'Where'. The timing of a lie, when it is told, can be crucial to its effect or success, but for me, it was all about context.

I thought again of the unimpressed lawyer I had assailed with questions. The courtroom is an arena where there can be no grey. It is a place that insists on the truth, the whole truth and nothing but the truth. Yet, deliciously, the result is that truths themselves can often be in short supply. If a court is society's highest forum of truth, then those who do battle within it are bound to be the first to symbolise our lies. When I discussed lying with others, lawyers were often the first profession cited in a list of liars. In defence of

---

6   Ibid.

my learned legal friends, the deeper I waded into the grey zone, the braver I thought they were.

Lawyers were not the only ones on people's lie lists. Journalists, politicians and bankers followed closely, because what counts is having the power to tell a story and the sphere in which you tell it, whether that is a television studio, a Parliament or a glass tower.

But if context can be about professions and places, it can also be linguistic. The words around a lie are just as important as the lie itself. Lies can be helped – or revealed – by repeated words, absent words and word whiskers such as a repeated 'um', 'ah' or 'like'. One missing word can puncture a whole message, or several used too many times quite quickly broadcast a motive. It seemed that no matter how hard I tried to look elsewhere, all my answers rested in words.

I should be more candid about this obsession. My mother is a former air hostess who brought us up surrounded by snippets of different languages. She is French/Italian, teaches French and met my English/Irish father in Beirut, Lebanon. He was a crossword fanatic, a book lover and a part-time poet. We lived in Luxembourg and Nigeria when I was little. I studied languages, became a journalist and am now a speechwriter. I even had a stint as part of the word police, when I worked for a few years as a news sub-editor at *The Times*. I have a paid-for dictionary app on my phone. OK, I'm an addict.

As a journalist, I knew the power of headlines, the dangers of libel and the perils of the odd missing 'not' – for instance in the phrase 'not guilty'. I currently work as a speechwriter for the executive committee at Shell, one of the world's largest public companies. My job is to find the right words for the decision makers who speak in the controversial forum of big energy. Those words need to be true to the facts – and true to the speaker. Context is crucial, and within this context I am now an even fiercer watcher of words.

This obsession with words, stories and how they are told has also meant that I have long hoovered up examples of interviews, press conferences and speeches by famous – and proven – liars. In those examples, the circumstances of their guilty admissions were just as key to the context as the words they did – or did not – use. These were lies that had been categorically proven, told publicly and told long ago enough that all the elements around the story had settled and the different viewpoints had coalesced.

For a classic case of right words, wrong message, Lance Armstrong's two-hour interview with Oprah Winfrey is a goldmine. After years of denials, the former champion was confessing tersely rather than humbly to taking performance-enhancing drugs – an impression that was reinforced by the pattern of his words, rather than their individual meaning.

In January 2013, the disgraced seven-time Tour de France winner agreed to do the 'no holds barred' interview, broadcast in two one-hour slots. The theme of the interview was truth – and he duly said variations of it thirty-seven times in 7,240 words.[7]

However, twenty of those were references to 'not true' – he was confessing to a specific, and tightly defined, set of things only. He said formulations of 'apology' and 'sorry' a total of thirteen times, but those were equalled by the word 'win' (thirteen derivations), then 'leader' (nine) and 'lies' (nine). 'Wrong', 'ashamed' and 're-morse' got one outing each but 'comeback' got seven. And what

---

7 'Full Transcript: Lance Armstrong on Oprah', https://armchairspectator.wordpress.com/2013/01/23/full-transcript-lance-armstrong-on-oprah/

about that corker, 'guilt' or 'guilty'? He does not say it once. But before I get an angry man in Lycra in hot pursuit, I must emphasise that this is speculative and illustrative only.

It was not just fallen stars I started to parse. I could hear everyday language masking truths all the time, in a host of subtle ways. In each case, these micro lies were determined by context.

I talked to teenagers – those who would let me. For instance, the 'honest' in 'to be honest' very rarely is – and this takes on a life of its own in text-speak on hand-held devices. In this wild zone governed by teenagers, it has become 'TBH' and morphed into a noun on social media, where 'a TBH' is a kind of watery pleasantry posted on each other's profiles in return for 'a like' – a heart symbol or the thumbs-up so popularised by Facebook. Hence the frequent plea: 'Like for a TBH,' which would then be reciprocated with the public statement: 'TBH you're amaze.'

If I say I am being 'honest', or 'H', in any one of these contexts, you will know that my message has as much depth and integrity as a grunt – or an algorithm. And if I thought a person could be only honest or dishonest, then an informed teen would doubtless say to me: 'TBBH [to be brutally honest], you need to rethink your absolutes.' If truth can be nasty or brutal ('TBBH no one likes you…'), at least the small lie of a TBH can be kinder ('…because TBH you're so pretty'). The setting is key. On the wrong platform, a declaration of honesty can be the worst fraud or the height of cruelty.

The more I parsed, the more I saw that linguistic context makes it easier both to trick someone and to be caught out. The trick comes from the expectation that context creates. The trap comes when expectations are not met.

Context, verbal or otherwise, had firmly qualified as the third part of my trio. Suddenly, I remembered being in the main conference room at *The Times*. It was another unsporting tale, a star athlete was about to speak publicly for the first time and the sports editor was unusually animated. This was the moment, he said. This would make a difference. It was about golf – and even to the deeply uninterested parties in the room (me), it seemed like a moment that should not be missed.

It had all begun years before in 1997 when a promising 21-year-old teed off at the Masters. The crowd knew immediately that they were watching something special. When he won by twelve shots, a tournament record that still stands today, they realised they had seen a moment of sporting history. Not only had he destroyed a field of experienced rivals, he was the youngest champion and the first African-American to put on the famous green jacket. Tiger Woods was special.

That year, he moved into the world No. 1 slot two times. By 2009, he had been world No. 1 all year for eight years, won his fourteenth major title and become the first billion-dollar athlete and an embodiment of the American dream who in April that year would be invited to meet President Barack Obama in the Oval Office.

However, that same year, the world suddenly saw a different side to a man who kept himself so hidden off the fairway that even his super-yacht was named *Privacy*. In November, the *National Enquirer* accused him of being a philanderer and liar. The tabloid had caught a tiger.

Days after publication and just after celebrating Thanksgiving with his family, sensation struck again. Woods crashed his car into a tree just outside his home. He was found by his wife, Elin Norde-gren. The couple at first gave different accounts of what happened, and in an irony that tickled commentators pink, speculation grew that his wife had set upon him with a golf club and chased him in a golf buggy after she found proof of his infidelities.

Over the next two weeks, Woods released three statements. The first said that the accident was his responsibility alone; the second apologised for his 'transgressions' as more and more women came forward; the third announced he would take 'an indefinite break from professional golf'. He dropped out of public view and straight into therapy. Two months later, he was back and announced a press conference. Would he find his way out of this most difficult of bunkers?

It is 19 February 2010. The press conference is on home territory: the PGA Tour headquarters in Florida. In front of him is an audi-ence of forty carefully selected people, including his mother, who sits in the front row. The cap he so often wears is off. The setting is orchestrated to the finest detail, but that does not help him. He walks in with the dread clump of a robot and the wary eyes of a nocturnal creature.

'Many of you in the room are my friends,' he begins.[8] Is that a plea or an instruction? 'Many of you in this room know me.' His mouth is dry, he stumbles over his words, his eyes are watery.

'Many of you have cheered for me, or worked with me, or sup-ported me, and now, every one of you has good reason to be critical

---

8 Transcript: http://edition.cnn.com/2010/US/02/19/tiger.woods.transcript/. Video: 'Tiger addresses private indiscretions in 2010 public news conference' (19 February 2010), www.golfchannel.com/video/tiger-woods-full-apology-press-conference

of me. I want to say to each of you, simply and directly...' There is a long pause. He seems on the verge of tears.

'I am deeply sorry for my irresponsible and selfish behavior.'

The words are personal, direct, humble. But as he extends his apologies, another theme starts to emerge. His reputation. He apologises to his friends, his family, his fans, his team and... his sponsors. The wider audience is repeatedly reminded of the wholesome circle of people around him. He addresses emotional subjects but proceeds to shut them all down one by one. Domestic violence, performance-enhancing drugs, a broken marriage? All off-topic. He confesses emphatically to infidelity ('I was unfaithful. I had affairs. I cheated.') but will discuss nothing else. To make matters worse, he then refuses to take questions. He may have apologised profusely, but the way he did it spoke only of insincerity and that was because of the context.

Hundreds of journalists had travelled from across the world for this moment, but they had to watch by video link in a building a mile away from the clubhouse and then were denied direct access to Woods. When he finished, he hugged his mother, then most of the front row, then went back through a curtained door. This was theatre, but it was bad theatre. The word 'reputation' did not feature once, but his was damaged and his career took years to piece back together.

Context is a killer – and an excellent way to spot a lie and judge what kind of lie it is, especially when a moment has been consigned to the past with a great, big rubber stamp on it that says 'false'. If the context that undermined Armstrong was the words he used in his admission of guilt, and for Woods, it was his words along with the setting in which he spoke, what about when someone's context is prepared to perfection over decades – and that is what undoes them? My third proven liar can still be found on YouTube, in action, denying her misdeeds in grainy footage from 2002.

Enter America's impeccable domestic goddess: Martha Stewart. She had forged a career on wholesome goodness, on proving that she was the right person to trust at the heart of every home. No one expected an insider-trading scandal to come steaming her way, and when the story emerged, she dealt with it the only way she knew how.

She agreed to address the allegations on her regular live cooking slot on *The Early Show*. Her condition was that the questions should be asked in her usual kitchen setting and there would be no separate interview. Her lawyers approved; it was her natural habitat and she would be questioned by Jane Clayson, the presenter who usually assisted her. Stewart was the mistress of telling people how to live their lives; her image was built on presentation and perfection, attention to detail. What could go wrong? One very sharp and pointed object.

She was betrayed by her own attempt to recapture her normal, homely demeanour. She should have given the questions the attention they deserved, but instead of answering them candidly, or in any meaningful way, she dismissively set about chopping a cabbage with a very large knife. All the audience could see was a quietly agitated woman wielding a blade, which she then waved at her interviewer as she tried to make light of the issues, insisting that she would be 'exonerated of any ridiculousness'.

A carefully constructed but fake kitchen was the worst place for her to dissimulate – in that environment, she was no longer a goddess but a mere mortal whose veneer had cracked and briefly revealed a ferocity that few had seen before. 'I want to focus on my salad, because that's why we're here,' she said, slicing away and laughing a little too hard.

She later admitted that the interview had been a mistake. It was the last time she would contribute to the programme – and she was indicted a year later. On 5 March 2004, she was found guilty of obstruction of agency proceedings, conspiracy and making false statements, and went on to spend five months in jail. She would, however, make a big comeback and retain the uncanny ability to diversify and grow her brand. At every step, it seemed her self-belief carried her through. She believed in her own story – and in this context, there would always be a happy ending.

The context of a lie has a final quirk. Our surroundings are not just capable of exposing our deceits but enabling and endorsing them too. I thought of all the places in which someone is positively encouraged to lie. Take the World Series of Poker, which every year features a gleeful winner surrounded by a mountain of cash. The game would certainly lose its appeal if the players could not lie. In this context, telling the truth is just another tactic.

Similarly, I thought of the devoted legions of crime-fiction fans, myself among them. How we cherish an author who can twist and turn a tale, whether they evoke a tiny English village with murderers in tweed, a Norwegian city with a surfeit of killers or the dark drains and blood-thirsty clowns of small-town America. When I read them, I think: trick me, as I flick hurriedly through the pages; lie to me, because in this forum, I want you to. Who killed Roger Ackroyd? I would be ruining a great story if I answered the title question, but suffice to say that in this tale Agatha Christie tells her readers one great big fib.

Equally, I thought of eager queues over the centuries to see ladies sawn in two. When the crafty prestidigitator confounds us, we pay for the pleasure, we crave the lie. We play along even though our participation is what makes the illusion work so well: we want the rabbit to disappear. But the moment we step outside the auditorium and the context changes, there is a silent understanding that tricks have to stop.

The How, the Where and the Why – I finally had my own way of weighing up lies, and by looking at them in this way I could see how big their presence was in our daily interactions. But this also showed me something else. I had separated the shadow zone of the spies and the grey zone of day-to-day white-lie-fibs on the basis that one involved transformation and the other was more prosaic. However, the more I looked at both zones, the more I could see that they involved exactly the same mind-bending abilities. I remembered my amnesia and my difficulty in understanding different versions of the same story. I saw that every time we lie, whether fib, fraud or felony, we use the same complex mental tools to do it. These were the tools I lost when I lost my memory but that I felt return as my brain healed.

Where does this ability come from, when does it all start and how do we do this thing we do – and do it so very well? I needed to go from big lies, to small lies, to very small liars. I steeled myself and prepared to enter the only marginally safer world of psychologists, scientists and toddlers.

CHAPTER 6

WHERE DOES IT ALL BEGIN? | *TODDLERS*

'Time really flies,' says the genial head of the Institute of Child Study at the University of Toronto, when I ask him how long he has been studying lying in children. Professor Kang Lee is surprisingly open, energetic and enthusiastic considering he specialises in such a delicate subject – but perhaps that is exactly why he managed to become a specialist in the first place. As soon as the video comes on, I realise how wrong I was to fear that he would be a haughty mega-brain with little time for questions.

He greets me with a megawatt smile that lights up the Skype screen. Behind him is a whiteboard full of mysterious hieroglyphs. He is in a hooded top, hair brushed into a spiky quiff, and has a youthful bounce as he speaks. Now I see why he answers his emails as Kang rather than Dr Lee – he is absolutely himself, no elevated status needed.

Kang is a leading figure in the study of children's lies. He has been at this for decades, his influential work is often quoted and misquoted, and he even had a hand in changing the legal system in Canada. I kept coming across his work as I started to look at little liars – every intriguing piece of research seemed to have his name attached to it in some form. Where did it all begin for him?

'I began my research on children's lying from 1995. When I first set my lab up, very few researchers were working on this topic.' It seems a gaping hole to me, but there was a surprisingly simple reason for this.

'There was a pervasive, common-sense view that children do not lie.' They did not lie? How could an educated society ignore this type of behaviour in its proto-adults? The answer is short. One word, two syllables. One of the great secret-makers. 'It was taboo.'

When Kang started his research, there were few others working on the topic – indeed, it has a patchy history. He credits the first study to one of the world's top taboo-busters: Charles Darwin. The polymath was the first to apply a magnifying glass to the subject in 1877 with his essay 'Biographical Sketch of an Infant',[1] which came from detailed notes on the behavioural changes of his first child William. At two years and eight months, Darwin notes a 'carefully planned deceit' involving a covert trip to the dining room and an outfit suddenly stained with pickle juice. What had he done? 'Nothing,' said William, 'go away!' The deceitfulness does not last, however, and Darwin notes that William 'soon became truthful, open and tender'.

Kang says that the Swiss psychologist Jean Piaget came next. Piaget picked up the thread more than five decades later with his studies on children's cognitive development. This was followed by the more systematic research on dishonesty in children by the Harvard professor Hugh Hartshorne and the priest Mark May, who published two volumes of their findings in 1928 and 1932. After that, he says, 'the field went very quiet', with only occasional reports:

---

1 'Biographical Sketch of an Infant', *Mind* (July 1877), http://darwin-online.org.uk/

When I came out of grad school, although people continued to believe children do not lie, the tide started to turn against this view in law and education and in policy-making. However, research on the topic was still rare. One reason is research ethics. It is such a taboo topic.

In email exchanges before our video call, Kang wrote that he encountered resistance on many fronts. He had several 'run-ins' with ethical boards as he moved from one university to another. When he left the University of California at San Diego to become head of the institute in Toronto, he hit another wall.

'My first application to the review board was turned down flat! I had second thoughts about the wisdom of moving there at the time.' The reason they gave was blunt.

'They said I should not study such a topic because it is not only unethical... but also useless.'

If research institutions did not dare to take a scientific approach to lying, who on earth would? Kang persisted. For him, there was more at stake than a new line of research.

'This view [that children did not lie] was so pervasive that the criminal courts in most parts of the world accepted children's testimonies at their face value. This led to many cases of miscarriage of justice.'

I started to think about young children as witnesses and how they might bring chaos to a courtroom. Why did they need children to testify?

'Mostly child abuse cases.' Kang's answer stopped me in my tracks. I had not thought about children's lies in this way: when it is their word against an adult's in a criminal context, and one in which events could give them great power – or none at all. In cases like these, innocent lies could cause as much damage as malicious ones. I thought of stories where, after years, it emerged that children had said what they thought they should say rather than the truth, or when they had misguidedly tried to cover up for someone else. I could not look at children's lies and ignore this dark side.

Kang explains that there were numerous high-profile cases in America in the 1990s. The problem came in the methods used to judge how reliable a child would be as a witness. The standard assessment was called the Competency Test and it hinged on testing whether a child grasped concepts such as 'oath', 'truth' and 'promise'. Some children with potentially vital information might be excluded because they did not seem to understand the full meaning of these words, while others, who understood without problem, could not be relied on to tell the truth. Kang's research and advice would prove indispensable for the Canadian courts. The key was getting young children to promise to tell the truth. They showed that making a child promise encouraged them to be truthful in a way that the Competency Test did not.[2] In 2006, the Canadian Parliament passed a law that led to a new legal procedure for admitting children as witnesses in the criminal court. This was based entirely on the research Kang and his team had conducted.

This was his moment. He showed the review board years of accumulated research that gently built on how to measure lying in

2 'The Competency of Children to Testify: Psychological Research Informing Canadian Law Reform', Nicholas Bala, Kang Lee, R. C. L. Lindsay and Victoria Talwar, *The International Journal of Children's Rights* (2010).

children. He conveyed the benign nature of his tests – and, crucially, he outlined the legal significance of the work. Luckily, this was enough to persuade even the unpersuadables.

He had overcome his biggest challenge, but the members of the review board were not the only ones he needed to get onside. Resistance came on two more fronts. Academic journals ('they took some convincing to publish our work') and, of course, parents.

'They thought participating in such a study would ruin their kids for life.' He flashes another broad smile. The bigger the challenge, the more enthusiastic he gets.

'But we were lucky that there were many enlightened parents. Once our work came out showing how normal it is for children to lie, parents started to be enthusiastic about participating.' More than 5,000 children have since participated in studies across several continents.

How do people generally respond to his work? Kang says that many of them laugh at first:

They wonder why I'd spend my career on something so trivial! My mom always asked me why I'd do such research and why the funding agencies would support my research. Only after I told them – and my mom! – about the new law in Canada did they realise that what I've been doing is meaningful.

But I still get a surprised look and laugh from people when I first tell them what I study. It's really fun, though, because once I tell them more about what I've found, they start volunteering their kids... or even their relatives.

Kang eventually broke through because his system is ingenious, simple, yet very careful. It is based on the work of the Stanford professor Robert Sears, who studied the conscience of children:

He did not study lying… but his methods were very clever. I thought it could be used for studying lying. Before me, Michael Lewis used a similar method. However, it took us about six months with many children to finally figure out how to do it properly. This is a method used regularly now by the field.

Kang's goal was to establish a reliable test – one that was as naturalistic as possible and caught spontaneous lies in children of all ages.

For the children involved, it was a guessing game, but its adult name is the Temptation Resistance Paradigm. The child was placed in a room with a supervising adult. A popular toy was put behind them and they were told not to look. Music associated with the toy was then played. Could they guess what it was without turning round? The children liked the game – principally because most of them were very good at it. Until, that is, it came to a certain dinosaur.

Barney the bright purple dinosaur is a star of children's television in America. But when it came to Barney, the music played was not associated with him – nor any other well-known toy. If the children wanted to answer correctly, they had to break the rules and peek. The goal was to identify when a child first started to lie, and to do that, the test itself involved video cameras and a small degree of trickery. A lie, to best catch a liar.

Under Kang's supervision, his third PhD student, Victoria Talwar, set up tests on a whopping 101 three- to seven-year-olds.[3]

The experiment boiled down to the following moment of temptation: the supervising adult left the room saying, 'Remember, no peeking.' The children now thought they were alone with the toy. The moment the adult returned was the one the experimenters were waiting for. They were about to find out if the child had given in to temptation and peeked, and then lied about it. But there was more. If they peeked and they lied, were they then any good at covering up their lie? At what age did children start telling successful lies?

The returning adult first asked if the child had peeked, then asked: 'What do you think the toy is?' Sure enough, it was a temptation too far for most – and it was hard to forget Barney's familiar face once they had peeked.

The paper found that 82 per cent of children peeked (there was no difference between girls or boys) – and 80 per cent of the peekers then lied about their behaviour. When asked what the toy was, 74 per cent of peeker-liars blurted out 'Barney' and gave themselves away. Only 16 per cent feigned ignorance. And just 10 per cent managed to name another toy to throw the adults off the scent. This 10 per cent demonstrated the most complicated level of deceit.

Kang's megawatt smile returns as he remembers one five-year-old girl's artful attempt to explain how she had guessed it was Barney.

'She said: "I didn't peek."' Kang pauses for dramatic effect. 'Then

---

3 'Development of lying to conceal a transgression: Children's control of expressive behaviour during verbal deception', Victoria Talwar and Kang Lee, *International Journal of Behavioral Development* (2002).

she said... "Wait a second! Let me touch it." And then, he says chuckling and miming what the child did to cover her tracks, 'she puts her hand underneath it. Then she feels it. Then she says: "It's purple!"'

Overall, younger liars had trouble maintaining consistent versions of the lie, while the six- to seven-year-olds managed to name another toy instead as proof of their innocence. It makes intuitive sense that the older children would be better able to maintain a deceit, but what Kang and team were showing was a pattern: proof that the ability to deceive develops in the same way as other skills.

This sent a shiver of discovery through me. Far from being a fault in the machine, being able to tell a successful lie was demonstrably a valuable stage in development.

Had Kang ever tried the tests on his own children? He smiles again.

'I have a teenaged son. I tried many new methods with him before starting real studies with other kids. It is always a good policy to do so because you need to make sure how kids react to our paradigms and whether they become upset.'

So, how did Kang junior behave?

'When he turned three, I put him through the paradigm and he peeked... and lied. After showing him the video which caught him red-handed... he still refused to admit it right away!' Kang was patient. He shakes his head as he remembers.

'Only a few days later, he admitted peeking.'

It is one thing for Kang to have video evidence of his son's misdemeanours, but what about other parents: are they any good at spotting when little ones lie? In a follow-up part of the test, the researchers judged how successful the children were at covering up their lies through the way they behaved. They showed the videos of the peekers and non-peekers to undergraduate students and parents who had not been involved in the tests. Could they spot a fibber just from their body language?

The tests showed that simply by judging the child's non-verbal behaviour, they could not. There was no significant clue that gave the children away, or to use the technical term: no leakage. The children gave themselves away when they tried to hide their deceit with words.

I would return to the effervescent Kang and his years of careful calibration, but first, I had to go back further in a child's development. If there is a pattern, when and how does it start?

I had scrutinised and practically stalked some spies and double agents, now it was time to give a few esteemed psychologists the same treatment.

As Kang said, it was Piaget who really got the ball rolling. His studies on cognitive development in children identified different stages in their learning and thinking.[4] The Swiss psychologist's work countered prevailing theories that children had blank minds, waiting to be filled with facts. He saw them as agents in their own worlds, accumulating and sorting knowledge through innate cognitive structures. They were not empty vessels lost at sea waiting to be given cargo and directions, they were pirate ships acquiring treasure and what was more, Piaget started sketching the map that showed their progress.

---

4 'Piaget's Stages of Cognitive Development', Saul McLeod (2020), www.simplypsychology.org/piaget.html

Piaget's theory came from his time at the Sorbonne, when he was working on adapting French versions of English intelligence tests for children. What intrigued him were not so much the results of the tests but the thought processes revealed by common errors. Children of the same age gave similar incorrect answers, suggesting stages in their ability to reason. Piaget found an unexpected answer in the children's mistakes.

Piaget devised simple tests and used them to identify the different stages. For instance, at what age does a child begin to understand that something can exist even if they do not see it? When explaining this conundrum, researchers cite a game of peekaboo. (A face is there. It is hidden. How marvellous, it has returned!) The surprise and delight the game causes in a very young child suggests that they do not realise the face is still there unless they can actually see it.

What Piaget then tested was at what age a child would start to look for an object if they could not actually see it for themselves. How to do this? Simple, he hid a ball under a blanket. When a child started to look under the blanket for it, they had graduated to a new stage.

To put it in Piaget-speak: when an infant encounters a new situation, they experience *disequilibrium* ('What is it?') prompting them to *assimilate* using existing knowledge – or *schema* ('Is it like something I know?') – and *accommodate* the new elements ('This is like a ball + I cannot see it') until they return to a state of *equilibrium* ('This is like a ball + I cannot see it = it is still a ball'). At this point, a child achieves *object permanence*; they find the ball and a game of peekaboo becomes a lot less fun.

Piaget called the first stage of childhood, from zero to twenty-four months, '*la période sensorimotrice*', The Sensorimotor Stage. Its name may sound like a terrible exercise bike routine, but it represents an almighty workout for the brain. The work being done on the mental infrastructure is phenomenal, with children developing rapidly from wild egocentrics to beings who understand that objects and events exist independently of them.

I was astounded. I thought about how often I had taken for granted that children just 'know' how to do things, that they just learn by copying and studying like an adult would. Instead, the brain was developing and regularly achieving wonders in an incredibly deliberate way.

Many have contested aspects of Piaget's work since, but there is now a widely accepted set of milestones in childhood development, charting when and how a child goes from laughing and pointing to seeking a hidden object and, in turn, learning to hide one successfully. It is a literally mind-boggling feat to go from basic sensory understanding to communicating, understanding others and acting on that information.

The further I delved into Piaget and stages in development, the more I came across a teasingly simple, yet frustratingly abstract term: Theory of Mind. This became my next quarry. I tracked it back to 1978, and what waited for me was slightly hairier than I had expected. It was all down to a chimpanzee.

Theory of Mind articulated the basis of human deductive skills at a time when psychologists were busy looking elsewhere for their models – and it began with a series of tests involving Sarah the chimp at a laboratory in Pennsylvania, USA.

What David Premack and Guy Woodruff wanted to know was:

could Sarah understand the role a person was playing and what they were trying to achieve? Could she read a situation and understand their beliefs, their intentions and even their mistakes? In experiments using actors and recorded scenes, they established that she could. To do this, they posited that she had established a theory about what was in another creature's mind. They wrote: 'An individual has a theory of mind if he imputes mental states to himself and others ... the system can be used to make predictions about the behavior of others.'[5] Their methods were subsequently disputed too, but their theory was highly influential.

Again, I thought about children and how they just 'knew' how to pretend play with an adult. This was Theory of Mind in action. When my nieces were younger, I could come up with all sorts of elaborate theatre, involving toy containers and magic sauces, and they would just play along. They could even tell me the colour of the invisible sauce. (Pinky-orange.) They could understand my beliefs, they interpreted my actions accordingly and they could briefly see the world as I wanted them to see it.

Interpreting behaviour is a mighty talent, whether it is displayed by a celebrated chimp or a giggling niece. The question for psychologists is: when does that mental gear change happen? When does the magic sauce start to take shape?

I went online and submerged myself in research papers. It was like being a trainee detective at a crime scene. All the answers were hidden away. Research-ese is almost as incomprehensible as corporate jargon, and it took me months, skimming through

---

5 'Does the chimpanzee have a theory of mind?', David Premack and Guy Woodruff, *Behavioral and Brain Sciences* (1978).

impenetrable sub-clauses, scouring footnotes and studying cast lists of contributors until I found who – and what – I needed. Once again, I followed a trail of excellent papers and this time, it led me to Alan Leslie, professor of psychology and cognitive science at Rutgers University in New Jersey.

Not only is Dr Leslie part of a groundbreaking team that transformed the study of autism but he has written extensively on the emergence of pretend play and he even gets a great review from Kang. 'It's a very small world!' Kang is delighted when I mention him. 'When I was a visiting scholar, I was actually in his unit in London. He was writing his seminal paper about pretence. He's very smart and he's funny.' These pioneers of pretence have a lot in common.

Dr Leslie is very much in demand but that did not stop him giving time to a journalist he had never heard of. 'I'm so sorry, it's been one of those weeks when even my interruptions are interrupted!' His voice is warm, Scottish lilt flowing away despite the fact that it is still early in the morning in New Jersey.

So, how did he crack the code? How did child's play lead him to deep, career-defining insight? Did it come to him in a flash?

He pauses. 'Well, it was one of those "flash" kind of moments.' It started with the first burblings of toddlers. 'Oddly, I came to focus on this by struggling with the problem of very early communication.'

He was studying under Jerome Bruner, professor of experimental psychology at the University of Oxford.

'Bruner was keenly aware that infants in the second year begin to communicate in a way that looks intentional or deliberate,' he says. 'I pretty much shared his intuition, along with probably every mother and father in history, but how to prove it?'

The problem seemed intractable then with the methods they had available. Then one day, during his time researching at the University of Edinburgh, it came to him. Pretend play could be crucial in understanding deliberate communication.

'Communications about pretend scenarios depart from standard communication – for example, I say to you, "The telephone is ringing"… and hand you a silent banana! If you understand my words literally, then you've *misunderstood* my meaning.' He pauses, possibly to allow me to catch up:

If you *do* understand me correctly… then you must have understood what I had in mind at the moment I uttered those words. You would have to employ your Theory of Mind, because grammar and a mental dictionary don't work here. There's really no other way to do this than Theory of Mind.

So, he says, if an infant plays along without question, it means that they are using Theory of Mind in order to communicate with others.

Part of his theory was that as soon as children can pretend themselves, they understand pretending in others. All this without a word ever being spoken about *how* to pretend.

He scribbled down the essence of his theory on the spot, but it was not until he moved to London in 1982 and joined the newly created Cognitive Development Unit at University College London that research alchemy happened. In the unit was Simon Baron-Cohen, fresh from Oxford, working under professor Uta Frith, who specialised in the study of autistic spectrum disorders.

Dr Frith was giving a talk on her work to date when she said that autistic children 'failed to develop spontaneous pretend play'. That was the lightbulb moment for Dr Leslie. His hand shot up, he said he thought he might have an idea and the rest is research history.

'I found myself with two very special colleagues. Within weeks we had become a brainstorming team.'

After three years of working together, they published the much-cited paper on autism: 'Does the autistic child have a "theory of mind"?'[6] The study found that children with autism were 'unable to impute beliefs to others and to predict their behaviour' and that this was 'a crucial component of the social impairment in childhood autism'.

Viewed in that way, the ability to pretend becomes something akin to a superpower – a social superpower. By playing a game together, children are not just communicating but sharing a profound, socialising bond. Once the components of pretence were laid out before me, I could see what a staggering talent it was. Pretending not to have seen something, like a famous purple dinosaur, was a significant achievement. So, what is the secret code? How do children begin to pretend, make things up, start progressing towards their first lie?

'The basic idea was that during the second year of life a special brain system grew and began to function in typically developing infants,' Dr Leslie says. 'This allowed the infant to begin appreciating the different perspective on a situation that another person might have.'

His model was a framework for pretence. It explained 'how the young brain could accomplish these feats by the relatively simple processing of a special type of information, which I called

---

6 'Does the autistic child have a "theory of mind"?', Simon Baron-Cohen, Alan Leslie and Uta Frith, *Cognition* (1985).

meta-representation'. So, on the one hand, there is the fact, the observable object; on the other, the pretence. But they are not separate, they relate to each other – something 'sensory' connected to something 'symbolic': a real banana = a pretend phone. Referring to one explains and sets the rules for the other. The real object does not cease to be real; it is transformed in a given context. Banana = phone. What is in effect mental transubstantiation, for a toddler is just another game.

I was dumbfounded. Like all great breakthroughs, it seemed perfectly simple once someone else had thought of it, tested it and explained it. But there was one thing that intrigued me. One tiny, coloured thread sticking out from his exceptionally clever papers. What was Mrs McDog's Farm, who was Sarah-Jane and why were they in a footnote?

'Ha ha, I'm delighted you ask! Sarah-Jane is my elder daughter, who is now very grown up and a professor of philosophy at Princeton University. But back then she was my very first subject in my studies of the emergence and development of pretend play.'

He had had to wait for a while. This was science at its most delicate. 'In her second year, I already had this idea about pretence and had already been keeping an eye out for signs that she might be about to begin pretend play... in a gingerly observational way... without wanting to implant any ideas... just keeping a chart.' And then it happened. They had just moved to London and 'it all appeared in a rush at twenty months'. Dr Leslie says that the emergence of the ability to pretend 'is one of the major developments in the second year of human life'. Sarah-Jane never looked back.

'I had to pretend play with her every day! I was allowed to eat something… and then it was "Daddy, Daddy! Let's go down the farm!" We spent *countless* hours sharing pretence, almost all of it under the rubric of what came to be known as Mrs McDog's Farm.' He laughs.

'It was a pretend world with scores of toy animal figures… characters with histories… et cetera.' I can feel that he is going back in time. 'Not quite Tolkien, but lots of lovely shared memories for us now.' He laughs again. 'Unbeknownst to Sarah-Jane, at the time I was slipping in little experimental scenarios that I piloted on her.'

I ask him what it is that marks out spontaneous pretend play from just moving objects around or happy fidgeting.

'It's the storyline.' His answer gives me a tingle of anticipation. Stories. An answer that lay in stories was exactly the sort of answer I was seeking.

'The natural thing is that human beings communicate with each other, share with each other and are interested in each other in a totally spontaneous way.' One person spontaneously engages and the other person spontaneously responds. 'They respond by *adding* something… something new… something created. That's how it goes back and forth. Theory of Mind is all about the storyline,' says Dr Leslie. 'And that is the crucial thing missing from the play of autistic children.'

He gets more passionate as he tells me what he tells his students. Just think of the cinema, he says. 'Movies are always about people and people's inner lives: people's hopes… and fears… and goals. What they know, what they don't know, what they falsely believe. Falling in love… things they hear… things they wish – it's *all* about Theory of Mind!'

The research on Sarah the chimp may be outdated, but the theory is present in so many of our interactions. Dr Leslie is on a roll. 'Relationships are between two minds – and the sharing, or the not sharing, of two minds.'

I am glued to every word he is saying.

'Joking, teasing, making up stories, amusing each other, that all comes out of the same package that pretend play comes out of.' He says pretend play is one of the earliest activities that comes under the heading of the 'non-serious... creative... humorous... kinds of play' we share with each other:

> Shared pretence is fundamentally communicative. You're communicating with the other person. Sometimes 'mind-reading' is used as a name for Theory of Mind. And it's all right as long as you realise that the name's kind of like a joke, because there isn't really such a thing as telepathy. Another person only knows your mind insofar as you reveal that to them... sometimes unintentionally, but very often, intentionally. You *intend* that they understand you.

He says you cannot rely on what is going on in the real world, because pretend play is only loosely based on the real world:

> You are creating this world that your mind is manipulating. And that's part of what is going on in the brain when babies start to pretend. It's a new power of thinking about the world that... I think other creatures don't have. It comes out to humans in a very early way. We're not just placed in the world as it really is... Already in the second year of life we can rise above the basic, literal world.

What he is describing is so close to lying and it happens so early on. I am stunned this appears at such a young age. He says that it allows us to take charge of our thoughts.

'That is the core of creativity and it's at the *heart* of our social life. It is a powerful, powerful... and positive toolkit... a dynamo that drives our reasoning ability and our connection with other people – a very intimate connection.'

His sophisticated theory about the simple structures that allow us to pretend is as much about science as it is society, art and philosophy. And of course, the ability to establish a theory about another person's mind is at the core of telling a successful lie.

Dr Leslie had given me gold dust. And he had certainly made me think differently about chimps. I had the formula, but if I wanted to get a handle on the different stages of lying development, it was time to go back to Kang, his troupe of young scientists and their carefully collected data.

In 2013, Kang repeated the peeking/purple dinosaur test with another of his students, Angela Evans, on an even younger age group. This time, they focused on toddlers only. It was time for the terrible twos – forty-one of them and twenty-four three-year-olds.[7] This younger group also showed that the temptation was too great for them: 80 per cent peeked and 40 per cent of the peekers lied. In total, only a quarter of two-year-olds lied, but the older or more advanced the children were, the more likely they were to lie.

So, if pretence emerged from eighteen to twenty-four months, lying followed hot on its heels – for some toddlers, at least. The

---

7 'Emergence of Lying in Very Young Children', Angela D. Evans and Kang Lee, *Developmental Psychology* (2013).

paper proposed that 'rather than younger children simply being more morally inclined to tell the truth, they may simply be less able to tell lies'. Lying thus becomes 'an early developmental milestone [showing] increased cognitive development'.

And if lying is an early milestone, then little liars, far from being a source of concern or shame, should be a source of pride. Indeed, Evans says that it makes her 'a little proud' when she catches her children (who were three years old when we spoke) 'telling a good one'.

She and Kang also conducted a more sophisticated test for those aged eight to sixteen. Would they too cheat when given the opportunity, would they lie about it and if they did, what kind of lies would they tell? They found that 54 per cent peeked, and of those, 84 per cent lied about peeking. The more advanced children told the better lies, but being more advanced did not affect a child's decision to lie.[8]

I was mesmerised by all these research papers. In a clear, methodical way, they were all showing more and more clearly how and when humans begin to lie, and what factors govern the types of lie told. A talent for understanding others – a socialising talent – played a large part.

If the ability to lie developed early on, what about the ability to choose not to lie? I dug out a paper by Kang and Victoria Talwar that applied the Promise Test to Barney, our purple dinosaur. I promised myself that this would be the final Barney paper I looked at.

'As young as three years of age, children already have a rudimentary

---

8 'Verbal Deception from Late Childhood to Middle Adolescence and Its Relation to Executive Functioning Skills', Angela Evans and Kang Lee, *Developmental Psychology* (2011).

concept of lies that are told for anti-social purposes and they evaluate such lies negatively,' reads the paper. 'With increased age, children begin to differentiate anti-social lies from honest mistakes, guesses, exaggerations and eventually, sarcasm and irony. Children also gradually take into consideration the social context in which lies are told and the intention of the lie-teller when evaluating lies.'[9]

The team wanted to know if this evaluation by the children affected the way they conducted themselves when they told a lie.

In a study of 150 children aged three to eight, the noisy purple temptation was once again placed right behind them and the supervising adult left the room. When they returned, they asked: 'Do you promise to tell the truth?'

The peeking results were not dissimilar to previous tests, but the 'promise' factor made the children tested less likely to lie, across all the ages.

I had my own temptation that I could not resist, even though I knew it would have horrified the teams involved in all the studies. Although the studies were based on different sets of children and varying conditions, the pattern I was seeing was so strong that I was desperate to group the results:

- Two to three years: 80 per cent peeked; 40 per cent lied.
- Three to seven years: 82 per cent peeked; 80 per cent lied.
- Three to eight years: 82 per cent peeked; 64 per cent lied (the 'promise' test).
- Eight to sixteen years: 54 per cent peeked; 84 per cent lied.

---

9 'Social and cognitive correlates of children's lying behavior', Victoria Talwar and Kang Lee, *Child Development* (2008).

I knew I was hacking away at delicate work, but when it comes to lying children, it seemed that once they can lie, about 80 per cent of them do, and when forced to make a contract with authority (the promise), the majority still lies. And finally, as we grow older and have better self-control, we might peek less but we still lie just as much about having done it.

The question that was buzzing around me like a crazed mosquito was why so many of the children lied. The paper elicited three stages of lying development based on the team's results and previous research. They came up with a development model that is still referred to today. This model made me gasp when I saw it. There in black and white was the 'Why' of the children's lies.

First come 'Primary Lies'. This covers the witching time of two to three years when 'children are first able to deliberately make factually untrue statements'. Their lies are infrequent. When they do occur, the lies are told to hide a transgression, protect the child's interests or present them in a positive light. The child does not take into account the perspective of the listener.

Then there are the 'Secondary Lies'. This is the gear change that takes place sometime during the ages of three and four. From four years onwards, most children 'will readily tell a lie to conceal their own transgression'. They also start to understand false belief in others and they can modify non-verbal behaviour to appear honest.

Finally come the 'Tertiary Lies', from seven to eight years. Children now become more consistent in their follow-up statements. This is when they stop blurting out things that could give them away. A normally developing child can now reason about 'complex interactions between mental states involved in sustaining a lie and act appropriately'. And what is more, the research suggests that as a child's abilities develop, so do their morals. They learn their rights and wrongs by trying them out in small degrees – and this moral sense surfaces early: from about three years old.

In 'Little Liars', his review of two decades of experiments, Kang says that early lying behaviour follows the same pattern irrespective of gender, country and religion. There are no easy giveaways. Children's non-verbal behaviour deceives the majority of adults, 'whether they are parents, child protection lawyers, social workers, police, customs officers or judges'.

Kang writes:

In-depth analyses of the videos of children's nonverbal behaviors reveal that those who deliberately tell lies attempt to mimic the behaviors of people who tell the truth (e.g. making direct eye contact with the listener when lying). When the situation calls for children to avert their gaze when telling the truth (because children have to ponder the answer to a question), they also deliberately avert their gaze when lying.[10]

This was almost exactly what Dr Watson had told me about language: that people try to tell lies as naturalistically as possible.

I now found myself studying every small child in my vicinity, watching their eye movements in wonder. The research showed that our brains generally develop in a way that allows us better to

---

10 'Little Liars: Development of Verbal Deception in Children', Kang Lee, *Child Development Perspectives* (2013).

interact with others, communicate and evaluate a situation and decide whether to share something, show something or hide it.

The behaviour of all these assembled toddlers and children was fascinating. It offered many clues but, of course, as none of them could explain how they did it, I wanted to go a little further. I wanted to see what their brains were actually doing when they lied. But I wondered how exactly would one set about lifting the lid on a little head?

From ancient Egyptian medical texts to the dissections of the Greeks and Romans and the detailed anatomical images towards the end of the Renaissance, humanity's finest minds have long been on a quest to map the human interior. When it comes to the mind, modern science has gone from early experiments on blood vessels in the brain (1920s) to flat images of its structure (1960s), on to mapping the brain as it functions (1990s) and even using fluorescent proteins to distinguish individual neurons (the wonderfully named 'Brainbow', 2007). However, despite the huge leaps in scanning techniques, the research is still young and the secrets of our brains are very old.

My two brilliant psychologists may have helped me, but they had given me a lot to think about too. Are we born with mental structures and what kind are they? How do we begin to communicate? Do babies deceive when they seem to turn crying on and off? Is their smile caused by a physical event in the body (wind), is it love or mischief in the making?

Studies by Kang's team and many others have linked deception to the brain's 'executive functions' – our complex cognitive processes.

One academic work describes these vividly as an air traffic control system. For adults, the queue of activities involved is long indeed: 'Without [these functions], we could not solve complicated problems and make decisions, persist at tedious ... tasks, make plans and adjust them when necessary, recognize and correct mistakes, control our impulsive behavior, or set goals and monitor our progress toward meeting them.'[11]

This network that is called upon minute by minute takes time to grow and develop. It is a big airport, so how do children learn to deceive before they even have more than a few planes up in the air? A team in Japan were the first to try to map brain activity when a child tells a more advanced type of lie – the one that depends on understanding the beliefs of another person. The team wanted to find out if a child relied on the same pathways as adults and if not, how did they manage it?

The executive functions are thought to be regulated largely by the front of the brain. The question the team posed is: would this region light up when a child told this smarter kind of lie? Now the team just had to find a reliable way to get their answers.

It is quite an achievement to get a child to go into the ominously named functional magnetic resonance imaging scanner. I remember the experience as rather like being strapped onto a trolley and eased into the hole of a giant, vibrating, shouting doughnut. They started with twenty-eight volunteers aged eight to nine years old and ended up with ten results they could use.[12] This makes the sample tiny, but the results are still enlightening.

In an adult, researchers would expect a lightshow of activity in

11 'Building the Brain's "Air Traffic Control" System', Center on the Developing Child, Harvard University (2011).
12 'Neural correlates of deception in social contexts in normally developing children', Susumu Yokota, Yasuyuki Taki, Hiroshi Hashizume, Yuko Sassa, Benjamin Thyreau, Mari Tanaka and Ryuta Kawashima, *Frontiers in Human Neuroscience* (2013).

the frontal lobe. However, in the scans obtained during the tests, that frontal area remained eerily quiet. There were no significant levels of activity in the prefrontal cortex. The activity was at the back of the brain (the parietal lobe). These under-tens seemed to be using their brains differently in order to get those deception planes in the air, while the rest of their airport was still being built.

The images show a dark globe, the walnut-like brain encased in a white outline. At the top right of this shadowy 2D brain is a small set of yellow pixels caught in the blue cross-hairs of the imaging machine. For me, this yellow burst is dazzling. If the brain finds unexpected ways to facilitate deception so early on, those pixels are a breathtaking display of how vital the ability to deceive is in human development.

From the ringing banana (pretending) to Barney (lying) to something akin to managing the skies above Beijing, laboratories across the world backed up the theory that playing, pretending and lying are fundamental steps in our development. But not just that. The ability to maintain a pretence or deceit is a staggering talent – a social superpower that when we are little, we think is a game, and when we are older, we dismiss. I now had the ardent belief that we should all spend a little time in Mrs McDog's Farm, because the ability to fabricate helps make us team-players, storytellers and – almost – mind-readers.

CHAPTER 7

GIVING THE GAME
AWAY | *THE FACE*

The man is staring me straight in the eyes. His eyes are open wide, his look is fixed. His teeth are bared. I briefly marvel at how straight they are, then immediately wonder how strong they are. Are they sharp too? His nostrils are flared. His expression is deeply alarming. I feel a wave of fear, the need to flee.

It is just a black-and-white photo of some 'dude' with sideburns from the '70s, so why is it having such a powerful effect on me?

The answer is that it is a very unusual photo. In it, a psychologist is perfectly mimicking the facial expression of a chimpanzee, baring its teeth. The more I research facial expressions, the more times I come across images of this charismatic face: plain background, eyes fixed on the camera, his face filling the frame. Sometimes his expression makes me uneasy, other times, his unrestrained smile makes me smile right back at him. I am looking at Paul Ekman, and in every single photo, he is looking right back at me, frozen in time, making one very specific facial expression. It is disconcerting, haunting and fascinating – such is the power of facial expressions, especially when my brain is telling me that they are 100 per cent authentic and 100 per cent staged at the same time. How does he do this over and over again – and why?

Paul Ekman recreating facial expressions in controlled conditions as part of his work in developing the influential Facial Action Coding System.
Published with kind permission of Paul Ekman

If the inside of a little head was fascinating, I wondered how much I could learn from the outside of a big head. I had seen how humans grow into social creatures: connecting, learning, deceiving; but what about the surface of us, the 'us' we present to the outside world? What role does the face play in our lies? It helps us, of course, but does it play a vital role in hindering us too? A friend had recently told me a secret and asked me to keep it. I agonised, then made the conscious decision to lie for them. It sat badly with me. I could feel the knowledge of it haunting my mouth, lurking around my eyes and even making me blush. I was a hopeless accomplice who even started to feel guilty about this secret. How is it that we can do something as sophisticated as lying, then be undone by a traitorous movement across our faces at a crucial moment? The face became my new hunting ground, and if I wanted to understand its secrets, there was only one person I could turn to.

Professor Ekman has transformed the study of facial reading and hidden emotions. His work finds itself everywhere from US government agencies to Scotland Yard, Disney's Pixar Animation Studios and even the Himalayas, where he was commissioned by the Dalai Lama to produce a map of human emotion. As if that were not enough, his team also became the basis of the American television series *Lie to Me*, starring Tim Roth. Ekman is the don of lie detection.

But how to track him down? Finding references to him is easy: he has a sparkling website and plaudits everywhere. Finding him is another matter.

In 2017, when I was on his trail, he was much in demand and most elusive. The sprightly 83-year-old had wound down his activities and chose his interviews carefully – after all, his knowledge would be a fearsome weapon if it were ever to fall into the wrong hands.

I had to jump through several hoops before we were booked in for a video interview. It then took me at least another ten minutes to wear him down and get him to agree to switch on his video.

'Here I am,' he says wryly, as his avatar (a Mexican Day-of-the-Dead mask) turns into the features I have come to know so well. Finally, we were face to face in real time.

Ekman's substantial body of work on reading the human body, particularly the face, started in 1954 and includes his quest in the late 1960s to find out whether the facial expressions of emotions were universal or culture specific.

To test the theory, he had to find the most remote tribe he could. As these tribes were dwindling in number, he had to go as far as the south-western Pacific, to the highlands of Papua New Guinea. There, he found the South Fore, a primitive stone-age tribe, completely removed from the rest of the world, with no access to neighbours, let alone books, radio or television. As Ekman puts it, it was 'visually isolated'. The tribe's reactions to a situation would be entirely their own, not one influenced by or mimicking any other culture.

It took more than one trip, staying with the tribe and working with interpreters, but eventually, they found a reliable method to get the data they needed. The team told the tribe simple stories that would produce a clear emotion (for example: 'you see friends you like'), asked them to look at a set of photographs and pick the expression that best suited how the story made them feel. Despite their absolute isolation, they identified with the same emotional expressions as the twenty-one other cultures the team had studied – all literate and aware of the wider world. That trip provided the scientific community with the strongest evidence to date that there existed a universal set of facial expressions.[1]

In his autobiography, Ekman describes his career as fifty years spent investigating facial expressions, gestures, emotion and lies. He continues:

Why these topics, which had been abandoned as fruitless by the academic establishment? In much of my life I have been a bit oppositional, some would say rebellious, so I am not surprised that I gravitated towards topics scorned by academia as the stamping grounds of charlatans and fools. My eyes told me they were wrong. I delighted in the opportunity to prove that.[2]

---

1 'Constants across cultures in the face and emotion', Paul Ekman and Wallace Friesen, *Journal of Personality and Social Psychology* (1971).
2 *Nonverbal Messages: Cracking the Code: My Life's Pursuit*, Paul Ekman (2016).

As I had learnt in my exchanges with Kang, it takes a maverick streak to specialise in deceit. When we speak, Ekman sums up his long career encoding facial expressions in one sentence: 'I was amazed that no one had done it yet, that it was there waiting for me,' he says, with a slight smile and a flicker of delight in his eyes, 'so I did it.'

Ekman made his mark working with his long-time collaborator Wallace Friesen to produce 'a comprehensive, anatomically based system for describing all visually discernible facial movement'.[3] Yes, every single expression. It took them a decade, but in 1978, the Facial Action Coding System (FACS) was born. FACS produced a set of coordinates that could be used to trace emotion. Distinct muscle movements involved in facial expressions were identified and listed as Action Units (AUs). Once they had caught them, they reproduced and photographed them, creating the unsettling catalogue of isolated expressions that I had stumbled upon in my research.

For instance, someone might frown as they try to take in the idea of a universal set of emotions, communicated facially in a universal way. This frowning movement would be AU4, or 'The brow lowerer', which comes courtesy of the superbly named *corrugator supercilii* muscle, which is small, pyramid-like and sits towards the front area of an eyebrow. It is a favourite among the Botox brigade. The photo of the aggressive chimpanzee expression is a combination of AUs: 10 (upper lip raiser) + 12 (lip corner puller) + 16 (lower lip depressor) + 25 (lips part). I just think of it as 'angry ape'.

---

3 'Facial Action Coding System', www.paulekman.com/facial-action-coding-system/

Describing the movement of a face only, they had created a tool to teach others how to read emotion better – even hidden emotion.[4]

'No one has done that before me, and no one's going to do it after me because once you've done it, it's done,' says Ekman, activating another subtle flurry of AUs on his face that certainly look like pleasure. 'There isn't another way to do it. You are simply describing the mechanics of how the face is constructed, how the muscles work.'

It is a staggering work of facial cartography that is still used today. From psychologists to animators and those who work in the facial rigging that brings 3D characters alive, FACS is both an inspiration and a vital resource. I thought of the terrifyingly emotional creature Gollum, brought to life from J. R. R. Tolkien's books in the *Lord of the Rings* films (2001–03), and sure enough, the animators consulted Ekman's work. Pixar's *Inside Out* (2015) animation is another lively embodiment of Ekman's work, and in making it, the production team collaborated with Ekman to turn emotions into five characters bouncing around the mind of an eleven-year-old girl.

In the long process of creating FACS, they identified more than 10,000 expressions, of which 3,000 were linked to emotion.[5] To try to grasp the scale of this, I picked up my smartphone. Emojis were introduced on mobile phones in Japan in 1999. By 2017, there were seventy-seven emojis featuring specific facial expressions, each with a unique numeric value. For Apple devices, they ranged from 'face with tears of joy' to 'neutral face' and yes, 'lying face' (code =

---

4 *Unmasking the Face: A Guide to Recognizing Emotions from Facial Expressions*, Paul Ekman and Wallace Friesen (2003).
5 Facial Action Coding System (1978, revised in 2002).

U+1F925; main feature = Pinocchio's nose).[6] I could see why it took them ten years to compile FACS.

Drs Ekman and Friesen later published a guide to recognising emotions and listed six big, universally recognised emotions: surprise, fear, anger, disgust, sadness and happiness.[7] They put these into families, to identify the spectrum of feelings and the minute signals involved:

> Surprise, for example, is an emotion with a big family. There is not one surprise facial expression, but many – questioning surprise, dumbfounded surprise, dazed surprise, slight, moderate and extreme surprise. The complexities of facial expressions are shown in photographs of how different emotions can blend into a single facial expression to show sad-angry expressions, angry-afraid expressions, surprise-fearful expressions.[8]

They produced a blueprint to allow everyone from nosey amateurs to professional sleuths to master facial expressions and identify when a subject was trying to disguise themselves. There was no equivalent to Pinocchio's nose, but there were whole fleets of mini-giveaways if you knew where to look: micro expressions.

According to Dr Ekman, these occur when we suppress a feeling, whether this is unconscious ('repression') or deliberate ('suppression'). These 'micros' are too speedy for the untrained eye, but

---

6 emojipedia.org
7 Ekman later includes 'contempt' in the list, however in The Atlas of Emotions, which he created with his daughter Eve Ekman and was a project funded by the Dalai Lama, the list was refined to five: anger, fear, sadness, disgust and enjoyment, atlasofemotions.org
8 *Unmasking the Face*, Ekman and Friesen.

the coding system meant that it became possible to train people to spot these. FACS created a Lilliputian world, where it is the small things that matter and any face becomes a vast geographical plain of information.

For two of the ten painstaking years it took them to complete FACS, they had a room set up in the lab, ready to pounce when the right AU presented itself and needed documenting. The lighting conditions had to be the same every time, which was 'dull as hell' for Dr Ekman, who had grown up taking portraits of his neighbours and later photographed dancers to earn money, but the science demanded it. They persisted even as the finances 'got tough' and five years in, the project was saved only by a last-minute intervention. Dr Ekman's quest to capture every last AU was so determined that if ever there was a doubt about which he had activated, he would put a needle into his face and electrically stimulate the muscle. This was a quietly horrifying idea, but it was not one that surprised me, considering the many unsettling practices I had come across researching the pursuit of emotion. A series of ghoulish images flashed in my mind of people being electrocuted for science, but this was not courtesy of an over-active imagination. Those twisted faces were real – and they came from nineteenth-century Paris.

The images were the fruit of the studies by the French neurologist Guillaume-Benjamin-Amand Duchenne de Boulogne. I came across them thanks to Ekman, who credits him with the first meaningful cataloguing of the facial muscles used in expressions. Indeed, he was one of two scientific revolutionaries who laid the groundwork for Ekman.

Ekman describes Duchenne as 'the great neurologist' and it was his work that was key in spotting a liar's smile. Duchenne used electrodes and early photography to chart the different muscles involved in facial expressions, whether they were 'the muscle of joy' or 'the muscle of lasciviousness'.[9]

To the modern eye (and certainly to my eye), the project's resultant photos are a disturbing gallery of emotion, particularly when the electrodes are visible and Duchenne is in shot, calmly bent over a tortured face, applying the electrodes with the help of an assistant. However, he was using electricity in a new way – precisely, carefully, exploratively. He made his subjects' faces move muscle by muscle, then captured them in 144 images, nine plates that would be a bedrock of research into facial musculature. He had produced what he called 'a living anatomy'. What puzzled me was how such a rogues' gallery could lead Duchenne to be identified with a genuine smile of pleasure.

The *zygomatic major* muscles play a key role in facial expressions, because they are the ones that allow us to smile. When Duchenne stimulated those muscles, he got what he expected: a large smile. What Duchenne did not expect was that this induced smile was totally unconvincing. This fascinated him. What was missing? He told his subject a joke, captured his un-stimulated response to it and made his discovery. When we feel genuine pleasure, we not only engage the smile muscles but contract the muscles surrounding our eyes. Now that I had a better idea about zygomatics, I tried the liar's

---

9 *Mécanisme de la Physionomie Humaine*, Guillaume-Benjamin-Amand Duchenne de Boulogne (1862).

smile. Sure enough, it even felt fake. No wonder Duchenne called it the 'false friend'.[10] The hunt for the liar's mask had begun.

Duchenne's frozen faces provided material for the second figure whose work anticipated Ekman's. He was a figure I would keep encountering as I talked to those who delved into the penumbrous human interior: Charles Darwin. Darwin set about demonstrating the evolutionary nature of expressions in *The Expression of the Emotions in Man and Animals* (1872).

Darwin wrote of 'the extraordinarily complex chain of events which lead to certain expressive movements'. He sent out questionnaires to laypeople and scientists across the world in an attempt to track the universality of expressions. At a time when the pre-eminence of the Victorian man was considered an established fact, Darwin was once again delving across other cultures, races and species.

He received reports that ranged from the anecdotal to the stringently scientific, and amassed information that stretched from pets, pigeons and livestock to his family, his contemporaries, the Dayak tribes of Borneo and the men working in the botanic gardens of Calcutta. These reports could not be considered cast-iron data points, but they were enough for Darwin and he deduced that the same set of facial expressions was indeed recognised across the world – and if this was so, then only an innate, inherited trait could account for this commonality.

He wrote: 'The young and the old of widely different races, both

---

10 Ibid.

with man and animals, express the same state of mind by the same movements.' There was a core set of recognisable features, even if expressions were tweaked and adapted in different ways.

'Many of our most important expressions have not been learnt, but it is remarkable that some, which are certainly innate, require practice in the individual, before they are performed in a full and perfect manner; for instance, weeping and laughing.'

He postulated that if it was accepted that kittens and cats arched their backs alike, and puppies wagged their tails for the same reasons as older dogs, why should it be surprising that our shrug is an innate gesture, reproduced across the ages for the same reasons? How do the deaf 'know' how to cry, and the blind 'know' what fear looks like?

The evidence was not just in our behaviour but in our anatomy. Darwin's work was ahead of its time not just in the material it presented but in the illustrations it used. He drew inspiration from Duchenne, even using some of his images, then combined them with portrait photography, family engravings and detailed anatomical diagrams. The book did not touch on lying but it opened a wide path for future lie detectors.

I thought again of Ekman, electrifying his face to catch those fugitive movements. When he turned on his video camera, I wondered if I would be able to see him scrutinising me – deciphering my motives in a blink just from my over-reliance on those zygomatics. But I was wrong. His gaze was much softer than I expected and despite being such a disciplinarian in research terms, his voice was gentle, he had a calm, deliberate way of speaking and a ready chuckle. Still, he ruthlessly dispatched any question he deemed unworthy with a one-word answer. He is, after all, a prodigy who had his first paper published in his early twenties.[11]

Did all that work manipulating his face have any effect on his behaviour outside the lab?

'Zero.'

On his interaction with others?

'Zero.'

Had he met any resistance to his line of work? People who balked at such a forensic physical study of the expression of emotion?

'No.'

I was struggling. 'None at all?'

'Not that I can recall.' This time I let the long pause roll on until he spoke. 'I think people who didn't like what I was doing ignored me. I'm sure there are people who thought it was a waste of time.'

I was beginning to get a sense of the willpower that drove a project like FACS. So where did this all begin for him?

He has written about his tough upbringing, being controlled during childhood, which in turn made him deceive his parents. I asked if he had an epiphany – a moment when the deception got too much.

'No.'

'It was just a gradual...?'

'Uh-huh.' I was beginning to wonder if Ekman was ever going to open the vaults and let me in. Then, finally, he started elaborating.

'I didn't start my career focused on lying. I started my career in

---

11 'A Methodological Discussion of Nonverbal Behavior', Paul Ekman, *The Journal of Psychology* (1957), pp. 141–9.

research… God, it was such a long time ago – I've been at this a very long time, but what I was after was trying to understand emotion not deception.'

He has spoken before about his mother's suicide when he was fourteen. The day before she killed herself, she had asked him to save her. But how could he, he asks? There was not even medication then for what he says was bipolar disorder.

In his autobiography, he writes: 'After her death I pledged to her and to myself that I would dedicate my life to helping people like her. I had no choice; I was obligated by my failure to save my mother from herself.'[12]

It was later that he would focus on lies.

'Deception came in when I got asked by young people being trained to be psychiatrists, how they could tell when their patient was lying about whether they intended to take their own life if they were given a pass from the hospital. That's what got me started.'

When Eve, his first child, was born he made a conscious effort to give up lying. Did he manage to keep that up as she got older?

'Yes, I think I very rarely tell a lie. The skill is to be able to avoid having to tell lies – and of course, I don't want to hurt people's feelings, so if someone says to me… "Do I still look young in this outfit?", you know?' He chuckles. 'I mean, that's flattery, I don't consider flattery a lie.'

And does he still avoid putting people in a position where they might have to tell a lie?

'Oh, very much so. Sure.'

---

12 *Nonverbal Messages*, Ekman.

Ekman first spotted micro expressions in the late 1960s, when he was filming those sessions with psychiatric patients to help doctors decode their deceit. In his best-known book, *Telling Lies*, he recalls one particular patient, Mary:

Once we had the idea that concealed feelings might be evident in these very brief *micro expressions*, we searched and found many more, typically covered in an instant by a smile. We also found a *micro gesture*. When telling the doctor how well she was handling her problems Mary sometimes showed a fragment of a shrug – not the whole thing, just a part of it. She would shrug with just one hand, rotating it a bit. Or her hands would be quiet but there would be a momentary lift of one shoulder.[13]

Mary was covering up her suicidal urges and lying to them, but it took a confession and filmed interviews to spot it. What they spotted was not the lie but the truth seeping out: 'Most often lies fail because some sign of an emotion being concealed leaks.'

Emotions, it seemed, were like an unruly classroom: they could be disciplined but they would never be truly quiet. And not only did they fuel lies, they complicated them and interfered with the thought process, jamming all those useful things like clear recall, intuition and problem solving. If my mental resources were being sucked up dealing with guilt, for instance, how could they be expected to manage my brain's air traffic control system? Darwin wrote about expressions that were innate but refined, practised and

---

13 *Telling Lies: Clues to Deceit in the Marketplace, Politics, and Marriage*, Paul Ekman (1985).

emerged in different ways in different places. I thought of how practised expressions could help an overloaded brain, shielding its true
intentions from casual investigators. What do I do when I panic and
try to hide something? I think I smile.

'Who's publishing what you're writing?'

'I'm sorry… I didn't hear that,' I reply, in a rush. Did he just say
publisher? Holy Christ. Had I lied to his team to get the interview?
At the time, I did not have a contract with a publisher. I doubted
that I would have taken the risk to fake anything with Ekman. But
had I?

'Who… is… publishing… what you are writing?'

On screen, I could see that my eyebrows had shot up in panic.
I tucked my hair behind my ear. I put my hand on my chin. DO
NOT TOUCH YOUR FACE, I thought. I had read somewhere that
touching your face meant you were reassuring yourself, perhaps
even protecting yourself against a threatening encounter. It was too
late. I was now fully resting my head on my hand. Then I smiled.

'We're negotiating.' I rolled my eyes dramatically. This was classic
masking – it's in Ekman's books. This was out of control. How could
I be stupid enough to lie to him? But while these thoughts flashed
through my brain, it seemed my mouth had carried on talking.

'It's been a long and tortuous process,' I continued, perhaps referring to the sensation of watching my own animated, red face ca-
reering from one ill-advised facial expression to another. He looked
at me. Then looked away. Then looked back. There was no escape.

'But you have an agent?'

Finally, breathing room.

'I have an agent.' Which was sort of true – not 100 per cent confirmed at that point but not 100 per cent false. My face was calmer, but I could see that my shoulders were still twisted awkwardly. When would this torture end?

He let me off the hook and started talking about the parlous state of publishing. Thankfully, my ridiculous fib was either not interesting enough to register or it had suddenly made me much more interesting.

In *Telling Lies*, he outlines the route to take when approaching a suspect face. The first step is to identify facial 'noise' and turn down the volume. This means filtering out all the facial expressions unconnected to emotion. This includes 'conversational signals' that emphasise speech or punctuate an exchange. Examples were the 'facial gestures' that accompany a question or a 'facial manipulator' such as lip biting and cheek puffing.

The second step is to consider the treacherous zones of the face – the ones that give us away.

Certain muscles are hard to move deliberately. For instance, trying to pull the corners of the lips downwards, without moving the chin muscle. Ekman calls these 'reliable' muscles, not because they are the ones someone could count on in dire straits but because they behave reliably: they are the ones that are hardest to manipulate and most likely to betray us. The forehead is home to the majority of these reliables because while lip corners may be tricky to manipulate, overall we have more control over the muscles in the lower region of our faces as they are the ones we need for talking and chewing.

The reliable forehead is where fear, terror, distress, grief and sadness all surface. But if those muscles provide reliable information, they are not guaranteed to give away every person. Some people move theirs differently, some are better at manipulating them and the muscles themselves can be triggered simply by successfully remembering an emotion. This gives actors and actresses, with careers full of summoned emotions, a distinct advantage. I thought of trying to FACS Daniel Day-Lewis or Viola Davis and knew I would not get very far. Jim Carrey's hyperactive face in the film *Liar Liar* is a masterclass of distracting movement.

Once a trainee-FACSer has established the zones that will give a person away, the third step is to identify 'masking'. I thought of depressed Mary's smile. If a liar's goal is to conceal an emotion, then the expression of an opposite emotion – or one that creates a lot of facial movement – is one to watch. (Ekman does not list eye-rolling here, but I bet it counts too.)

Another thing to watch out for are 'antagonistic muscles'. These can shut down a facial expression at speed but can also make an expression unnatural. Ekman writes that a smile of pleasure 'can be diminished by pressing the lips together and pushing the chin muscle up', but what sort of signal does that send to someone who is watching carefully? He calls an interrupted expression a 'squelch'.

Once all the distractions, escaped emotion and masking or blocking have been identified, it is time to get more tactical and mark out terrains in the face for special attention. The eyes, for instance, are tricky. So much for all those torrid novellas that refer to them as the windows of the soul. Not only do they fail to shed much light on the soul, they are well practised at cloaking it. Ekman identified 'five sources of information' emanating from the eyes. Two of these are potential deceivers: the muscles around the eyeball and the gaze, which, thanks to Kang, I now knew even children could manipulate when they needed to. These are pitted against three 'autonomic' signs of emotion: increased blinking, pupil dilation and tears.

The mouth area can also reveal us in different ways, despite our greater ability to manipulate it. The subtlety of Ekman's science shows itself in his finely tuned description of the lip movement that is a giveaway for incipient anger:

> One of the best clues to anger is a narrowing of the lips. The red area becomes less visible, but the lips are not sucked in or necessarily pressed. This muscle action is very difficult for most people to make, and I have noted it often appears when someone starts to become angry, even before the person is aware of the feeling.

I take a cold, hard look at my facial expressions on the recording of the video call, when I (white-) lied to Ekman. At twenty-seven minutes and thirty-two seconds, I am about to say: 'We're negotiating' and that whole set of unfortunate movements is happening across my face.

Ekman is looking at me. I am distracted, looking warily at the tiny image of my face betraying me in the corner of the Skype screen. I think it is safe to say that I could never be a spy.

Ekman's basics for detecting deception are dense with information, but chief among the rules is to remember our own biases when engaging in detective work. Even though Ekman has an armoury of insights and technical know-how, he is at pains to remind wannabe sleuths that there is no categorical sign of lying – again, no Pinocchio's nose. I remembered the toddlers and the elaborate precautions it took to measure their lying behaviour. The lie must be neither prompted, encouraged nor distorted. Lie spotting comes from a combination of factors, not least remembering our own perspective and the mistakes we might make.

Ekman calls this the 'Othello Error' and for anyone facing a suspected liar, it is salutary to bear the jealous general in mind. When might we too fall prey to vanity and trickery; misjudge fear and desperate denials; smother Desdemona? It is one thing to study a person's changing facial signals and find motive; it is quite another to remember why we ourselves are looking for that motive. Context really can be a killer. Just as an expected reaction can mislead, so too an inexplicable reaction might be the key to understanding a whole story, but its significance might escape us. I remember a friend telling me how she planned a birthday surprise for her partner, only to be confronted with incomprehensible fury at the moment of revelation. It was only much later – and too late to save the relationship – that she realised it had been the wrath of a liar who loathes being tricked, who has to control their own story above everything else.

My friend still likes to surprise her partners but says that she is now much better at choosing them.

Ekman had taught me a lot, but there was a very important part of the face that I had left until last to explore fully. One that has already been very present in this chapter.

From the inscrutable Sphinx to Mona Lisa's mouth and O. J. Simpson's troubling flashes of delight in court, the smile has long perplexed and perturbed us and rules non-verbal communication. In my exploration of the mountainous proposition of the face, I felt as if I should pause and check my crampons and climbing kit before I began the ascent of the smile. After all, Ekman smiled frequently throughout our interview, but I could never quite forget that chimpanzee expression.

According to Ekman's work, a smile is recognisable from a distance of up to 300ft and is the expression it takes the least time to decipher. Infants can summon a smile before they are twelve months old and we find them very hard to resist: smile at me and I smile back; your behaviour influences mine – and this one is a powerful exhortation.

Our smiles are sensational misleaders. They signify happiness but can mean so much more. I wondered how many different smiles I would find if I tried to classify them. My smartphone at the time came up with twenty-four smiley-face emojis, from 'grinning face with big eyes' to 'beaming face with smiling eyes' and 'face with tears of joy'.[14]

Ekman has identified more than fifty different smiles. In *Telling*

---

14 'Smileys & People', emojipedia.org/people/

Lies, he lists a mighty eighteen genuine smiles. The first five are: the positive 'felt' smile (the Duchenne smile); the fear smile; the one laced with contempt; the one we hide ('the dampened') and the miserable one. To differentiate between those last two, he says to look for an echo of emotion around the eyes: if they are 'smiling' too, it is a positive emotion being turned down ('dampened'), if not, it is a negative one being amplified (misery guts).

Then there are 'the blends': enjoyable-anger, -contempt, -sadness, -fear, -excitement and -surprise (think Jack Nicholson in almost any role); then the smiles that recruit a gaze: flirtatious (smile + a high-speed, sideways glance) and embarrassed (gaze down or to the side); the 'Chaplin', an unusual smile extension that distances the smiler by adding an air of irony, which few people can achieve bar its namesake; and the four co-operative smiles that show complicity or soften a blow: compliance, co-ordination, qualifier or listener.

Against all these, there is the liar's smile. Not one that conveys elements of genuine emotions, positive and negative, but one that is 100 per cent pure fraud. The alligator smile. But Ekman is ready for this one too. He outlines four clues that could be summed up as echo, asymmetry, timing and brow.

It goes something like this. As Duchenne found, a liar's smile does not produce the same echo from the muscles around the eye, particularly the brow muscle. The 'felt' smile is also more symmetrical, therefore asymmetry is a clue to fakery. Thirdly, the smile may be too abrupt, appear out of sync with events or disappear in awkward stages. And finally, the reliable muscles of the brow will do their thing and give the game away by revealing any potential fear or distress.

I remembered another story I was told as I worked on the book. A divorcee recalled the moment she found herself flicking through her wedding album. Her sadness turned to masochism as she also went through the big pile of photos she had left out of it. She told me it was as if her hands knew exactly the image she was looking for, even if her mind did not. And there it was – a still moment, a face, caught in the background amid the jamboree in the foreground as the newly-weds swept past. It was the face of someone who, she found out later, had betrayed her, someone who would be part of the reason for the eventual divorce – and in that photo, she suddenly saw the treachery written on her face. The divorcee called it 'that empty smile'. It was a haunting lie that left only the most discreet signs of betrayal in its wake. There was a reason she had not put it in the album, but it took her years to find out why: it was something about that smile.

When Ekman wanted to broaden his work on psychiatric patients in the 1970s and test his theories about facial 'tells', he knew it would be difficult to find subjects who were genuinely motivated – and able – to lie for science. He had to identify a group of people who not only would put their moral reservations on hold but were disposed to lying in certain circumstances, when the situation was upsetting and the stakes and emotions were high. Where would he find this cohort and how could he stop them being put off by the graphic images needed to provoke strong emotions? One group of people came to his mind immediately. He picked student nurses and set about giving them some brutal work experience.[15]

15 'Detecting deception from the body or face', Paul Ekman and Wallace Friesen, *Journal of Personality and Social Psychology* (1974).

He knew that if anyone was going to be able to face the goriest maiming then turn to a victim's family and soothe them, it would be a nurse. They were shown two films that they had to describe, as they watched, to an interviewer who could see their faces but not the screen. One was a pleasant ocean scene, the other, a harrowing combination of burns and amputation. They were told to convey this as a pleasant flower scene. The research allowed Ekman and team to mine several seams of information, including changes in voice pitch and gesture.

The team measured the false smiles using the absence of movement around the eye and signs of disgust or contempt (wrinkled noses and tightened lip corners). The results showed that these two did indeed provide a 'very strong' indication of the nurses' gory lie. And this was despite their strong motivation to hide it (the dean of their college had asked them to participate and they feared for their future careers if they failed to be convincing).

These signs of the false smile, however, are subtle, and when videos of the lying nurses were shown to others, they could only hazard a guess at who was lying. As with parents when faced with lying children, they had a 50/50 chance of getting it right. They might as well have kept their eyes closed. The nurses passed their lying test with flying colours.

If a benevolent nurse can do it, how does it compare to a murderer? As with everyday lies, it is the high-stakes examples of fraudulent facial expressions that best show the mechanisms at work. I did not want to delve into dark psyches, but I kept remembering Ian Huntley's childlike expression when he appealed for the two lost girls. Do murderers give themselves away in different micro ways, and what would a face hiding knowledge of evil look like?

Professor Leanne ten Brinke spent years assiduously applying facial theories to liars who sit on the extreme end of the Lie Scale. For her research, she scoured the world for people making the most impassioned plea of all to strangers: televised appeals for the return of a missing relative.

She ended up with footage of fifty-two 'pleaders', of which half were subsequently convicted of murdering that missing relative. It was a rich, and chilling, source of comparison. In the majority of cases it was parents pleading for the safe return of their missing child.

The team coded the facial muscles at work, frame by frame, each time coding the pleader's face twice – once for the upper face, once for the lower. They ended up with a total of 47,244 coded frames.[16] That is a long time spent in bad company.

Dr ten Brinke's slight physique, and lively, elfin-like face is a surprise considering the dark territories in which she has dwelt. Indeed, early in her career, she found ways to make sure she kept her distance from her quarry.

'I started my psychology career in a forensic psychology lab. Studying offenders, studying these murderers.' But after interacting with them, she decided she was not cut out for that work.

'I found these people fascinating, but they frightened me. Watching it on video, I was able to find it fascinating – but not terrifying.'

The study found that the deceivers were more likely to raise their brow muscles (the expression of surprise, or AUs 1 and 2, in FACS-speak) as they tried to replicate sadness.

---

16 'Darwin the detective: Observable facial muscle contractions reveal emotional high-stakes lies', Leanne ten Brinke, Stephen Porter and Alysha Baker, *Evolution and Human Behavior* (2011).

In genuine pleaders, it was the subtly different grief muscles at work in the brow (the frown, AU4) and the mouth ('lip corner depressor', AU15).

The guilty all kept their brow muscles raised for a longer proportion of their plea than genuine pleaders, and they were also more likely to activate the zygomatic (AU12) without any echo in their eyes – Duchenne's 'false friend', the lying smile.

Another of the studies[17] looked more broadly at the physical behaviour of the pleaders and found that: 'on average, deceptive pleaders blinked nearly twice as quickly as genuinely distressed individuals'. What causes the increased blinking? It is not just the 'cognitive load' of telling these types of elaborate and sustained lies but the arousal that occurs when masking big emotions.

One case that caught ten Brinke's attention was a plea, broadcast from a town just sixty miles away from her university base in Halifax, Nova Scotia, Canada, in 2008. She was in the middle of her research and 'furiously searching databases for emotional pleas to the public... when on came the local news'. When she saw Penny Boudreau's desperate plea for her missing twelve-year-old daughter Karissa, it stopped her in her tracks. Something was 'off'.

Ten Brinke has been chatty so far, sitting back in her chair, smiling and stroking the dog that plods in and out of frame. At the mention of Boudreau, she tenses, sits forward, focuses hard.

'It was like... she doesn't look like the genuine people that I've been watching. Specifically, she didn't express a lot of genuine

---

17 'Cry me a river: Identifying the behavioral consequences of extremely high-stakes interpersonal deception', Leanne ten Brinke and Stephen Porter, *Law and Human Behavior* (2011).

sadness. Her sadness looked more like surprise.' She tenses even more as she starts to show me what Boudreau's expressions were like.

'I thought it's not quite right,' she says, remembering her reaction to the appeal. 'It doesn't quite feel like you're sad.'

It is easy to imagine ten Brinke staring at the screen, studying the woman before her, gripped by the conflicting signals. She raises her shoulders as she relives the moment:

What do you do with that? I told my PhD adviser at the time and I think he got in contact with the police, but I don't know how helpful any of our insights were to their investigation. Or if they even heard them. And to be fair, at that point, we didn't have strong data to back ourselves up.

It was just a hunch, but it was a hunch that proved correct.

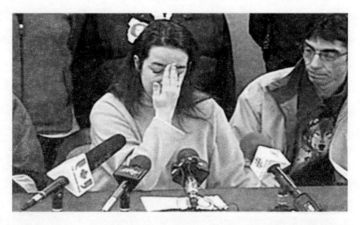

Boudreau's second public appeal. Bridgewater, Nova Scotia, 1 February 2008.
Source: LighthouseNOW News

With ten Brinke's work in mind, I too could watch the video of Boudreau, and – without knowing anything about the case – sense that something was wrong in the footage of her public appeal.

Boudreau's eyebrows are raised throughout, her expression keeps shifting, she hides her face with her hand. Her confusing behaviour, including even the briefest flicker of disgust and a smile, belies her tears.

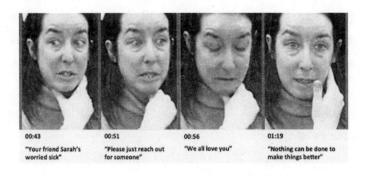

00:43
"Your friend Sarah's worried sick"

00:51
"Please just reach out for someone"

00:56
"We all love you"

01:19
"Nothing can be done to make things better"

It turns out that what she is masking is shocking knowledge. Just days before, she had carried out the premeditated murder of her child and disposed of her body, leaving it in a pose that suggested a sexual attack by a stranger.

Boudreau was arrested in June 2008 after undercover police officers tricked her into re-enacting how she had killed her daughter. She is now serving a twenty-year sentence for the murder.

The research confirmed what Ekman calls Darwin's 'inhibition hypothesis' concerning dark, sweeping emotions: those that are hard to fabricate voluntarily are just as hard to inhibit voluntarily.[18]

---

18 'Darwin, Deception, and Facial Expression', Paul Ekman, *Annals of the New York Academy of Sciences* (2003).

What Darwin wrote in passing was being proven by modern liars. It is only now that science and technology are giving the world a substantially better handle on these lucid insights from the nineteenth century.

I ask Ekman if he still works alongside crime agencies:

I do much less of that here [the US] than I used to, just because there's nothing new under the sun. I've already told them, and given them, most of what I thought they could use. So unless there's some special new case, new problem that wasn't there a few years ago, there's no need.

He tells me that he still does some work in the UK with the Metropolitan Police.

'I am very interested in anything I can contribute to counterterrorism... but I think I've already done that and I don't think I have anything new to offer. But I'll find out when I'm over there because people in Scotland Yard know I'm coming.'

When I mention Aimen Dean, Dr Ekman says only that he has been approached several times by government agencies (he will not say which ones, nor from which country) to train agents in the art of deception.

'A lot of bloodshed has been spared by undercover people,' he says:

It's clear that they are extremely useful and they help us avert great tragedies. But I just couldn't see training people to be good liars, because I knew that if I developed a really good training programme for that, I wouldn't be able to control who it was used on and it would have more malevolent use than benevolent use.

Has he ever been tempted to share his tricks?

'I could make considerably more money than I've made by running a School for Liars, teaching people how to beat the polygraph. I could do that very well.' But he will not – and he repeats this several times.

It's always been important to choose what not to work on and what to work on. You have to be pretty careful about that and not mislead yourself about it, so that you don't end up doing things just because it's fun. Or just because you can, or just to find out if you can. You've got to think ahead. Who's going to use it? What are they going to do with it? Do I want to develop that knowledge?

A lot of what he tells me is a reflection on his life's work, the sheer power of what he has created:

Because of all the people who are using the expertise I've developed so far, I have no control over them. And they aren't all good people. They aren't all people who are using it for reasons I would agree with. But, once it's out there, it's not your child any more.

He guards the keys to the temple of lie-hiding closely, and though

I was (finally) allowed to pass through, he will not allow me, or – it seems – anyone else, into the inner sanctum.

'There are a few secrets. A few discoveries that I've never published. And never mentioned. And I've kept secret.' He is suddenly more animated. 'Some of the most powerful ones,' he laughs, a full, candid laugh that shows his teeth. 'I wouldn't betray them under torture.'

What could those secrets be? How to tell a perfect lie? How could I have talked them out of the man who can beat the polygraph? From Ekman, I learnt the extent to which lies, like every aspect of human nature, are about balance. We can tell them, and we do very well, but the facial expressions that communicate them are subject to a force that is often beyond our control: our emotions. Everyone has a different tipping point of when a lie becomes too much, and sadly – or gladly – I was learning that my threshold was rather low. If we could tell perfect lies, then society would not function, but most of us cannot because we are betrayed by our prime zone of communication, our faces. We do not need to eradicate all lies to stop them overwhelming society; our emotions do that for us. If we ever do tell a lie that is unkind, unfair, unjust or just plain wrong, we feel it and we tend to show it.

Ekman is firm about many things, but he is firmest of all that he does not want to tip the balance. And if he really does know how to do this, how to create the infallible lie, then we should be glad that he is the one man guaranteed to be able to hide it.

CHAPTER 8

GOING VIRAL | *THAT WOMAN*

I t was the beginning of a new decade, January 2020, and everywhere I looked, I could see documented deceits of every size and
scope. Conspiracy theories upon conspiracy theories. Doctored
photos unstitching reality. Deep fakes. Presidents attacking world
truths with impunity. Premier league footballers lying in the face of
video evidence. Movie moguls who shouted down the small voices
of lone actresses; lone actresses who came together and slayed a
whole studio with a hashtag (#MeToo). Who was telling the truth?
How would history tell all these stories? And wasn't it all relative?

In the space of just a few years, lies had become almost a lingua
franca of social media, public discourse and politics. Anyone with
the power to pronounce something had the power to pronounce it
'true'. This made finding a good, modern example tricky.

I needed a lie, from beginning to end. The cycle of a deceit from
its start to its peak and subsequent collapse. This cycle should not
be too short – I would need some good material – nor should
it be too long and complex. It should be a clear lie that could have
been avoided. A transgression of everyday proportions. Yet to understand its impact, it should be one that was played out on the
world stage. Even better if it involved a treacherous face and I could

apply my new collection of Ekman tricks. My final criteria were that I needed something simple, yet human and provable. Something memorable.

In my forty-ish-year-old brain, there was one such lie that stood out. One I saw for myself. It happened more than twenty years ago, yet it came back to me in bright colours – tricksome, troubling and still confounding.

In fact, it was a corker. And it was not too far removed from the contemporary themes of #MeToo. But there was no one shouting 'me too' back then – this was all about what the man had to say. A man more powerful than even Harvey Weinstein.

This man is an oratorical master. An audacious figure whose lie dominated a year of politics, whose sex story was the first to go viral on the internet and whose famous denial still scores millions of views on YouTube.

I will never forget the first time he lied to me.

I feel conflicted to write this about his particular deceit, but it was almost a work of art. A perfectly formed illusion. There before me was a true savant. Bill looked me in the eyes, took his time, smiled warmly – and lied to me.

But it was not just me he was talking to, a young student watching him on a shared television. No. He was talking to 'the American people'. All 276 million of them.[1]

It was 26 January 1998, and William Jefferson Blythe III Clinton was about to embark on his odyssey of public denials and public

---

1 'Population, total – United States (1998)', https://data.worldbank.org/indicator/SP.POP. TOTL?locations=US

confessions. It was a stunning moment of guile. But old technology meant that once seen, it was gone, lost in news bulletins and headlines, only to resurface badly remembered.

Did he really look me in the eyes?

Had he allowed for the possibility of guilt?

Was his wife there?

But today the digital age has changed everything and helped to rewrite our collective memory. It has certainly helped me with mine.

So, I held my breath, opened YouTube and typed in 'bill clinton denies'. And there he was. Ready and waiting, frozen in time in the Roosevelt Room of the White House. It was a moment of crisis, he was about to bet the house, would he win or would he lose? If I wanted to get to grips with adult lies, this clip was an excellent place to start.

The news had broken nine days earlier, with claims online that *Newsweek* had pulled a story at the last minute that involved the President and a White House aide. The internet was just beginning to connect all our lives, it was transforming the way we saw the world and Drudge Report had the scoop of its life. Digital media was about to outfox traditional media for the first time.

It was a scandal that could have toppled a world leader already being investigated over a suspect land deal and a sexual harassment case.

What would he do?

President Clinton had just made a gracious, courteous speech about education proposals. He thanked everyone in the room, he lauded responsible parents, he praised his wife, who was standing next to him but out of shot of the video camera.

White House press conference, 26 January 1998.
© Harry Hamburg/NY Daily News via Getty Images

As I watched it again, I felt like I was being seduced. Yes, Bill, whatever you say – I'd vote for you. Community learning centres, smaller class sizes… yes, yes, yes. His eyes sparkled, he looked lean and fit, not a word was out of place.

I marvelled at Houdini in a box sealed with chains. How would he get out of trouble? He carries on, thanking supporters, donors, friends, family. The whole room is his. It takes six minutes and seventeen seconds for the presidential cavalcade to come screeching to a halt with one word.

'Now.' There is just a heartbeat between words and the world is rapt.

'I have to go back to work on my State of the Union speech,' he says, reminding us that there are bigger things at play than a putative affair and possibly, even, a hidden blue dress. 'But', he pauses, 'I want to say one thing to the American people.' What is it, Bill, what is it? Surely you have more than one thing to say?

'I want you to listen to me.' Who, me? I am, Bill. I trust you. That is when he got me.

'I did not…', the camera begins to zoom in. 'Have. Sexual. Relations. With that woman…' He punctuates each word by hitting the lectern with his finger, he looks stern, defiant as he upbraids each and every one of us for daring to doubt him. But the words 'that woman' sounded wrong. Why was he suddenly so unchivalrous? Why brush her off like that? Was it because he felt insulted, because it was not true – or more, because he was fighting for his political life? He had to make her sound unimportant, to distance himself from 'Miss Lewinsky', as he then called her.

His lawyerly words so close to the truth were also so close to a lie. Would he have the gall to issue a full denial in front of a whole nation? Would he dare confront such a steaming, hot topic with such cold fakery? Mrs Clinton, wearing a bright yellow, I-will-not-be-ignored outfit, looks on – standing by him, as she would continue to do.

'I never told anybody to lie, not a single time. Never.' Three denials. 'These allegations are false.' Four. 'And I need to go back to work, for the American people.'

And there it was. He was innocent. All the journalists, all the committees, all the prosecutors: they were wrong. He reminded his audience that everything he did, he did it for them and nothing should get in the way of his work. That he should be brought so low to have to deny the allegations spoke only of his nobility. How on earth could this man be lying?

I was in the student common room when I first saw it. I remember my friends and I all looking at each other. 'Did he just…?'

What had happened? The word 'never' rang in the air. The President of the United States had just denied something. On television. Guarded by his two most loyal lieutenants: his wife and Al Gore, the Vice-President, who had been due to give the key speech that day. It felt like it was a big moment.

Who was this mysterious being he had evoked? And why was her name prefaced by the words: 'that woman'? It felt like a hit-and-run. We had just been told something, without being told anything at all. It nagged away at me for a long time, because although I felt as if he had persuaded me, my subconscious told me that it was not true.

The YouTube clips gave me a lot of material, but it was not enough. If it had had such an effect on me, catching it once on television, what was it like to be there, in the Roosevelt Room, on the day in question? I needed to find someone who was around at the time. I needed a member of Team Clinton.

Eventually, through contacts of contacts, I found someone. He was unsure at first. Who was this strange woman so fascinated with lies, and why did she want to pick his brain? Over the course of a few months, and more than a few emails, we agreed some ground rules and, on the condition of anonymity, he spoke to me. As with Foxtrot, the secret agent from Chapter 2, I have given him an assumed name courtesy of the NATO alphabet.

Meet Oscar, the White House official.

Oscar has gravitas, but he is modest, soft-spoken and easy to talk to. I wonder how much he will really be able to tell me. I had established that he would have been at the White House for some of the Monica Lewinsky 'cycle'. But would he remember that day? Was he even in Washington, let alone in the building? He was. And not just nearby. He was inside the Roosevelt Room.

Oscar speaks slowly, deliberately, with emphasis. I dare not interrupt. He tells me how the door opposite the Oval Office opened, and in came the Clinton group.

'I don't remember the order they came in, but I do remember being very surprised that Hillary Clinton looked... [emphasis] *radiant*.'

Having rewatched as many different versions of the press conference as I could, I knew what he meant. Nothing in her bearing gives away any sense of trouble. She seems at ease, in her element, in control. She is so radiant that Oscar later says he remembers her wearing not yellow but gold.

First Lady Hillary Clinton introduces the speeches on education, 26 January 1998.
Courtesy of the William J. Clinton Presidential Library

'But...', says Oscar slowing even more. 'The President looked like he had been up all night... crying. He was... *Washed. Out.*' Oscar tells me that what struck him most was the transformation when it was the President's turn to speak.

'When he came to the podium and the lights were on him, he looked like his normal self. I was struck by that. The ashen face, the stricken look that he wore when he came into the room... it was *gone* when he was speaking to the camera.'

And as Oscar stood in the Roosevelt Room that day, did he know it was a big moment?

Yes, he says, of course. 'We felt the deep seriousness of the moment.'

And did he believe the President? Oscar goes on to describe Bill Clinton as 'a genius', a 'smart politician' who could be 'brilliant' and had an 'amazing ability to connect with people'. At this point, I already know Oscar is a loyalist. So how far will he go?

'I'll tell you the obvious. I did not believe him.' Again, I find that I am holding my breath. 'Based on what I saw in the Roosevelt Room on the Monday... before his State of the Union address... and the way he looked when he entered, I did not believe him.'

So, the man behind the scenes, the man with the background knowledge that evaded 99 per cent of Clinton's audience on that day, this man sensed the same lie I did. But it seems that we were united by something else. We sensed it, but we could not believe that Clinton would dare to do it. So what about the others around him in the White House team? Was it conspiracy – or did we all fall for the same trick?

'I don't know whether [those] who said they believed him... truly believed him.' Oscar pauses a lot when he talks. Some pauses are so long that I worry he will come to a stop, end the interview, leave. But he continues.

'I don't know how many of his Cabinet-level appointees and senior-level White House staff he spoke to personally... eye to eye, face to face... and I don't know what measure of charm and persuasiveness he was able to bring to that moment... but they said they believed him.'

And were the White House teams told how to deal with the issue? Oscar remembers an email going out to one team that could be summed up as: 'Don't. Say. A. Word.'

'It was not that [they] knew anything, just that if the President had put himself in a position where he was risking impeachment and removal from office... [any comment] would be grossly inappropriate.'

Oscar goes back to the day after the speech. Clinton had just finished his State of the Union address when he passed through a group of Oscar's colleagues, who were once again in the Roosevelt Room. That day, the room had been turned into a TV viewing area for staff. Clinton stopped to talk to them. He was fired up and full of energy.

Each word jumps out as Oscar slips into the Clinton lilt and repeats what he said.

'He said: "You gotta keep gettin' up... comin' to work... and doin' your job every day." And then he said: "This... will... turn." And then he left.'

It is another Sphinx-like Clinton phrase. I can only guess that he meant he thought it would all go away.

Oscar says: 'There was the feeling... I had the feeling. But I also think the feeling was shared... that if this [story] is true, he's outta here.' No one believed he would take that risk.

And what was the reaction in the room when Clinton said the line that had so caught my attention – 'that woman'?

'I wasn't really in a position to feel the reaction. Except I can tell you when the President is at that podium, you can hear his voice and shutters clicking. There were just cameras shooting… clicking, clicking, clicking away. It was very obvious it was a significant moment. And he was speaking forcefully.'

And did Oscar have one, lasting impression of the President on that day?

'He didn't seem, *to me*, to have the fire and anger of someone who had been falsely accused.'

Indeed, with the benefit of Oscar's version of events, subsequent records and many, many replays of the YouTube clips, there is one glimpse that suggests Clinton might have had alternate emotions on the day.

Courtesy of the William J. Clinton Presidential Library[2]

---

2   Courtesy of the William J. Clinton Presidential Library (26 January 1998), www.youtube.com/watch?v=HdoWvIe_rxA. His speech starts: 17 mins, 38 secs; the pause: 20 mins, 48 secs; 'that woman': 23 mins, 59 secs.

Three minutes and ten seconds into his speech, Clinton is clapped by everyone in the room. He has to stop, wait for it to finish. For a fraction of a second, the performance halted, he loses eye contact with the audience. A different man suddenly inhabits the charismatic shell. It seems like a flash of shame in response to the applause.

In a heartbeat, it is gone. He stumbles over a word, then the star performer remembers his lines, looks up and continues.

What would he do next, faced with these difficult events? Like every skilled teller of tales, the President waits. The tide 'will turn'. Meanwhile, he keeps his audience entranced. Again and again, he fends off accusers with his charm, his legal skills and his words.

It was seven months later that he testified before the grand jury. The allegations had not gone away and his conduct was being investigated. In his testimony, he reached once again deep into his lawyer's armoury. Even the word 'sex' was undressed several times during the legal to-ing and fro-ing. No word was safe.

What exactly did 'sex' mean?

He was about to outdo himself. Clinton was asked about a statement made by his lawyer, repeating Monica Lewinsky's legal testimony that 'there is absolutely no sex of any kind in any manner, shape or form, with President Clinton'. Was this statement 'utterly false'?

Surely anyone would wither when faced with such legal incisiveness and specificity? Not this President. He took the word 'is' and like an errant dance partner, spun her round several times until she looked like a different word entirely.

'It depends on what the meaning of the word "is" is,' he said, and set about arguing the terribly fine line between 'there is not and never has been' and 'there is not at this precise moment'. Nuance would be too blunt a word to describe it. Pushed on this point, he said that his lawyer's statement 'was well beyond any point of improper contact between me and Ms Lewinsky', so anyone 'generally' speaking in the present tense would be telling the truth. 'Is' was undone.

A recording of the President's testimony would not be released to the public for another month, but that evening, 17 August 1998, he broadcast a public confession on national television. His neat little jig around the truth was coming to an end. Once again, he spoke to the American people. This time, he really did look them in the eyes.

He confessed to a 'physical relationship' that was 'not appropriate' with an intern, whose full name he now remembered. It was wrong, he said, and he 'deeply regretted' misleading people. However, out of the 542 words he used, not one of them was 'sorry'.[3]

Come on, Bill, you think. You are very good at this stuff, but you're going to have to give something up. The presidency perhaps? Not a chance. What about giving some ground, or even uttering one of two tricky words? 'Lied' is hard, because the word 'liar' eats into the very fabric of being a leader. So what about 'sorry'? Would the misleader finally confront his own misleading?

Three weeks later, at a breakfast for religious leaders, he declared that he had searched his soul and found 'genuine sorrow'. This man, who was totally in control of his repertoire, was now hovering yet again so close to a word without actually saying it.

---

3 'August 17, 1998: Statement on His Testimony Before the Grand Jury', UVA, Miller Center, https://millercenter.org/the-presidency/presidential-speeches/august-17-1998-state ment-his-testimony-grand-jury

'I agree with those who have said that in my first statement after I testified I was not contrite enough.' So, would he apologise?

'I don't think there is a fancy way to say that I have sinned.' He was bold enough to call himself a sinner, but would he go further? He then deployed a religious text, a passage from the Yom Kippur liturgy: 'Now is the time for turning ... And this is always painful. It means saying I am sorry.' He said sorry, but he was quoting.[4]

Three months later, on 11 December, he finally did it. Choosing the Rose Garden of the White House for the final scene of his *commedia dell'arte*, he said: 'I am profoundly sorry for all I have done wrong in words and deeds. I never should have misled the country, the Congress, my friends or my family. Quite simply, I gave into my shame.'

A year in press conferences, Bill Clinton, 1998. January: 'These allegations are false'; August: 'I take responsibility'; September: 'I have sinned'; December: 'I am profoundly sorry.'[5]

Details would emerge that showed not just the extent of the liaison but, yes, sexual relations conducted in the President's study and study hallway, just off from the Oval Office.[6] It defies belief that this

---

4 Courtesy of the William J. Clinton Presidential Library (11 September 1998), www.youtube.com/watch?v=B2_EzLLIPNg
5 Stills taken from videos courtesy of the William J. Clinton Presidential Library on YouTube.
6 *Washington Post*, https://www.washingtonpost.com/wp-srv/politics/special/clinton/icreport/6narritii.htm

is an area just a few steps away from the Roosevelt Room, the scene of his original, robust denial.

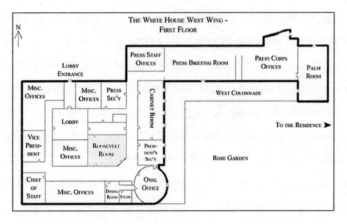

Location of the Roosevelt Room in the West Wing of the White House.
Source: Wikipedia

If he had said 'sorry' in January, perhaps the effect would have been different, but it was too late, the line was too fine and the evidence that was being presented against him was too much.

He was impeached eight days later for perjury and obstruction of justice. However, it would be rash to underestimate his powers of persuasion. The 'comeback kid' lived up to his nickname. He was acquitted on 12 February 1999 and served his full second term until 2001. He had waited it out and, just as he predicted, it had indeed 'turned'.

This extraordinary year-long cycle is made more extraordinary by the circumstances. For one thing, the White House machine collided with the media and the new, public internet in a way it never had before. There were many firsts. The report of the investigation by the independent counsel Kenneth Starr was the first such document to be published in full online. The document that would become known as the Starr Report was a detailed account of the sex scandal, as prepared for the House of Representatives. In 222 pages of unflinching legalese, Starr put the case for impeachment.[7]

There was also the first panic that the internet might crash because so many people were trying to access the same material simultaneously. And it was the first time that excerpts of audio tapes from an investigation were made available online for anyone to listen to freely. The tapes were recordings of a young intern telling an older confidante about her love affair with her boss. Hours and hours of detail that Monica Lewinsky thought was being heard privately.

One sample:

Lewinsky: 'We were getting off, and I'm like, all right, "I love you, butthead". I called him butthead.'

Linda Tripp: 'You didn't.'

Lewinsky: 'I did.'

Her supposed confidante recorded more than twenty hours of conversations, kept them and later submitted them as evidence.[8] This was the unprecedented, public and permanent detailing of a lie.

And it was a lie set apart from others even further, because of the liar's persona. Clinton was not a revolutionary pitted against the establishment; he was an insider, who every step of the way showed how well versed he was in political deportment.

---

7   'Referral from Independent Counsel Kenneth W. Starr in Conformity with the Requirement of Title 28, United States Code, Section 595(c)', www.govinfo.gov/content/pkg/GPO-CDOC-106sdoc3/pdf/GPO-CDOC-106sdoc3-2.pdf

8   'Tripp-Lewinsky Tapes', C-SPAN, www.c-span.org/video/?115463-1/tripp-lewinsky-tapes

So when this man denies 'relations' with 'that woman' in a legal forum, then on a national stage, he elevates his misdeed to a much rarer status. Add to that subsequent misleading testimony the claims of conspiracy, a performance Olympic in nuance in front of a fearsome grand jury, the televised confessions and the world's first viral internet story, and the Monica Lewinsky cycle is distinguished from all other public lies and peccadilloes.

And now, even though I know he lied, when I rewatch that first denial, he hoodwinks me every single time. I want to see goodness, heroism, truth – everything his manner transmits – so I participate in the deception. It seems that the most convincing lies require teamwork – whether we know it or not – and it turned out that in my small way, I too had been part of Team Clinton.

But what about the #MeToo aspect? What about the other alleged women? Surely, there is more to this lie? Monica Lewinsky talked of herself as the 'patient zero'[9] of public shaming and she was indeed exposed in a way few before her had been – but she tells her tale as one of great love, great passion and great regret.

I asked Oscar if the President's potential secrets ever weighed on his mind.

'I do stumble and I stammer when I get to the point of... how do I reconcile my affectionate recollection for President Clinton... knowing that he had this tremendous character flaw?'

The stories have sat heavily in his memories:

---

9 'The price of shame', Monica Lewinsky, TED2015 (March 2015), https://www.ted.com/talks/monica_lewinsky_the_price_of_shame/transcript?language=en#t-241064

Until recently, it seemed like... OK, it's a dalliance with an intern but now it seems... because we just know more, since #MeToo, that it was bigger... And more of a problem than his supporters, including me, ever really honestly admitted. So... there's a reckoning as we learn more about ourselves as history goes forward and we have more guilt than we want to admit.

Oscar's words ring with regret. Suddenly, he sounds weary. He broadens his focus to talk more about group lies and the wilfully blind behaviour that gave rise to #MeToo.

But how much do we lie by simply not saying something?

We didn't call it out. We forgave things – or more like, we tried not to see things and we ignored things and we gave people a pass... or we pretended it wasn't going on and then, there's a reckoning and we realise that we had a moral blindspot that we carefully cultivated. A blindspot, so that we wouldn't have to talk about it or reckon with it or call out our friends and colleagues.

But isn't that just avoidance?

'Avoidance, that's exactly right. It's avoidance! It's *swerving* away from a moral question that could make us awkward – or obliged to confront a colleague... or a group... or an institution.'

Oscar certainly is not swerving now. I wonder if I too am an enabler by focusing only on the man, not the woman – the liar, not the lie-ee; the person in charge of the story. The lie remakes the world of the person who is lied about – and that is what makes lies awkward, awful and awe-inspiring. A simple selection of words, uttered in the right order, at the right time and a situation is transformed.

Seventeen years after the lie cycle, Monica Lewinsky would transform the story again with one of the opening lines of a TED Talk she gave.[10]

'At the age of twenty-two, I fell in love with my boss.'

She uses her talk to make the case for compassion in an age of 'technologically enhanced shaming'. To watch it is to see the other side of a lie, to see what it is like for someone caught in its distortions.

Watching her open, expressive face as she revisited 1998, I remembered that feeling of vertigo. Our experiences could not have been more different but I remembered what it feels like to have your version of yourself taken and brusquely rewritten. It took me straight back to when I was exposed as the main suspect in the mystery of my cardiac arrest – the horror, shame and fear all came flooding back.

How did she feel, when she saw her handsome President dismissing her publicly the way he did? She refers to it in passing.

'The attention and judgment that I … personally received … was unprecedented. I was branded as a tramp, tart, slut, whore, bimbo, and, of course, "that woman". I was seen by many, but actually known by few.' The power of those two puny words is etched into her face more than a decade later. His lie, her shame.

She calls for the crowds on social media to be 'upstanders' not 'bystanders' and talks about the power of empathy and compassion:

---

10 Ibid.

[It's] time to stop tiptoeing around my past, time to stop living a life of opprobrium and time to take back my narrative. It's also not just about saving myself. Anyone who is suffering from shame and public humiliation needs to know one thing: you can survive it. I know it's hard. It may not be painless, quick or easy, but you can insist on a different ending to your story.

His lie, her truth.

Now the 'that woman' moment is almost a quarter of a century old, it is a salutary reminder of the power of digital media and what it does to perpetuate, amplify or distort a story. When it comes to little lies, I need only think of my own social media accounts, where I grab moments and retell them the way I want to, and where mine and most people's profile photos are of a beauty unmatched by the asymmetric reality of our faces. The legacy of 'that woman' brought me to a very awkward point in my exploration of lies. I had learnt that for lies to be good for us – to heal us, protect us, hold us together – there had to be a balance between the white and the grey lies and the much darker ones. But now I was faced with a beast. Could it be that our communication tools have become too powerful and modern media too toxic to preserve that healthy balance?

CHAPTER 9

DIGITAL WARFARE | *MARIA*

O f all the mountains of words that have been written on the challenge social media poses to society, the quote that captures it best is this: 'The real problem of humanity is the following: we have Paleolithic emotions, medieval institutions and god-like technology.' It is not my quote, and it is not even one I found myself, but it is chillingly accurate.

In fact, it runs through everything I would learn about the digital dynamics of today's world. To illustrate it, there is only one place I can start, and it is with the story of a bison.

The howl is what really gets me. It is a silent howl but as I study it, I can imagine what it sounds like. In the flick, flick, flick of photos on my screen, I can see it changing and growing. It is being bellowed from the depths of what can only be described as a human bison.

The three bearded men stand side by side, facing down the security guards. Behind them, the portraits of politicians past stare sternly out of their golden frames. One of the protesters, eyes glazed with defiance, wears a red cap emblazoned with a politician's name; the other, a hoodie. The man in the middle wears a bison headdress. He is bigger than the other two, his torso is bare and covered in tattoos of Norse symbols. This confusing vision of a Native American

Viking carries a spear with an American flag tied to it. His face is painted with the Stars and Stripes. From his shoulder hangs a megaphone. He wears thick black boots and black gloves. This man would later be identified as Jacob Chansley or, as he became known, the QAnon Shaman. He is standing like a rebel leader at the heart of the Capitol building, crying the word: 'Freedom!' This is modern America on 6 January 2021. This is make-believe made real.

A storm of anger had just swept up the steps of the Capitol, through those halls of history and onto the many seats of democracy – including the Vice-President's seat in the Senate Chamber.

The protesters had broken through the flimsy police lines. Hundreds of them climbing the stairs, the buttresses and the walls to get in. They smashed windows. They broke furniture and ripped away podiums. They found and rummaged through the office of House Speaker Nancy Pelosi, photographing documents and leaving taunting notes. There was tear gas and shooting.

That day was the day a joint session of Congress was meant to have certified the result of the American presidential elections: the contest between the Democrat Joe Biden and the incumbent Republican, Donald Trump. This would normally have been a formality, but 2020 was no normal election. After numerous counts and recounts, the winning margin of 7,058,637 votes, or seventy-four electoral college votes,[1] still counted for nothing to many on the Trump side.

For those who stormed the Capitol, it was outright theft.

---

1   'US election results 2020: Joe Biden's defeat of Donald Trump', *The Guardian*, https://www. theguardian.com/us-news/ng-interactive/2020/dec/08/us-election-results-2020-joe-biden-de feats-donald-trump-to-win-presidency

They chanted as one.

'Stop the steal! Stop the steal! Stop the steal!'

'This is our house! This is our country!'

'Yooooo-Essss-Ayyy! Yooooo-Essss-Ayyy! Yooooo-Essss-Ayyy!'

The chants sound spontaneous. They must have been terrifying for the members of Congress caught in the upper chamber, because this mob seemed to have a chilling unity of purpose. This was no coincidence. Research would later show that the chants had long been repeated and perfected on social media. Parts of the crowd had come to Washington prepared, organised and armed.

But where did it begin? When did the warm air first rise, hit cold air and stir the storm to life?

On the day itself, many blamed President Trump, who, rather than conceding as past Presidents and candidates had done, refused to accept even the possibility of defeat.

Could it have been his words alone that caused it?

Earlier that day, at the Save America March, thousands had gathered to hear their Commander-in-Chief. Behind the stage, framed by flags, was the very building from which he would soon be evicted: the White House.

It is mesmerising to watch the scenes on playback, one report superimposing pro-Trump tweets from days before on live footage of the very actions they called for.[2]

The tweets fly. The passion is high. And on the stage, separated from the raucous crowd by screen, Donald Trump prepares to speak to his tribe.

---

2 'How pro-Trump protesters stormed the Capitol', Rohit Kachroo, ITV News/Centre for Capturing Digital Hate (12 January 2021).

He walks towards the podium slowly, deliberately, pointing at the crowd, clapping them, mouthing 'thank you', raising his fist in a sign of solidarity. He comments on the size of the crowd – and asks whether the 'fake news media' would show how big it really was. Size has certainly been a recurring issue of Trump's, and indeed it proves difficult to find a reliable estimate of the size of his crowd.

To a yelping, whooping throng, he picks up on his favourite themes: 'All of us here today do not want to see our election victory stolen by emboldened radical-left Democrats, which is what they're doing.' He takes a quick breath, but his words seem to keep charging on, without pause. 'And stolen by the fake news media. That's what they've done and what they're doing. We will never give up, we will never concede. It doesn't happen. You don't concede when there's theft involved.'

The crowd is rapturous. It seems to be the word 'theft' that does it.

Many have called him a buffoon and a rambling orator. From my experiences as a speechwriter, I think his speech is chillingly well executed. He sticks to his theme. He repeats phrases that then get repeated by others like an incantation. His speech builds and builds. He is absolutely in tune with his audience. He connects with them directly, on a personal level – and his words incite emotion, belief and even action.

From his plinth, Trump excites the crowd even further.

'We will not let them silence your voices. We're not going to let it happen. Not going to let it happen.'

The crowd chants: 'Fight for Trump!'

'Thank you,' he replies.

Later in the speech, he encourages them yet further.

'Because you'll never take back our country with weakness. You have to show strength and you have to be strong.'

Then, he rounds off his 74-minute speech with an instruction, presented as a team activity.

'We're going to walk down Pennsylvania Avenue, I love Pennsylvania Avenue, and we're going to the Capitol … [and] we're going to try and give them the kind of pride and boldness that they need to take back our country.'

He did not join them, of course. But he did not need to. Parts of the crowd were already marching towards the barricades on the west side of the Capitol. Some had gathered earlier on the east side of the building. They were ready – and before Trump had even finished his speech, the first barricades were breached.[3]

A week later, Trump would be impeached by the House of Representatives for 'incitement of insurrection'. It would be his second impeachment, which was a first for an American President.

But could his words on the day have been all that was needed to start the storm? Or was it all of his words and actions leading up to that moment? After years of rallying cries, and his unrelenting fight against authority, antecedents and measurable truth, he spent the weeks after the election urging his supporters to head to Washington and protest against the result.

He certainly knows how to create bad weather, but could it be that the storm started elsewhere? Perhaps in another regime, led by

---

3 'How a Presidential Rally Turned Into a Capitol Rampage', Lauren Leatherby, Arielle Ray, Anjali Singhvi, Christiaan Triebert, Derek Watkins and Haley Willis, *New York Times* (12 January 2021), www.nytimes.com/interactive/2021/01/12/us/capitol-mob-timeline.html

another 'strong-man leader', but one who comes in a very different guise?

The Election Integrity Partnership (EIP) is a research group that includes a team from Stanford University. It studies electoral disinformation in America.

In a report on the source of allegations of vote-rigging in the 2020 election, the group writes:

> This narrative [of the delegitimised election] is worth examining not for its content, but to understand how it weaves together a wide swath of discrete events into an overarching meta-narrative, involving both influencers and ordinary users in the process. The meta-narrative becomes a scaffolding on which any future event can be hung: any new protest, or newly-discovered discarded ballot, is processed as further confirmatory evidence.[4]

A 'meta-narrative' – now I really was getting into the dark sophistication of digital lies. If the events leading up to Clinton's impeachment in 1998 marked the first time a digital story turned viral, the events leading up to Trump's second impeachment seemed to be a case study in digital warfare. The battle over the truth is very different when there are suddenly so many different published 'truths' to fight for.

At first glance, digital lies are something that happen up close, they are immediate and amorphous, but the more I tried to step

---

4 'Laying the Groundwork: Meta-Narratives and Delegitimization Over Time', Renee Diresta and Isabella Garcia-Camargo, Election Integrity Partnership (19 October 2020), www. eipartnership.net/rapid-response/election-delegitimization-meta-narratives

back and look at them as a phenomenon, the more I started to worry about modern lies. Or at least, the modern tools that enable lying.

Have we gone past a point of no return? If lying can be seen as a social superpower, is social media its kryptonite? The evidence shows its users – us – in a bad light. The digital landscape is changing so fast that it still feels like we are only building frontier towns in a territory we know little about. The 'www', the world's new Wild West, is fertile ground for information – and disinformation. Our data footprints leave traces of lies everywhere, from the white lies of enhanced selfies to the dark reaches of troll land.

One day we may look back and censor ourselves, the servers may fail and delete us, but at this very moment, we seem to be willingly testifying for and against ourselves on a daily basis. Even if I am cautious, I still share huge amounts of data every minute of every day. Where am I? My phone will tell you. What am I doing? Call me using video. What is my guilty passion? Just ask Amazon.

In 2017, Seth Stephens-Davidowitz, a former data scientist at Google, published *Everybody Lies*, a book based on aggregated Google search data. What he found is that the questions people typed into their search engines in the privacy of their homes were rather different to the answers they would give when speaking to others – for instance, on social media or when answering surveys. As he puts it:

> Google was invented so people could learn about the world, not so researchers could learn about people. But it turns out the trails we leave as we seek knowledge on the internet are tremendously revealing.

In other words, people's search for information is, in itself, information. When and where they search for facts, quotes, jokes, places, persons, things, or help, it turns out, can tell us a lot more about what they really think, really desire, really fear, and really do than anyone might have guessed.[5]

His book includes many provocative revelations including the prevalence of racist views, the link between violent films and violent offences and what he calls the truth about abortion. One area he explores in brief is the question of how many men might be secretly gay in the more conservative states of America. Survey results are unsurprisingly unhelpful on this topic, as are Facebook profiles, but an analysis of searches on American pornography sites certainly suggests an interest in explicit gay male material that is far greater than those who admit to it. So how to get closer to the truth?

One ingenious way is to look at the number of Google searches asking a very specific question. In private moments, wives across the whole of America have been asking: 'Is my husband gay?' In fact, the phrase 'Is my husband...?' is 10 per cent more likely to be completed with the word 'gay?' than it is with the second most common word: 'cheating?'. Stephens-Davidowitz found that in twenty-one of the twenty-five states where this question is asked most frequently, support for gay marriage is lower than the national average. The two states where the question was asked most often? The deeply conservative states of Louisiana and South Carolina.

While we may be able to use our digital words and images to

---

5 *Everybody Lies: What the Internet Can Tell Us About Who We Really Are*, Seth Stephens-Davidowitz (2017).

mask ourselves in the most simple ways, the way we use the internet shows us as we really are. The billion-dollar question is who controls all the data? Who controls all this truth? It seems a strangely disproportionate power to leave in the hands of those blandly dressed billionaires in Silicon Valley. Perhaps the answer to addressing the vast quantity of digital truth and lies out there is to determine who is responsible for them. The frontier towns could do with a few sheriffs. From the latest court cases unfolding across the world, this is a battle that will continue in decades to come. But even if these digital tools are deeply problematic, I could not ask for a better way to see modern lying behaviour in action.

To get a sense of the scale, the world's population was 7.83 billion at the start of 2021. Of that number, a staggering 5.22 billion use a mobile phone, 4.66 billion use the internet and 4.2 billion use social media. That is more than half the world tapping, posting and sharing.[6]

Suddenly it seems that every new generation has its own code for interactions, anyone with access to a network can be their own publisher and every published fragment can be spread exponentially and at great speed. There is little to stop the small ripples of a white lie becoming tidal waves of deceit – propaganda, even. This was what was bothering me. I was happy to go dark in exploring lies as long as they led me to some truths. What would I really find if I entered deep into what is often called the 'echo chamber' of social media?

Back to the meta-narrative, Trump and 6 January. The EIP did

---

6 'Digital 2021: The Latest Insights Into The "State Of Digital"', We Are Social (27 January 2021),
   https://wearesocial.com/uk/blog/2021/01/digital-2021-the-latest-insights-into-the-state-of-digital/

an excellent job of mapping the spread of an idea – from the first seedling to the forest fire.

The EIP broke it up into four phases. The first is to introduce an idea – in this case, that there was a deep-state, leftist conspiracy to topple the Republican administration in America. However, the 'strong-man' leader most closely associated with this initial idea was not Trump, it was Vladimir Putin – and the year was not 2021, it was 2019. The article identifies the first outings of this idea in a series of opinion pieces in Russia Today or RT, the state-owned media network. Not only do the pieces introduce this idea; crucially, they pin it to one punchy term: the 'color revolution'. Note the American spelling.

This packaging of a complex idea with a simple label (or eventually hashtag) means that the convoluted notion of a conspiracy becomes much easier to disseminate. To do this successfully, the EIP showed that the people behind the initial idea need one thing more than anything: time. And so it was that the articles in RT started to appear as early as August 2019. This is Phase One, it lasts a year and the EIP calls it 'Introducing the Narrative'.

Phase Two, which the EIP calls 'Mainstreaming', is essentially when the idea, now rumbling on in the background, finds a conduit into mainstream media – social and otherwise. In this case, it was Trump's former speechwriter turned commentator Darren Beattie.

He appeared in a range of broadcasts that presented the idea to a much wider world. Sample message: 'What's unfolding before our eyes is a very specific type of coup called the Color Revolution.'

He repeated it on the Trump-supporting Fox News in mid-September – and that was when the 'Super Spreaders' came into play. Phase Three. These are 'active users', spreading content to dozens of groups simultaneously, in this case, over a three-week period that pushes the idea to the fourth and final phase, 'Normalization'.

As the report puts it:

An October 7th 'Q-drop' (a post from the actor that goes by 'Q' in the QAnon conspiracy theory community) pushes the term into a large, aligned new audience: the cluster of online communities dedicated to following Q, which has previously spent years suggesting that the President is battling Deep State forces. Group super-spreader dynamic continues, but the term now enters the casual vernacular of a broader right-wing audience.[7]

The academic tone in which this process is presented emphasises just how much cold calculation goes into 'seeding' a virulent idea and into generating 'spontaneous' behaviour years later. It is not hard to see how this might have led all the way to the so-called QAnon Shaman howling 'Freedom!' in the heart of the Capitol. On that day, they were jubilant. After all, he and his fellow rebels had stormed the building of their own free will, hadn't they?

This vast mobilisation of ideas was explained to me patiently on a Sunday morning by one of the most extraordinary people I have met in my pursuit of lies – and the truth behind them.

I have met champion liars and champion lie-spotters, but the effervescent woman talking to me on a video call, in such an animated fashion that I remember it as if we had been face to face, is a truth champion.

---

7 'Laying the Groundwork: Meta-Narratives and Delegitimization Over Time', Diresta and Garcia-Camargo.

Maria Ressa is an award-winning journalist who was CNN's bureau chief in Manila and then Jakarta, went on to head the news division of ABS-CBN, the largest media organisation in the Philippines, and now runs Rappler, the multimedia news website based in the Philippines, which she founded with a group of like-minded, digitally skilled journalists in 2012. Rappler's investigative work has put Ressa squarely in the sights of another 'strong-man' populist leader, Rodrigo Duterte, President of the Philippines.

In 2018, she was one of a group of journalists who jointly won *Time* magazine's Person of the Year, under the headline 'The Guardians and the War on Truth'.

Chillingly, another of the winners was Jamal Khashoggi, the Saudi journalist killed that year at the Saudi consulate in Istanbul. Allegedly, this was an assassination approved by the Kingdom's Crown Prince Mohammed bin Salman, whom Khashoggi had been reporting on and investigating. The Crown Prince has long since denied this charge.

Ressa's work has been recognised many times. In April 2021, she was awarded the UNESCO/Guillermo Cano World Press Freedom Prize and in October that year became the first Filipino to win the Nobel Peace Prize, jointly winning with the Russian journalist Dmitry Muratov for 'safeguarding freedom of information'.

She also has a sheen of celebrity, one that hopefully protects her as much as her standing and reputation. She is represented by human rights lawyer Amal Clooney, has been interviewed on air by the unlikely figure of Prince Harry, the Duke of Sussex, and in 2020 was the subject of a multi-award-winning documentary film, *A Thousand Cuts*, directed by Ramona S. Díaz and focusing on President

Duterte's war of attrition against the press. Through Ressa, I would learn that in the Philippines, the art of political, social-media warfare is way ahead of America.

With her profile and her determination to 'call out injustice' no matter the personal cost, Ressa had made a very powerful enemy in Duterte – and before I could learn more about her, I had to learn more about him.

It was in 2016 that Rodrigo Roa Duterte swept to power with hardline promises to wipe out crime, corruption and, ultimately, dissent. He was seventy-one and before he became President, Duterte had been mayor of Davao City in the south of the Philippines on and off for nearly thirty years. His rule was controversial and bloody, his approach was that only violence could stop violence and he earned himself the nickname 'Duterte Harry', from Hollywood's most famous tough-guy cop: *Dirty Harry*. He may have transformed the city from the chaos of the 1980s and made it one of the safest in the Philippines, but reports were rife of a death squad operating on his behalf. As a Human Rights Watch report puts it, '[he] was very clear about his intention to eliminate crime by eliminating criminals.'[8] To illustrate this, the report uses a quote of Duterte's that refers to the 1,000 people allegedly executed while he was mayor.

'If by chance that God will place me there [the presidency], watch out because the 1,000 will become 100,000. You will see the fish in Manila Bay getting fat. That is where I will dump you.'[9]

Duterte has thrived on his direct, uncensored approach and

---

8   '"License to Kill": Philippine Police Killings in Duterte's "War on Drugs"', Human Rights Watch (2 March 2017), https://www.hrw.org/report/2017/03/02/license-kill/philippine-pol ice-killings-dutertes-war-drugs

9   Ibid.

shock tactics ranging from encouraging his supporters to take the law into their own hands to admitting sexual assault as a teenager and murder as an adult. He frequently makes sexual references in public and he caused a storm in 2016 for the way he referred to the death of a female missionary who was raped and murdered in a hostage siege in 1989 when he was Davao City's mayor.

'I was angry because she was [gang] raped, that's one thing,' he said. 'But she was so beautiful, the mayor should have been first, what a waste.' It is still shocking to reread this. It is in keeping with his other public comments.

He also called not only President Obama but Pope Francis 'sons of whores' and showed his middle finger and told the 'hypocrites' of the European Union 'f*ck you'. (My asterisk.)

When it comes to journalists, this President is no less combative. After a journalist was murdered in 2016, he said: 'Just because you're a journalist you are not exempted from assassination if you're a son of a bitch.'

The Philippines has long been a dangerous place to be a journalist, but global reports on the state of journalism during Duterte's rule make sobering reading. The Committee to Protect Journalists found that in 2020, the Philippines was one of three countries with the most journalists 'singled out for murder in retaliation for their work'. It says that three were murdered in 2020 alone.[10] The Philippines now sits 138th in a list of 180 countries ranked in the 2021 World Press Freedom Index.[11]

But for Duterte, it was not always so. He is solicitous towards those

---

10 'Murders of journalists more than double worldwide', Committee to Protect Journalists (22 December 2020), https://cpj.org/reports/2020/12/murders-journalists-more-than-doubled-killed/

11 '2021 World Press Freedom Index', Reporters Without Borders, https://rsf.org/en/ranking

he believes are on his side and his encounters with the press were not hostile by default. Indeed, Rappler followed him closely on the campaign trail in 2016, and in the past, he has thanked them for the extensive coverage which he said helped him to win. Ressa interviewed him several times, once when he was still mayor, on 26 October 2015.

Now I have learnt more about him, it is unnerving to see them sitting face to face, less than a metre apart. The interview takes place at a hotel, chosen by Duterte, in Davao City. In photos of the interview, he and his small entourage are seen being welcomed, with a few of the senior Rappler team watching warily from the sidelines.

As the cameras roll, Maria is polite and careful, but although her voice is soft, her questions are unflinching. She asks him about his rule in Davao City.

Rodrigo Duterte interviewed by Maria Ressa before
he announced his run for the presidency.
Source: rappler.com

'So, no qualms about killing killers?'

'Yes, of course. I must admit, I have killed,' he says. 'Three months earlier I killed about three people.' His face is impassive.

He sits spread-legged, facing her. She leans in and holds his gaze, unwavering.

And how would he fix the problems of the Philippines?

'When I said I'll stop criminality, I'll stop criminality. If I have to kill you, I'll kill you. Personally.' He speaks quietly, deliberately. His voice does not change whether he is talking about committing murder, running 'a dictatorship' or how much he loves his country. Contrary to the size and ferocity of his ambitions, he is small in build and casual in appearance. He has a roguish charm, answers every one of her questions and his calm demeanour is as unsettling as a hand grenade. It is quite an encounter. Ressa's voice is even quieter at the end of the interview, but her eyes have a new shine to them. Is it fear – a premonition of what is to come?

In the article accompanying the interview, Ressa wrote that to understand Duterte's appeal, it was important to understand the context.

'Institutions are weak at best and law and order is patchy in many parts of the country. Violence is part of the political landscape, and it gets worse during elections.'[12] She writes that the worst election-related violence in the world happened in the Philippines in 2009, when fifty-eight people were massacred, including thirty journalists, the largest number ever recorded killed in one incident.

It was Ressa who helped to break the story of the massacre when she was at ABS-CBN, using photos and information sent to them by a 'citizen journalist' – an ordinary citizen, reporting the events they saw in front of them as they happened. She believes it was likely to have been a soldier, shocked by the killings and using his

---

12 'Duterte, his 6 contradictions and planned dictatorship', Maria Ressa, Rappler (26 October 2015), www.rappler.com/nation/elections/duterte-contradictions-dictatorship

phone to take a few hasty, dangerous photos of the corpses laid out on the ground. A man in the frame stands pointing at one of the eight visible bodies, another has a machine gun, one of the vans in the background has blood on its open side door. Everything in the image speaks of events that are fresh.

As head of news at ABS-CBN, Ressa had been encouraging citizen journalism as a way to make the news more democratic and to encourage engagement, debate and even positive activism. Suddenly, ABS-CBN had in their hands the harrowing, unedited truth from the ground – and they got the news before any official account was given. When events like this take place in election time, it is not hard to see the appeal of a no-nonsense, tough-guy leader who promises to wipe out corruption and stop these kinds of atrocities.

Ressa would go on to form Rappler (a combination of 'rap', to talk, and 'ripple', to make waves) in a bid to 'evolve journalism and use new technology to harness citizens for nation-building'.

The question is, what could Rappler and Ressa go on to do to provoke someone as unshockable as Duterte?

I first met Ressa at Chatham House in London in 2018. It was an event to award its annual prize for the improvement of international relations, and that year, the winners were the Committee to Protect Journalists. I was in the audience, she was a panellist.

She is small in person, talks quietly but passionately and listens intently. She is also a giant of courage, will and perseverance. She has a conviction that somehow shines through every one of the tough stories she tells. We must have spoken for about ten minutes only, but I could not forget her afterwards. I knew if I really wanted to understand truth and lies in the digital world, I had to speak to her again.

I could not have picked a busier period. By the time we were agreeing dates for the interview, she had had the documentary crew following her around for a year, she was doing a string of events to publicise the film's launch, she had just started writing a book herself, she was fighting nine active criminal cases brought by Duterte's government – and she was running Rappler. But still, true to her open nature, curiosity and enthusiasm for other people's work, she made time to speak to me.

'I wanted to make sure I talked to you because books are incredibly important! When the world is atomised into meaninglessness... the only thing that gives meaning is when you string those moments together. And *that's* what books do... *That's* what the [documentary] film does.'

Her hands punctuate everything she says. She leans in close to the camera many times as we talk. She has an open, expressive face and smiling eyes that convey delight, but more often convey soft and hard sadness. The students of Paul Ekman would love her face. She is wearing a Princeton T-shirt (she grew up in America and studied molecular biology and theatre at Princeton, then won a Fulbright scholarship to return to the Philippines and study political theatre). She is so open, candid and authentic that it feels fake and vaguely insulting to keep using the distancing family name 'Ressa' so, just like Kang, she will be Maria from here on.

'You need the context, you need continuity, right?' She stretches out an imaginary shape in front of her – a story that stands strong because it is a true story. She shakes her head. 'And it is so much easier to manipulate us without context.'

When she says 'atomised into meaninglessness', she is referring to social media, to the millions of digital fragments flying around the infosphere. Because if the physical might of the Duterte regime is fearsome, his digital armies are just as deadly. Orchestrated online attacks were becoming a very real horror in the busy virtual world of the Philippines.

Maria calls Duterte one of several 'digital authoritarians' – and it seems that the digital tentacles of the Duterte team had been reaching out long before he moved into the presidential palace. Indeed, during his time as mayor, Davao City became the first 'smart city' in the Philippines, harnessing as much data as possible from the public services and creating a live 'dashboard' that brought together infrastructure such as traffic management, crime prevention and the emergency services. At the time, the city itself had a particularly active social media community so it was not surprising that Rappler first identified the use of 'Twitter bots' (fake, automated 'robot' accounts) in Filipino politics, four days after Duterte declared he would run for the presidency.

'From midnight to 2am on November 25, 2015, more than 30,000 tweets mentioning Rodrigo Duterte were posted, at times reaching more than 700 tweets per minute,' Maria wrote in an article. 'That's more than … all the tweets about any presidential candidate over the previous twenty-nine days.'[13]

But it was not his digital manoeuvrings that first made Rappler focus hard on how his regime operated. One of his election pledges was to tackle the illegal drugs trade ravaging the cities. Maria says she was stunned by how quickly Duterte moved on the drug gangs

---

13 'Propaganda war: Weaponizing the internet', Maria Ressa, Rappler (3 October 2016), www.rappler.com/nation/propaganda-war-weaponizing-internet

when he came to power. Within the first month, 293 people were reported killed by police or vigilantes.[14] She shakes her head, discussing a spate of deadly acts with the emotional distance of a war correspondent.

> I think I knew in 2016 that we couldn't follow the government line in terms of the number of people killed. And you know, we used the government's own numbers against it. Even now though, we've come under such attack and they have pounded social media so much that people have no idea how many people have died.

When she talks about 'pounding' she makes a slamming fist gesture to show the effect of the social media barrage. Maria herself has faced death threats, imprisonment and battalions of internet trolls for investigating Duterte.

In a sense Rappler is under siege from the very thing that made it so strong: social media. The Rappler newsroom has been the backdrop for many interviews Maria has given – and it is a zone of ceaseless activity. The team, which is now more than 100-strong, is young, predominantly female and perpetually clutching or working at some kind of digital device – whether they are streaming a report on a smartphone turned news camera using a telescopic stand or editing videos or researching furiously on their laptops. Maria is often seen flipping between different digital devices – one laptop, two smartphones and a Bluetooth earpiece and microphone.

When we talk, it is on Zoom, and she has one of the platform's

---

14 'War vs drugs: Cops kill nearly 300 suspects in 24 days', Bea Cupin, Rappler (25 July 2016), www.rappler.com/nation/140853-pnp-war-illegal-drugs-death-toll/

virtual backgrounds covering her own real one. ('Sorry, my family's behind me! Do you mind?') Before we started, I briefly glimpsed a row of photos on top of the piano behind her, a window open in front of her, light streaming in. It is late afternoon in Manila. In Maria's virtual meeting room, there is now a beach scene filling the frame and the waves roll in on a loop as we talk. At one point she will get up to answer the intercom, taking her laptop with her, so that suddenly my interviewee, the palm trees and the ocean are all moving together. It is as disorientating as it is funny. She is candid about herself, completely open about what she is doing and when, but a fierce protector of even a glimpse of her loved ones.

When the Rappler team started covering the drug raids, they used 'crowdsourcing' to find the location of a killing as quickly as possible. This meant using as many different reports of an incident as they could find on social media and combining them to confirm the details. Rappler's use of citizen journalists added to its edge – and its popularity. Having verified a killing thanks to the virtual crowd, the young reporters would then speed off on the back of a moped, digital camera in hand, live streaming where possible – truth hunters, in constant motion.

What they kept finding were not signs of armed resistance but bodies splayed in the streets, often surrounded by a stunned group of relatives and onlookers. The corpses were left as a warning, a fulfilment of Duterte's election promises, but, as one report puts it, the police learnt quickly to collect the bodies as soon as possible.[15] In the Philippines, if you are aged sixteen to sixty-four, you spend the

---

15 *Fake News, Real Consequences*, Series 3, Episode 19, CBSN Originals (27 June 2019).

most amount of time on social media per day than anywhere else in the world (four hours and fifteen minutes in 2021).[16] This meant it was not a clever move to leave the evidence of asymmetric warfare bleeding on the streets, just waiting to be captured on camera, posted and shared.

The best way to get a sense of the scale of what happened in the first few years of Duterte's presidency is to use that most disputed of commodities: data.

Duterte was sworn in on 30 June 2016. Between 1 July 2016 and 26 September 2017, the Drug Enforcement Agency of the Philippines stated that 3,906 suspected drug users and dealers had been killed in police operations. That is almost nine people a day. According to reports amassed by Human Rights Watch, that figure was actually more than 12,000.

By 30 September 2020, the government agency put the figure at 5,903. Again, local human rights agencies had a different figure. The UN reports that the total number of deaths in that time may well have amounted to more than 27,000.[17] That is more people than would fit in the Philippine Sports Stadium, the largest in the country.[18]

'You know the crazy thing is I thought by this time it would be better. Right? I mean, I started talking about Facebook and Duterte

---

16 'Digital 2021: Global Overview Report', We Are Social, https://wearesocial.com/uk/blog/2021/01/digital-2021-the-latest-insights-into-the-state-of-digital/

17 'Philippines: Events of 2017', Human Rights Watch, www.hrw.org/world-report/2018/country-chapters/philippines; 'Philippines: No Letup in "Drug War" Killings', Human Rights Watch (14 January 2020), www.hrw.org/news/2020/01/14/philippines-no-letup-drug-war-killings; 'Philippines: Events of 2020', Human Rights Watch, www.hrw.org/world-report/2021/country-chapters/philippines

18 'In Photos: A glimpse inside the Philippine Sports Stadium', Josh Albelda, Rappler (15 April 2015), www.rappler.com/sports/89985-in-photos-glimps-philippine-sports-stadium/

and demanding an end to [presidential] impunity in 2016!' Her eyebrows knot in frustration but her voice stays level.

'And it's 2021, so it hasn't improved.' She smiles. It is a disarmingly sad smile that surfaces many times during our interview.

She refers to Duterte's 'creeping dictatorship' and says that journalists have to shine a light on it. 'That's what journalists do. We call it out. We hold it to account.'

And so Rappler kept on digging.

'We began to see the pounding on social media.' Again, Maria makes the fist gesture and swipes down.

Originally, in August of 2016, we didn't know what it was. But we noticed immediately, because we *live* on social media, we noticed that our followers – the people who would normally have conversations on Facebook – were now being pounded to silence, because the first people that would go on a thread would spread hate.

These accounts would toxify the discussion and discourage both those speaking up and others joining in.

In October that year, over a week-long period, Rappler published three in-depth articles into how the Duterte administration had been 'weaponizing the internet'. Maria wrote two of them. In the first, she focused on the techniques deployed in an online assault. The foot soldiers in the propaganda war were 'bots' and fake accounts.

Maria describes bots as: 'program[s] written to give an automated response to posts on social media, creating the perception that there's a tidal wave of public opinion'. She writes that these programs can generate thousands of posts per minute. The fake accounts are 'manufactured online identities' and they can be lucrative. The Rappler team found that the people behind these accounts could earn up to P100,000/month[19] (close to £1,600/month at the time).

Maria's follow-up article focused on how much a platform's algorithms could affect the behaviour of its users by deciding what they see on their feeds. Rappler looked at Facebook in particular, the most popular platform in the Philippines. By 2019, there were almost 68 million Facebook users, out of a population of 108 million, and almost 97 per cent of internet users were accessing the platform.[20]

'Facebook's algorithms … cater to our weaknesses, what psychologists call cognitive bias – when we unconsciously gravitate towards those who echo what we believe.' The problem, she writes, is that the algorithms 'don't distinguish fact from fiction'.[21] Untruths were being amplified because so many people were repeating them. Considering the vast number of Facebook users, Maria argued that this meant these algorithms were shaping reality.

The final article looked at a specific set of fake accounts designed to 'manufacture reality'. Rappler identified twenty-six fake accounts on Facebook that together extended to a network influencing at

---

19 'Propaganda war', Ressa.
20 'Number of Facebook users in the Philippines from 2017 to 2020, with forecasts until 2026', Statista, www.statista.com/statistics/490455/number-of-philippines-facebook-users/; 'Facebook usage penetration in the Philippines from 2015 to 3rd quarter 2020', Statista, www.statista.com/statistics/490518/share-of-the-philippines-internet-users-using-facebook/
21 'How Facebook algorithms impact democracy', Maria Ressa, Rappler (8 October 2016), www.rappler.com/newsbreak/facebook-algorithms-impact-democracy

least 3 million other accounts.[22] With this many apparently different voices all presenting the same 'truth', dissenting voices such as Maria's and Rappler's begin to seem like the lying minority. This fake, virtual world was not just one big lie, it was millions of tiny ones together.

It is one thing to see headlines and have a sense that propaganda wars are being fought on a new terrain; it is quite another to be this deep inside the digital world – not just a wilderness of mirrors but a refracting, distorting, spinning maze of lies. This made my chest tight. The safe harbour of a tiny lie was being used to create illusions big enough to change the outcome of elections. Digital lying behaviour seemed to have no redeeming features whatsoever – and white lies particularly enabled huge deceits. Was this digital distortion the natural culmination of a species hardwired to tell stories unreliably? Would we lose ourselves in our lies? I hoped that Maria could show me that there was still hope for our digital lives. Meanwhile, she carried on with her story – and it took me deeper into the maze.

Rappler had now truly stuck its head above the parapet, and the troll army – and its commanders – took notice. Now the 'pounding' got personal. Maria says that she was getting more than ninety hate messages per hour on Facebook.

When Maria describes this to me, she refers to a recent study by the International Center for Journalists, the University of Sheffield and Rappler.[23] The report on fighting online violence analysed more

---

22 'Fake accounts, manufactured reality on social media', Chay F. Hofileña, Rappler (9 October 2016), www.rappler.com/newsbreak/investigative/fake-accounts-manufactured-reality-social-media
23 'Maria Ressa: Fighting an Onslaught of Online Violence', International Center for Journalists (2021), www.icfj.org/our-work/maria-ressa-big-data-analysis

than 57,000 posts and comments published on Facebook between 2016 and 2021, and almost 400,000 tweets directed at Maria from December 2019 to February 2021.

'It actually showed you the goal [of the attacks]. Almost 60 per cent of the attacks were about "liar!", right? About credibility,' says Maria. 'So they were aiming to cut down credibility.' She slices the air repeatedly with her hand.

'And then 40 per cent were very personal. Misogynistic, sexist, super nasty, threats, you know… and then, I'm going to say that 16 per cent were violent…' In her savagely understated way, Maria then evokes what the scale of the attacks must have felt like: '…but 16 per cent of almost half a million is still a lot.'

I remember when I first started researching Maria, I very quickly came across negative posts. One example was on a YouTube video of an interview she did with CBS News.

Normally, I would glance at comments beneath a post, then move on. This time, I scrolled down. The comments were seemingly endless, and they all repeated the same kind of thing: 'She is not fighting fake news, she IS fake news!!!' Over and over. It was like a roomful of voices. Outraged view upon outrage. But there was no one there at all. Common sense told me that these were not normal, spontaneous replies. They were similar lengths, focused on the same details and were unnervingly accurate in the points they picked to attack. They had to be choreographed. This was a mild incursion for the troll army, but even so, it showed itself as garrulous, raucous and insatiable.

The online violence report calls this 'networked gaslighting'

– when Maria exposes disinformation, she herself is accused of disinformation. It lists the many ways in which she was being attacked.

'Death threats. Rape threats. Doxxing. Racist, sexist, and misogynistic abuse and memes.' There were so many different techniques that I was learning a new vocabulary. I looked up 'doxxing', which is the public posting of private information, like a home address, as a threat to a person's safety. The term comes from 'dropping dox' on someone – meaning 'documents'. In Rappler's case, it was Maria's email address and the exact address of their offices.

The report says that Maria is attacked for being a journalist, a woman, an American citizen. They demean her. They question her sexuality. They attack the colour and texture of her skin. One called for her to be 'publicly raped to death'.

To see that much manufactured hatred brought together in one report is revolting. The original posts are meant to provoke a reaction, and in me, they certainly do.

'It's funny, you know,' says Maria, using the one word I would not associate with any of this, 'the biggest attack that they've done… that they keep doing, is actually on my skin – because I have really dry skin, I have eczema. So it's really personal, right?' She strokes the skin on her face lightly as she speaks. This is such a raw subject. That sad smile is back.

'At the beginning of this, which must have been 2019 when I got arrested, they put my face on a scrotum, like a hairy scrotum…' Now, her face is still. Her voice is low. 'I wake up to it. It's dehumanising… but that's the goal of it.' She leans in even closer to the screen, now clear-eyed with purpose. 'And you know, I think the key part is: own your truth. Whatever it is that they try to hit you with.' She pauses. 'So whatever it is they do, I feel like…' she nods as she says: 'What doesn't kill you makes you stronger. And that's what they forced me to do.'

To get a sense of the vicissitudes of having such a high public profile in the Philippines, this storm of revulsion surrounds someone once voted the 'sexiest woman alive' in the Philippines by *Esquire* magazine.[24] That was just over ten years ago. Maria's face looks almost exactly the same but the spotlight being shone on it has changed.

If Stephens-Davidowitz talks of online searches as a truth serum in *Everybody Lies*, this digital mobilisation has created an astoundingly powerful lie machine. These are mechanised lies put in the hands of real users and propagated with minimal effort, because sharing an emotionally charged post requires only the merest flicker of a decision. One click, one tap, and before you know it, you have connected once more with all your 'followers'.

In a presentation in 2011, Maria talked about the chemicals that are at work in our brains:

Are you addicted? Chances are, to some degree, you are. Your dopamine levels, the chemical that causes addiction, increases when you're on social media. It's proven in fMRI – Functional Magnetic Resonance Imaging studies, in brain scans! Remember, our emotions are really just chemical reactions, and social media is tweaking your emotions by changing the chemical levels in

24 'The Sexiest Woman Alive… From Every Country on Earth', *Esquire* (11 October 2010), www.esquire.com/entertainment/g654/sexiest-women-world/

your brain. Because your emotions are heightened, your expectations and the way you behave shifts.

She described the high that she felt herself when she first broke a news story on several different platforms. She thought it was the journalist's adrenalin of meeting a deadline, but later found out through her research that it was caused by elevated levels of dopamine and oxytocin. The latter is known as the love hormone and studies show that it increases when we connect with others online.[25]

This means that when we share a post, we feel more pleasure than responsibility – the thrill of being part of something bigger. I recognise the feeling, even if I hate what it means in practice. This is the 'cognitive bias' Maria refers to, the echo chamber.

The online violence report puts Maria at a unique point in the geography of digital hate: 'Ressa is an emblematic case study in the global scourge of online violence against women journalists, which operates at the intersection of viral disinformation, networked misogyny, platform capture, press freedom erosion, and contemporary populist politics.'

Among the most frequent hashtags aimed at Maria were #liar, #Rapplerfakenews and #presstitute – a favourite term of one of Duterte's female bloggers. But another theme had started to emerge.

In May 2017, #ArrestMariaRessa began to surface. Indeed, Maria says she needed only look at social media to find out what the

---

25 'The Internet and New Media: Tools for Countering Extremism and Building Community Resilience', Maria Ressa (2011).

government was going to do next. It took less than two years for that hashtagged wish to be fulfilled in reality.

In February 2019, plain-clothes policemen turned up at the Rappler offices and arrested her. The moment is captured in the documentary *A Thousand Cuts*. Maria exudes an other-worldly calm as she is led out of the offices. Every member of her team seems to be filming it. The documentary crew film them filming it. Her neat pastel blue suit seems a polite rebuke to the burly men in T-shirts leading her away. The charges were based on the relatively new law of cyber libel. Maria spent the night at the National Bureau of Investigation, then was released after posting bail. She was arrested again six weeks later on charges of being a front for a foreign owner. She calls this 'lawfare'.

By the time I speak to her, in March 2021, she will have posted bail ten times in less than two years. As she puts it, she has paid more in bail and bonds than Imelda Marcos, who, as the wife of the country's former dictator Ferdinand Marcos, has had corruption cases filed against her across the world.

'I came [back to the Philippines] to study theatre's role in bringing about political change. And here I am thirty-five years later!' She rocks back with a loud laugh and claps her hands. 'Right?!'

After Maria's night in detention, she emerged back into the spotlight of the media, pale, her eyes watering with the strain, but still standing firm. She made a statement that contains a line she repeats often and which would become the title of the documentary.

'What we're seeing is death by 1,000 cuts of our democracy … We at Rappler… we will not duck, we will not hide, we will hold the line.' #holdtheline is now the hashtag that her supporters use in response to every new attack. If she were convicted of all the charges she faced in March 2021, she would spend the rest of her life in jail. So how does she withstand the barrage?

I'm so busy. I study it, and I study it… I study it… so it almost seems separate from me. Because, I have a company to run and we've actually done well, and even under the pandemic, we've grown. I hired twenty-one more people last year, we've found a sustainable business model. I guess I'm actively searching for a solution. I do believe that facts are critical.

But if her objectivity helps to keep the attacks at a distance, how does she stop her emotional response? She looks away from the camera, thinking.

'At a micro level, as a person… if you live lies… even if you call them white lies… if you cannot embrace the worst truths… then you *cannot* progress… you *cannot* grow… you *cannot* be your own best person.' She shakes her head lightly as she says this.

'I mean, it's my formula for dealing with the worst case, which is to embrace the worst that could happen, right?' She holds her hand up and closes it like a claw. 'Embrace the worst case… Embrace your fears. I think, at an individual level, living in illusions doesn't work.'

She is certainly extraordinarily matter-of-fact about the challenges she faces. She jokes about how she always wanted to splice *Star Trek*'s Captain Kirk (led by his heart) and Mr Spock (led by logic). It sounds like *Star Trek* needs a new lead character, because those two traits are exactly what Maria combines. They are also how she overcomes the worst of the virtual and real campaigns against her.

When I ask her how she deals with smaller, day-to-day lies – social reality not social media – her answer is all about balance.

She recognises the white lies that have to be told in management – both of teams ('you can't be as open as I am as a person!') and family secrets ('families have tons of that!'), and there are things she will not disclose to protect others, but her main, driving force is the pursuit of truth.

I ask her if she has any regrets about her quest for truth.

She stops. Considering the question. Going back in time. She ends up in East Timor, towards the end of the 1990s, during the fight for independence. One of the people who worked with her team was pro-independence.

I remembered her talking about this in a speech in 2019:

It was in the final days of the Indonesian military's scorched earth policy, when they were killing pro-independence supporters. My team and I were leaving the capital, Dili, to head to Suai, about four hours away. We were about halfway there when we stopped for gas, and a source came running to our car. He asked for a ride back to Dili because he said he was being hunted. He feared for his life.[26]

Now I can see the events etched onto her face:

---

26 'Watch: Maria Ressa delivers commencement speech at 2019 Columbia Journalism School graduation', Rappler (23 May 2019), www.rappler.com/world/global-affairs/231333-video-maria-ressa-commencement-speech-columbia-journalism-school-may-2019

So, I didn't lie… I didn't lie to him. What I did say was that we couldn't take him with us because he would make us vulnerable to attacks. So we were driving deeper into where the anti-independence militia with the Indonesian military were attacking and they were actively looking for him. So we couldn't take him in the car. And I… I rationalise it as a decision for my team and for the story. But this guy died because we didn't take him with us. I made arrangements to pick him up in the evening, on the way back, and bring him back to the capital. So… I think about that all the time.

Her shoulders slump, her face is still and sad, she shakes her head and looks away.

When it comes to her own protection, she appears matter-of-fact, almost as if she sees the attacks as part of the job. When it comes to her team, though, she shields them with all her might, just as she does her loved ones.

'I'm more protective of some of our younger reporters. For example, Pia Ranada, you saw in the film, she had to stand up to bully Duterte.'

Ranada was given access to Duterte throughout his campaign to become President. He even wrote her a thank-you note when he won and they remained on good terms until January 2018, when a Rappler piece investigating corruption in his senior team sent him into a fury.

An official statement said he considered it a betrayal from someone he treated 'like a granddaughter'. He banned her from the presidential palace, then squared up to her at a crowded press conference, telling her: 'Your articles are ripe with innuendo and pregnant with falsity.' In a busy but listening room, he goes on in a low voice to rant about the 'fake news' of Rappler, then tells her: 'You are not only throwing toilet paper… you are throwing shit at us.'

Maria says he did that to her, and she was only twenty-six.

Duterte just attacks me verbally but I'm not in the same room. When he banned Pia from the palace, he also banned me – I don't go to the palace, right? So they mean to do this. They mean to use the power of the office. It's asymmetrical warfare against one citizen, one journalist.

It is only later in the interview that I begin to get a sense of the kind of emotions Maria shuts away. If she had not found ways to do this over time it is hard to see how she could carry on as she has done.

'I think the reason why the attacks… why… I feel… a lot of anger. I've gotten very good with anger management.' She smiles – there is no sadness in her smile this time, but it is a smile that disappears fast.

'Yeah. Because it's unjust. And the reason why I became a journalist in the first place is to look for justice. Right? And this is *skewed* so… The world is upside-down.'

This urge to hold the powerful to account is at the very core of Maria's life. She has done it throughout her career. And when I ask her what drives her, her answer is simple.

'It's drawing your lines – and I say this over and over… I can't say it differently. You have to know that line, that if you cross it, you're not you.'

So what is it that makes her 'her'? Where did she start her quest for truth and justice?

'Your timing is… I just wrote chapter one!' Maria is referring to her new book *How to Stand Up to a Dictator*,[27] which she gets up at 5 a.m. every day to work on. Her first chapter is on the first chapter of her life. She laughs loudly and rocks back in her chair again. In the midst of all the heavy subjects, I have found a source of genuine delight. Her first adventures must seem safely in the distance now, but tellingly, they hold as much drama and threat as the situations she would encounter throughout her life.

She tells me about the death of her father before she was one and how her mother left for America to find work and married again, this time to an Italian American. There was a family feud and in 1973, the year after Ferdinand Marcos declared martial law, her mother returned to get her and her sister. She was ten and her sister was eight.

'They took us… kidnapped us from school. And… I remember the date, we landed at JFK on 5 December.' They had flown over Alaska to get there and it was the first time she had seen snow. 'When we got to Toms River, New Jersey… imagine it's like you close one door and then you open another. They speak different languages and they are very, very different cultures.'

I tried to imagine her first day at school.

'I was four foot two, the shortest, only brown kid in the class, and I thought that Americans were so *rude*. Like they were aggressive. I felt sorry for the teacher!' Again, she rocks back with laughter.

---

27 *How to Stand Up to a Dictator*, Maria Ressa (2022).

'So, part of it was being an outsider. It's great training for being a journalist, right?'

I begin to see exactly how Maria's courage – and her curiosity – were forged early on in her life.

'I grew up as an outsider, I spent *years* really trying to understand all of the implicit messages that you see when you hear an accent...' Even then, she was grappling with data sets and trying to understand the truth of a situation. 'Like a New York accent is different from a New Jersey accent... you know, the accent in England, in Scotland, in Ireland... I didn't have those cues because I didn't grow up there.'

She pauses, reliving those years.

'And I saw the bullying part. That happened when I was younger – and that's why now that I'm in my fifties and a President tries to bully me it's like: "You don't!"' She laughs again. 'I mean... When you succumb to a bully, the bully gets stronger!'

And that is when I see it. She is courageous, she is hungry for information but what really keeps her going is a very simple, clear and unwavering characteristic: optimism. She remains luminous even in the darkest of places.

It seems that the reason her opposition to injustice endures is because it is a soft opposition. As she later puts it, she likes the story of the bamboo that sways in a storm and survives, rather than the mighty, unyielding oak which gets uprooted. No matter how many allegations blow in a gale around her, she believes that the truth will survive.

'And I do believe... I trust... you know, someone will be there.' The pitch of her voice raises. 'Because I think that people fundamentally know what's right. What's fair. What's just!' Her hands are open. She is leaning in close to the screen again.

'My best friend from college would say I'm naïve... but that's OK!' Her pitch raises even more. 'I'm really old now! I still believe in my ideals, that's pretty good!'

Maria is giving me a ray of hope, but before I can rest easy on this unexpected, sunny ledge, she has gone back into the maze.

She says that what is happening in the Philippines should be seen in context because the Philippines is a testing ground for what happens elsewhere. If Filipinos spend more time on social media than anyone else in the world, they also spend the most time online – an average of eleven hours a day. The global average is just under seven hours.[28] Maria compares the seeding of ideas in the Philippines, like the 2017 hashtag that called for her arrest, to the assault on the Capitol building in Washington in January 2021. She says that when she sees the impact of online disinformation across the world, she does not understand why the world is not panicking.

'It is critical right now because the distribution platform for facts, which is what journalists write, the distribution platform for facts is biased against facts.' The platform algorithms serve up sensational titbits that then have to compete with strait-laced facts – and the facts lose out almost every time.

She calls this a crisis, which she then sums up in the quote that I found so powerful. It was the American socio-biologist Edward O. Wilson who encapsulated humanity's problems so pithily:

---

28 'Digital 2021: Global Overview Report'.

'Paleolithic emotions, medieval institutions and god-like technolo-gy.'[29] She counts each one on her fingers as she says it.

That's why I keep saying that an atom bomb has gone off in our information ecosystem. It is just like the end of World War II. You can see the direct impact, and yet, it isn't the way we analyse the world. Our biology is... being... *used*... against us. We are being insidiously manipulated. And that changes the world!

She has said most of these extraordinary sentences with the quiet intensity of someone used to repeating things slowly to people who have not grasped the gravity of a situation. But now, the pitch of her voice rises again and her eyes widen.

'Did we not know this before?' There is a flash of anger in her eyes. 'This actually proves these...' for once, she is searching for her words, 'unscrupulous... money-hungry... manipulators. They're largely countries doing it for political gain... or platforms them-selves who are making money hand over fist, even during the pandemic.'

Now is such a crucial time, she says.

'If there are no facts, you can't have journalism, you can't have de-mocracy, you can't have any... meaningful... human... endeavour.' She emphasises each word. 'Look at the *huge* existential problems that we're dealing with.' Again, she counts out three crucial things.

---

29 'Looking Back Looking Forward: A Conversation with James D. Watson and Edward O. Wilson', Harvard Museum of Natural History (9 September 2009), https://hmnh.harvard. edu/lecture-video-year/2009-2010

'Climate… pandemic… and *truth*! So you go back to lies. Lies and truth. It is fundamental to our survival.' Watching her talk like this, I can see that the lie machine faces a mighty warrior – especially as this warrior knows how to bend like bamboo in a storm.

She keeps apologising for her long answers, but she is fascinating. The further she goes into the maze, the more closely I follow her.

'Storytellers, journalists, we've always known emotions are the key drivers but … television can only go so far [because] at least we still have a shared reality.' She draws a rectangle, marking out the borders of her screen:

You show an ad on television, everyone sees the same ad and we have a starting point for discussion. The same with the facts, right? And then it's your interpretation. Well now… the shared reality has been completely torn apart – it's built into the design of social media. It actually polarises by design. And it's just that one tech thing of growing… growing your network by recommending friends of friends… and then, and then… once you do that, radicalising you! Sorry… I will shut up, but I think they're all connected!

The image of the ex-radicaliser Aimen Dean on Facebook flashes unbidden in my mind. Maria's first book, *Seeds of Terror*,[30] was about how al-Qaeda's tactics shifted from relying on its own core membership to embracing local conflicts such as those in the southeast Asia region and, in this way, spreading its influence. Maria sees

---

30 *Seeds of Terror: An Eyewitness Account of al-Qaeda's Newest Center of Operations in Southeast Asia*, Maria Ressa (2003).

a strong parallel with the mass recruitment of views in the polarised virtual world. She says that those with even mildly radical views are being exploited:

> And now look at the right-ists coming together all over the world... but they're being *used*! Just in the same way that al-Qaeda used the home-grown groups who were fighting for their own independence, or for their own reasons, in each of our countries, and united them... kind of put an artificial... fight against the West. That's what happened with Jemaah Islamiyah [the Islamist group behind the 2002 Bali bombings, which killed 202 people]. Al-Qaeda co-opted them but they were never part of them.

The problems started with the shift from journalism to technology as the 'gatekeepers of the public sphere'. The trusted third party that was a journalist, relaying back the world's truths in print or online, suddenly gave way to something very different. Platforms and publishers multiplied and changed – and so did their intent, but few noticed the impact of this at first. ('We drank the Kool-Aid!') Maria says that the social media platforms 'got too greedy' and this is what made it so easy for digital authoritarians.

'They allowed them to use the mechanisms of advertising... with micro-targeting... and really turn it into quite a sophisticated behaviour modification system. We are all Pavlov's dogs in this and we're seeing it in country after country after country.'

The salivating, domesticated dog waiting for food is an arresting image. If social media was once designed for social good, that has certainly changed over time.

'The dominos began to fall in 2016. And I would say it was Duterte. After Duterte, a month later you had Brexit, after that, all of the different elections where we elected the digital authoritarians and then countries where there were already authoritarian-style leaders, then used social media.'

She says that conspiracy theories could never have taken hold the way they have if platforms were held accountable for identifying lies and for publishing facts.

'Our technology has become godlike, the people who are wielding it are not gods, they're so flawed, they are not taking responsibility for what they are doing.'

I ask her if the pandemic changed anything in social media, if the renewed attention on science and facts had any effect.

'Well… in the end… when lies kill, they were forced to act… and they did, right?'

I think of Donald Trump's tweets that were labelled as misleading during the pandemic and then his Twitter ban after the events of 6 January 2021. It was as if someone had taken away his loudhailer – or more, emptied his giant auditorium, unplugged the electric screens, stripped it of its chairs and locked the doors for good.

If this is a step in the right direction, what are the steps that will lead out of this worrisome, hyper-tech maze? I look around at the examples Maria has given me and all I see is disinformation. I think I might finally have reached the heart of the maze. At some points, as I made my way down its paths, it even crossed my mind that I should doubt Maria. (#LYINGFAKENEWSQUEEN!!!) I suddenly feel very alone in my exploration of truth and lies. Again and again, I had come up against the question of what – and who – can I really trust? In a perfect demonstration of the power of the lie machine, its whispers had reached my ears. I realised that I was doubting this trusting figure just when I needed her most.

Thankfully, Maria does not let other people's doubts stop her. Her view on trust is simple: 'You prove to me I can't trust you… otherwise, I'll trust you!'

And while I am still hesitating about which path to take next, she has sped on. She has been busy not just identifying the nature of disinformation and how it is applied but finding solutions that could result in something akin to mass re-information. For her, the best way out of the maze is to find an organised way to take down its walls.

In 2020, she co-chaired the steering group for the international Forum on Information and Democracy, which focuses on information chaos and the need to balance freedom of opinion and expression with the right to reliable information.[31]

'We were looking at systemic solutions to tech's problems,' says Maria, adding with a big smile: 'The smartest minds were working on this – and I learnt a ton!'

They looked at how to increase transparency, regulate the technology corporations and 'reverse the amplification of sensational content and rumour by promoting reliable news and information in

---

31 'Working group on infodemics', Forum on Information and Democracy (2020), https://informationdemocracy.org/working-groups/concrete-solutions-against-the-infodemic/

a structural manner'. The report balances many aspects such as the need for openness against the importance of data privacy.

In a time of pandemic, they were studying the 'infodemic' – or as the World Health Organization puts it: 'an overabundance of information, some accurate and some not, occurring during an epidemic'.

In her foreword to the report, Maria does not hold back.

Facebook is now the world's largest distributor of news. Except there's a catch: lies laced with anger and hate spread faster and further than the boring facts of news. They create a bandwagon effect of artificial consensus – for the lie. You repeat a lie a million times, it becomes a fact. Without facts, you can't have truth. Without truth, you can't have trust. Without these, democracy as we know it is dead.

Again, she uses the parallel of the end of the Second World War. She refers to the thirty-eight countries supporting the forum's work and what it reminds her of: 'Seventy-five years ago … the world got together to find multilateral, international solutions to prevent humanity from destroying itself.'

The warning is stark. I think of the maze and ask her if there is any good at all in social media today. Maria rocks forward, smiling and raises her index finger to punctuate what she says.

'So… yes!' She gives me two examples of good.

One… I think social media actually showed us that some of the assumptions about the way we look at the world, the way we set up power dynamics globally, are *wrong*. This is one platform that unites 3.2 billion – if you connect Facebook and WhatsApp together – 3.2 billion people around the planet. The same exact platform with the same methodology that unfortunately manipulates people in exactly the *same* way regardless of culture, regardless of nationality, so it proves to us… right?… Despite the weapons that they use, it proves that we have a lot more in common than we ever thought. I've always felt that. I've *always* felt that!

So despite the fact that the social media platforms encourage division, they are actually a great unifying force. I have to admire her ability to step back and see the bigger picture. She says that it was at CNN that she learnt to 'take local and make it global':

I spent my first twenty years as a journalist taking the Philippines, Singapore, Malaysia and kind of… explaining it to the West. Because you always know that you have multiple audiences. So the skill part was all about being able to take the truth that was *here* and… make you *care* about it in… London… or in New York.

She believes that the hunger for local truths still exists.

'I actually think that people haven't changed that much… I hope,' she crosses both fingers, 'if this doesn't last that long.'

We are not quite out of the maze just yet.

Her second example of good in social media is that there is a lot of significant, positive work underway. She refers to the Forum for Information and Democracy, to the European Union's Democracy

Action Plan, to the UK's Online Harms Bill and to Section 230 of the Communications Decency Act in the US. Change is certainly being formulated. She just wishes it were happening faster.

'A lot has to change within the platforms because they went too far down the road. It's like with human rights violations, it will take time to change world viewpoints forged by hate.'

The maze of the lie machine has left me deeply disoriented, it has shown me just how significant the relationship is between truth and lies for sentient, social creatures and it has made me worry about our virtual futures.

The balance between truth and lies is so key to the human psyche and to functioning societies that when something intervenes in that balance, when something is allowed to interrupt the delicate ecosystem of telling, it risks unbalancing healthy society. Prehistoric emotions undone by godlike technology. When the lie scale no longer functions, when there is no 'box of truth' to relate to and every type of deceit has the effect of a black lie, we lose ourselves. We lose the social connections that make us 'us'. And the worldwide lockdowns keep showing us how vital those are – and what a strange bedfellow technology can be when the comfort we need is human.

But if the digital world has ushered in new evils, its potential for good has not been diminished. The very fact that Maria and others like her are there holding the line, day after day, is proof of the power of the human spirit in the face of adversity – and our need to tell the stories that we believe are true.

And as for Duterte? Duterte's ratings have remained high. He is seen as a leader who gets things done and in the 2019 senatorial elections, normally a test of any sitting President, his supporters won by a landslide. Even after a year in which, according to Maria, lockdowns have allowed Duterte to 'consolidate power', polls still show how popular he is. One, in October 2020, put his popularity at 91 per cent.[32] The next general election is on 9 May 2022 – and although the constitution only allows for one six-year term in office, Duterte's daughter is waiting in the wings and at the time of writing there was speculation that she could well make her father Vice-President, protecting him from prosecution.[33] Sara Duterte-Carpio took over from him as mayor of Davao City when he became President, and is known as 'The Iron Lady of the South'. It seems, just like the *Dirty Harry* films, that there is at least one sequel to come. Social media is already alive with a #RunSaraRun campaign and #Daughterte2022.

And for Rappler? For now, Maria is busy with her teams, developing its design.

'We're building a tech platform. Because I think technology in the hands of journalists is completely different. Number 1, we don't treat lies like facts!' Today's Rappler is designed to be read on a phone, rather than a computer. A palm-full of information rather than a page – active news and engagement. Maria wants to incorporate the emotional authenticity and immediacy of social media, the 'context', as she calls it, with the trusted facts of traditional news media. Whatever the format, Rappler's goal remains the same. It

---

32 Pulse Asia Research (5 October 2020), www.pulseasia.ph/september-2020-nationwide-sur vey-on-the-performance-and-trust-ratings-of-the-top-philippine-government-officials-and-the-performance-ratings-of-key-government-institutions/

33 '"Duterte Harry" and daughter plot a Philippines dynasty', Philip Sherwell, *The Times* (6 June 2021), www.thetimes.co.uk/article/duterte-harry-and-daughter-plot-a-philippines-dynasty-9rjg9gxjn

aims to hold power to account, hold its head up high and most importantly, hold the line.

Maria may admit to feeling more pessimistic than she once did, she may be under siege and deeply worried that the world is not acting fast enough, but her relentless quest makes me hopeful. We have not lost ourselves in lies – we have lost sight of how powerful our communication tools have become. By now, I had spent more than seven years looking at the balance between good and bad lies. But this was different. Where direct human interaction benefits from the softening effect of white lies, so digital interaction needs a balance between lies and truth.

After our interview and the exchanges that followed on the encrypted platform Signal, one phrase of hers keeps coming back to me: 'I do believe… I trust… someone will be there. Because I think that people fundamentally know what's right. What's fair. What's just!'

CHAPTER 10

THE LIES WE MISS
| *MOST OF US*

I left the maze of the digital lie machine in both a horrified and hopeful state. What I found in there was not what I expected. But if it marked me, it also made me see how our tendency to tell and believe little lies is powerful enough to sustain an enormous, almost monstrous enterprise. This left me with a final set of questions about our small, daily deceits. First, how many do we tell in an average day, particularly when we are not plugged into social media? Then, why are we so bad at spotting them and so quick to believe them? And finally, how on earth can we trust ourselves to report any of this in a reliable fashion?

One excellent starting point is twenty-five years old, and it is analogue not digital: a diary. The psychologist and author Bella DePaulo has spent decades studying our everyday deceits. Her influential paper in 1996 sought to document how often we tell those shape-shifting little lies, the lies of 'ordinary social life'.[1]

On her website, she is clear about her methods. 'No polygraphs,

---

1 'Lying in Everyday Life', Bella DePaulo, Deborah Kashy, Susan Kirkendol, Melissa Wyer and Jennifer Epstein, *Journal of Personality and Social Psychology* (1996); 'Overview', Bella DePaulo, www.belladepaulo.com/deception-research-and-writing

brain scans or any other bells or whistles.' After all, why bother with fMRI scanners and truth serums if you can get people to keep a diary for you? The team recruited seventy-seven college students from the University of Virginia, Charlottesville, and seventy local people. The students were aged seventeen to twenty-two, the locals, eighteen to seventy-one. The participants were to conduct a normal week in their lives, carry the pocket-sized diaries with them at all times and record any of their own verbal and non-verbal deceptions. To encourage openness (and lessen the taboo), an in-depth session was held with the participants where it was established that lies were considered 'morally neutral' and that everyone involved in the study was a 'co-investigator'. They were being neither judged nor scrutinised; instead, they were helping to put together an exhaustive and groundbreaking piece of research. Lying was defined by De-Paulo's team as any intentional misleading.

The diaries were anonymous, motive was not documented and, to better understand the kinds of lies told, the type of social interaction was later recorded by the diarist in each case, as well as the 'seriousness' of the lie and the length of the interaction – the thinking being that the more time they had with someone, the more opportunity they had to tell a lie.

After a week, the 147 diarists recorded a treasure trove of 1,535 lies – although seven said they had not told a single lie. Students reported more lies than non-students. They recorded two lies a day, as opposed to just one by the non-students. In both groups, the most common lies were about feelings and opinions. A week later, participants said that most of their lies had remained undetected. The lies were told least in face-to-face interactions and to those closest to the diarist.

The team looked at how many of the lies told were 'other-oriented' (or altruistic, as in: 'told her she looked well') versus 'self-centred' (for the benefit of the liar, as in: 'led a girl to believe that I was a model with a New York agency' or 'lied about my husband being fired').

Of the reasons given for lying, the highest number of self-centred lies told (66 per cent) were student men lying to each other, revealing a hint of young Silverback among the participants. Overall, female students told slightly more lies a day than male students (2.04 vs 1.84), but this levelled out when the number of interactions was taken into account – the opportunity. Female students simply had more interactions.

As to the nature of the lies told, DePaulo writes: 'They did not put much planning into their lies, they generally did not regard their lies as serious, and they claimed that it was not all that important to them to avoid getting caught telling their lies.'[2] The diarists rated the seriousness of their lies as an average of 3.2 out of nine. Lies, the report concludes, are a fact of daily life.

This study on white lies is still referred to today – and perhaps the act of noting down lies in a small diary they carried around with them was just the sort of confidential yet intimate record needed to capture this fast-moving, ever-changing and controversial form of

---

2 'The Many Faces of Lies', Bella DePaulo, in *The Social Psychology of Good and Evil*, Arthur G. Miller (ed.) (2004).

behaviour. Certainly DePaulo's matrix proved an excellent way of assessing the little lies we almost do not realise we are telling.

To get a little more shading, DePaulo followed up the study with another in 2004: 173 people, again a mixture of students and local people.[3] This time the team were after the most serious lie they ever told and the most serious ever told to them. It was not behaviour over a week, it was recollection over a lifetime. The team recorded 235 serious lies in detail. Most were about affairs and 'misdeeds', the minority were about violence, danger and identity. The students described lies that were told on average about three years ago, the locals described lies told about twelve years ago. Participants rated the seriousness of the lies they related as 6.8 out of nine.

And what did the shading show DePaulo? That nearly two-thirds of the most serious lies were told in close relationships – the relationships we are most desperate to protect. She concludes: 'Lies are told to close friends, lovers, parents, and children, and by presidents to the entire American public, not because the liars do not care about the targets of their lies or what those targets think of them, but because they do.'

What is striking about the lies that DePaulo captures in her butterfly net is that far from undermining society, they reinforce social structures, they protect established relationships. The most frequent of our lies, the 3.2 (out of nine) lies, were told easily to those more distant personally from the participants, one to two times a day. The graver 6.8 lies were told with a gap of many years and weighed on those who told them – or were told them.

---

3 'Serious Lies', Bella DePaulo, Matthew Ansfield, Susan Kirkendol and Joseph Boden, *Basic and Applied Social Psychology* (2004).

As to the number of white-lie-fibs we tell on a daily basis, if we take it from this study that it is one to two 3.2s, then it is a mind-stretching feat to imagine how many small modifications to the truth would get caught in my altogether more unyielding butterfly net. DePaulo's involves any intentional misleading, my net, anything that has been changed or transformed in the telling. How many of those do we do a day?

The problem with self-reporting is the 'self' part. No matter the lengths to which a team goes to obtain reliable data, we tell and retell stories, we embellish, we forget. We also lie to ourselves. Stephens-Davidowitz's book *Everybody Lies* is excellent on this. He uses an example of the now ubiquitous streaming service Netflix. One lesson it learnt about its customers came in its very early days and it was this: 'Don't trust what people tell you; trust what they do.'

Netflix learnt this lesson when it introduced a function that allowed users to create a queue of films they wanted to watch in future. Subscribers duly jumped at the chance to list their 'must-see' films. What Netflix noticed, though, was that when users were reminded of their list of films, they rarely clicked on them. Their chosen 'aspirational, high-brow' films were just that, aspirational. After ignoring their own queue of suggestions, what they chose to watch was 'the same movies they usually want to watch: lowbrow comedies or romance films'. People were 'lying to themselves' about the kinds of films they watched. Netflix's answer? Every time a user logged on, it would welcome them with a list of suggested films based on millions chosen by similar customers. 'Not what they claimed to like ... but what they were likely to view.'

This issue of how much we lie to ourselves captures one of the criticisms directed at the lie diaries. How could the diarists be relied on to provide accurate data on intentional misleading when some might well be unintentionally misleading themselves?

For instance, could a person be tempted to lie to themselves, just a little, when it came to assessing how good they were at telling those day-to-day lies? Perhaps they chose not to notice that the people they lied to knew they were lying – and were, in fact, lying right back to them? And what about the seven slightly fishy participants who said that they did not mislead anyone in a week?

Still, factoring in a certain degree of 'unreliable narrator', the diaries were brilliant because they involved people studying their own behaviour in a natural environment, confiding in the person closest to them (themselves), then analysing their behaviour and sharing it for the greater good (science).

These two studies made me hungry for more information. I wondered if someone had devised a way to help fibbers better spot their own fibs – those we tell without any sense that we are telling them, those we miss.

Like a frenzied magpie, I swooped when I finally found some more treasure glinting in another scientist's carefully constructed nest.

Robert Feldman is an author, professor of psychology at the University of Massachusetts, Amherst, and another polymath who has turned his talents to studying lying. He conducted a study in 2002, based on evidence that people altered their behaviour to make positive first impressions. The study paired up 242 psychology students who did not know each other. One (the 'self-presenter') was told to either get to know the other person or to come across as likeable/

competent to them. They were told that the goal was to measure social interactions. It was only after the encounter that they learnt the research actually focused on deception. It was another case of a lie to best catch a liar.

The self-presenters were then asked to watch the footage of the session and identify the number and kind of lies they told.

Sure enough, those who sought to appear more likeable or competent told more lies. In fact, more than 60 per cent admitted to using verbal deception and doing it an average of almost three times in a ten-minute conversation. The greatest number of lies in one session was twelve. The paper is cautious about the 40 per cent who claimed not to have lied, because '[they] may have been lying about not lying'.[4]

It was a staged setting, of course, with behaviour that was strongly guided by the researchers, but the treasure I saw sparkling away was this: the students were telling lies without realising it for socially positive reasons, and – just like Kang and his troupe of toddlers – they needed hindsight, recorded interviews and a degree of trickery to spot exactly how many they had told. In those conditions, the lies students tended to tell each other jumped from one or two a day to three in ten minutes.

This socially positive element fascinated me. Could there be something in the way we interact that tells us when to deceive and when not to? And if there is a 'thing' that does this, could that be why we do not recognise these small deceptions as deception? I thought back to Dr Watson, in his complicated rooms in Christ

---

4 'Self-Presentation and Verbal Deception: Do Self-Presenters Lie More?', Robert Feldman, James Forrest and Benjamin Happ, *Basic and Applied Social Psychology* (2002).

Church, Oxford. He had mentioned 'politeness phenomena', and I wondered where in the world I could find the best example of this.

I was now in full magpie mode – and this was how I found *nunchi*. It was on a scrap of paper. An old document from 1993 that had been photocopied and immortalised online. Somehow, one of Google's tentacles had found it as I pushed the search engine harder and harder to find examples of codified lying behaviour far removed from my own, mostly European, experiences.

It was a pamphlet for American 'instructional personnel' about how to understand Korean Americans.[5] On its cover was a crouching tiger – and it was a hidden beauty. Forty-seven pages of gold dust, from history to religion and social mores, every possible cultural pitfall was laid out in black and white. But it was *nunchi* that I would take away with me, and its inseparable companion *kibun*.

'When one is overjoyed with another person's magnificent generosity or when one faces sad affairs, it is considered a virtue to hide one's own feelings. In this case, Koreans can detect whether others are really pleased with them (or dissatisfied) by what is called *nunchi*.'

Bingo. If there is a widely recognised term in a culture for reading the hidden aspects of a situation, then there is also an expectation that aspects will be hidden. In English, there is no translation for *nunchi*. I quickly read up on it and started talking to anyone I could find who might be able to tell me more.

Nunchi translates literally as an 'eye-measure' and it refers to a deeply sophisticated, intrinsic part of Korean culture. My crouching

---

5 'Multiethnic Reminder: The Korean Americans', Harold Chu (1993). Reproduced with permission by the Education Resources Information Center.

tiger guide put it as follows: '*Nunchi* is an ability to guess or sense another's feelings, sentiments and thinking by perceiving the environment and atmosphere that surrounds a situation.' I started to see that it was much more than tact, emotional intelligence or even using one's smarts: it was about gauging a situation, respecting and reinforcing social structures, connecting – carefully. Indeed, Korean parents even chide their offspring with the question: 'Don't you have any *nunchi*?'

The eye-measure is paired with *kibun*: a sense of a person's inner feeling. As the guide puts it: 'In interpersonal relationships, keeping the *kibun* in good order often takes precedence over all other considerations.' Between them, *nunchi* and *kibun* preserve the equilibrium that is the very spirit of Korean politesse. This is a subtle but powerful artform.

In my investigation of this enigmatic pairing, I found another linguist who could help me navigate a grey area. However, even my Korean specialist had to perform grammatical gymnastics to convey the exact meaning of both words.

Soonja Choi, professor of linguistics and director of the Korean studies programme at San Diego State University, kindly tries to take me through the nuances, but I still have to opt for a variety of brackets to turn *nunchi* into something I can understand: 'One should have *nunchi* (= read current situation [that includes understanding the current social context and reading other people's thoughts and feelings] correctly) to behave properly and in a socially appropriate way in a given situation.'

I steeled myself and asked her about the finer points of *kibun*. Professor Choi says that *kibun* relates to the addressee's state of feelings and that it is important to read other people's *kibun* correctly, act appropriately and maintain its flow in a situation.

So what does this sensitivity to the flow of other people's emotions mean for truth-telling? If, in Korea, it is paramount to have *nunchi* and to preserve another's *kibun*, then the path between the two must be strewn with acceptable little lies, accommodations and avoidance.

Professor Choi is firm that *nunchi* is a positive term, not linked to lies or falsehood, which sheds an entirely different light on the lower reaches of deception.

'Yes, in some cases, having *nunchi* may lead one to say something that is not truthful, and that's accepted.' She says it often means 'not saying "x" or refraining from doing something because it may hurt the listener or it may be inappropriate'.

This extends to not announcing bad news and not telling a superior when they are wrong, and it changes where different deceits sit on the Lie Scale. It would take a multidimensional rotating model to capture how lie scales overlap in different cultures.

Back to my beloved crouching tiger guide: what makes it stand out from the vast trove of documents on the world's mores is that it tells both sides of the story. It presents the tranquil, ordered side of interactions in Korean society, as well as the moments when there is a passionate, unguarded boiling over of emotion:

The Korean method of social intercourse, to pretend to like something though it is bad and to pretend dislike though it is good, has different implications than the method of the American who publicly dissects and analyzes everything. And yet, when Koreans get angry and lose their tempers, they do not hesitate to reveal their feelings in angry words or fistfights, regardless of onlookers. Paradoxically, they change from lambs to lions.

In business dealings the lamb/lion dichotomy is one to watch out for. The guide rounds off its explanation of *kibun* as: 'Businessmen try to operate in a manner that will enhance the *kibun* of both persons. To damage the *kibun* may effectively cut off relationships and create an enemy. One does not tend to do business with a person who has damaged one's *kibun*.'

Business dealings across nations become a little tricky if truth-avoidance is encouraged by one party but considered a red flag by another. In Korean culture, admitting failure, or worse, losing face, is so stigmatised that Silicon-Valley-style straight talking, flat hierarchies and unforgiving glass meeting rooms would prove most troublesome.

Across the Korea Strait in Japan, the word *wa* is the attitude of group harmony encouraged in the workplace. Here, consensus-building and diplomacy are more important than truth-telling, and indirect language is used to avoid confrontation. The art of saying 'no' without saying it is a fine one, and results in nuanced words such as *chotto* in Japanese. Just one of its translations is 'a little', which is most useful when you want to avoid a thumping 'no' but is sure to wrong-foot an inexperienced Western negotiator.

The importance of these shifting mores is the ensuing misunderstandings. A business counterpart may think they are being lied to when in fact they are being treated with respect – a respect that shaves the sharp edges off the facts.

We more reserved nations in Western cultures may bow and curtsey beautifully, but our politeness can be treacherous. Just think of the way the British use the word 'quite', as in 'quite good'. Is it positive or negative, dismissive or simply delicate? We should make room for 'quite lies' just above 'white lies' on the British Lie Scale. And as for the modifier 'pretty' in American English, suffice to say that it too can be *quite* deceptive.

A guide for the direct Dutch, explaining British double-speak, and pinned on the wall of the European Court of Justice, explains that the phrase 'with the greatest respect' does not mean 'I value every word you say', it means: 'you are wrong'. Meanwhile, another guide on international relations counsels that it is not worth asking a Finn to embellish information for the sake of a meeting: they will not do it. In Finnish culture, your word is your bond and no professional half-lie passes muster.[6]

Deceit is codified differently in different languages and by different cultures. The politeness factor is a reminder of how valuable our deceptive talents can be, whether we call the acts involved courtesies, misdirection or lies. It also begins to explain why we might be so bad at spotting lies – not only are the more low-level ones frequent and almost unconscious but they are camouflaged by varying degrees of politeness culture across the world.

And these grey areas are not restricted to speech. If body language can betray us, it can also be completely confusing to those who engage with us. Our distracting, cross-cultural gestures can make dishonesty – or even honesty – difficult to spot.

---

6 'I understand, up to a point', Charlemagne column, *The Economist* (September 2004); 'Where The Truth Lies Across Cultures', Carol Kinsey Goman, *Forbes* (August 2013).

Cross your fingers in almost all parts of the world and it means good luck, unless you are a child and then it is a broken promise, the sign of a white lie; in Vietnam, it is a vulgar evocation of a woman.

Equally, look me in the eye when addressing me and I might have you executed if I am queen in a certain place at a certain time; avert your eyes when I am interrogating you in a modern police station and I might find you guilty. Show me the soles of your feet (with or without shoes) and I might think you over-entitled in New York, or perhaps presidential in Washington; in some parts of the Middle East and Africa, you will be profoundly insulting me.

A thumbs-up almost everywhere is good, but in Iran it is a serious insult; underwater, in the world of scuba, it means: 'I'm going up', which in some cases might not be good at all. Finally, the 'horns' hand gesture (raising your little finger and your index while holding down the other fingers with your thumb) might mean 'rock on' in the US music scene and represent the Texas Longhorns American football team, but in Italy it means '*cornuto*' ('your spouse is cheating on you'); in Buddhism and Hinduism, meanwhile, an almost identical gesture is a mudra that fends off evil and negativity.

If there is a host of small reasons we miss lies or are culturally primed not to recognise them, what about the bigger, darker lies? Why do we miss those? History shows that our quest to expose an impure heart has long been elaborate, painful and deeply questionable. Exhibit A is the Egyptian feather test, in which only after death could the purity of a heart be tested when it was removed and weighed against a feather belonging to Maat, the goddess of truth. Exhibit B is the medieval trial by ordeal, such as the swim tests for witches in which the suspected woman was bound and thrown into water. If she sank, she was innocent but likely to drown; if she floated, she was guilty and would be killed. Exhibit C is the lumpy bumpy techniques of phrenology in the nineteenth century, where heads were shaved and measured to determine a person's psychology, pathology and even criminality. Even Exhibit D, the modern polygraph test, is often met with deep scepticism.

Ekman told me nonchalantly that he could easily teach people how to beat it, and in *Telling Lies*, he writes: 'The polygraph exam does not detect lies, just signs of emotion … [It] fail[s] not only because some innocents still fear being falsely accused or for other reasons are upset when tested but also because some criminals don't believe in the magic of the machine.'

Ekman does not come out against the polygraph, but he is vocal in pointing out its shortcomings. He adds: 'There is very little scientific evidence about [the polygraph's] accuracy. Of more than 4,000 published articles or books, less than 400 actually involve research, and of these no more than thirty to forty meet minimum scientific standards.'[7]

So, without having to weigh a heart against a feather, spend years at spy school or be perennially suspicious, how much can we simply rely on our first impressions to judge good character?

In 2005, a team at the Princeton University psychology department asked more than 800 students to look at photographs of politicians they did not recognise from Senate races across America between 2000 and 2004. They found that the instantaneous decisions we make about faces significantly influence our judgements.

---

7   *Telling Lies: Clues to Deceit in the Marketplace, Politics, and Marriage*, Paul Ekman (1985).

The students were given one second to choose between two faces. Asked to determine the politicians' competence, based solely on their faces, they predicted the outcome of 71.6 per cent of the races. This meant that in one second, they were making the same decision as a majority of voters who would have spent a lot longer than a second considering how to vote.[8]

In another paper, the same Princeton team showed that people made up their minds about a face after just 100 milliseconds. I remembered that Ekman found a micro expression flashes across a face in less than 40 milliseconds,[9] which means that someone barely has the time to betray themselves before we have made up our minds. It would seem that our inner detective is just a bit too quick off the mark. The Princeton team added insult to injury by finding that any increased time simply boosted the participant's confidence in the judgements they made, rather than changing the evaluation. In other words, we are hasty and we are stubborn.

But perhaps there was more to this? I thought about the divorcee and the 'empty smile' photo that had haunted her lightly for years before she found out why. Could there be a difference between a conscious first impression and an unconscious one? I went back to the person whose instincts left such a lasting impression on me. The elfin psychologist who had spotted the lie of a child killer.

Dr ten Brinke now runs the Truth and Trust Lab at the University of Denver and has a theory about lie spotting, which she set about testing based on previous findings in forensic psychology,

---

8 'Inferences of Competence from Faces Predict Election Outcomes', Alexander Todorov, Anesu N. Mandisodza, Amir Goren and Crystal C. Hall, *Science* (2005).

9 'Micro Expressions', www.paulekman.com/resources/micro-expressions/

neuroscience and primatology. She calls it direct and indirect lie detection.[10]

In laboratory conditions, six people were told to 'steal' $100 from an envelope; six were told not to. All twelve were promised cash rewards if they then successfully pleaded innocent, whether guilty or not. The team's goal was to see if people watching their pleas were better at spotting lies subconsciously, rather than consciously.

The videos of the would-be thieves were shown to seventy-two undergraduates, who were asked to separate the liars from the innocent. The seventy-two did this first with a straightforward yes/no verdict (making a 'direct' judgement), then they were asked to look at still images of the subjects and associate them with words referring to honest or deceitful behaviour, for instance 'valid' or 'untruthful'. This was the 'indirect' judgement and it was done using an Implicit Association Test, a test designed to assess unconscious bias.

The direct results confirmed that when we apply a conscious thought process – the high-speed yes/no verdict – we fare no better than chance: in fact, the students only correctly identified the liars 44 per cent of the time. The students fared much better in the indirect test (with women doing better than men). This kind of indirect test cannot be measured in easy percentages, but the responses were enough for the team to find that 'automatic associations were significantly more accurate than controlled, deliberate decisions'.

Dr ten Brinke uses her results and previous studies to conclude that although we are good at sensing lies, accurate unconscious

10 'Some Evidence for Unconscious Lie Detection', Leanne ten Brinke, Dayna Stimson and Dana Carney, *Psychological Science* (2014).

assessments are distorted 'by conscious biases and incorrect decision rules'.

Examples of the false but persistent premises (or rules) are the notions that liars fidget more, avert their gaze or look up to the right when they are constructing a fiction, all of which have been disproven by research. Another thing that might dull our detection is cited in the paper: 'Humans often live in conditions of such abundance and safety that they lack the motivation and suspicion necessary to detect deception.' What this clever subliminal research shows, however, is that if this factor mollifies suspicion, it does not remove it entirely.

I felt a jolt when I realised that perhaps we are bad at spotting lies because most of them pose no threat to us – in fact, they help us as social creatures. Our failings as natural detectives do not make us more vulnerable, they make us better at connecting with others. If we could see all the little lies all the time, we would be very reticent to engage at all. I thought of the friends who had deleted their social media accounts for this reason – all they saw were lies.

And perhaps it is not just that we are bad at spotting lies but that we actively look for the truth? I remembered another thing Dr Watson told me when I went to see him in Oxford. 'We take it as the default case that someone is telling the truth, and how would society work if that were not so?' We depend on the reliable behaviour of others for the smooth functioning of society, and this makes us predisposed to see honest motives and means we are as likely to miss a lie as we are to discount it without realising it.

I knew I was jumping from doctor to doctor, but I suddenly thought of a piece of research from another doctor in a previous chapter. Like a true top investigator, I had overlooked it. Now my pulse was racing. I went back into the bulging archive I had built up and saw that it had been there all along, just waiting to be found: the Truth Bias.

Dr Angela Evans, one of Kang's gang, had followed up a study of adolescent lying behaviour by testing the effects of what is known as 'the truth bias' on a very specific group of people: those who spent their days in the trenches, studying every facial twitch, learning to interpret every strategy, mood or whim of a child – parents. Would they be any good at spotting their own child's lies?

If adults are bad at reading non-verbal clues in young children (the Kang tests had showed a 50 per cent success rate of adults spotting a lie), do they fare any better when faced with an adolescent? Dr Evans used the videos from tests on children aged eight to sixteen to see how parents and others compared at spotting adolescent lies.[11]

The results of those eighty parents, compared with other parents (seventy-two) and non-parents (seventy-nine), showed again that none of them had better than a chance guess at getting it right. And not only were none of the groups better at guessing, what differed was the parents' scores. It may have been a marginal difference, but of all the potential lie-spotters, parents did worst, showing a bias towards believing that all children were honest – and that their own children were most honest of all. What a perfect illustration of why we might be bad at lie spotting. We protect our significant relationships by shutting our eyes to little lies. They may be a sign of development, they may keep social circles spinning, but they remain

---

11 'Can parents detect 8- to 16-year-olds' lies? Parental biases, confidence, and accuracy', Angela D. Evans, Jasmine Bender and Kang Lee, *Journal of Experimental Child Psychology* (2016).

undetected because the truth is that if we acknowledged how much we lied, then we would stop trusting each other. So we tell ourselves little lies about the little lies we tell.

Dr ten Brinke's observations about threat levels in day-to-day life led me to one last question. (So I suppose I told a little lie when I said I had only three at the beginning of this chapter.) If fibs are generally a benefit rather than a threat, does living in more threatening conditions change how many we tell? Or is it simply, as Bella DePaulo found, a question of opportunity?

If I wanted to gauge the effect of increased levels of threat, it happened to be a very good time to do it: it was the middle of the Covid-19 pandemic. All I had to do was find a way of measuring if this changed the way we fibbed.

The idea of using a pocket-sized format, used to record daily interactions, made me wonder if I could do the same with a smartphone. After all, I seemed to have mine welded to my hand at all times. Getting hold of other people's data was another matter. I thought back to my spies. Foxtrot probably had people he could ask and methods for forensically mapping behaviour, but what interested me was the voluntary reporting of lies because that still seemed the best way of catching the little ones.

I had barely escaped the digital maze, so I was wary of turning back, but as I saw it, Twitter seemed the best way to capture glimpses of lying behaviour. I had already tried to take the temperature in 2017 by running a Twitter poll, so I would, very carefully, try to do it again.

Although the two Twitter polls were four years apart, the number of impressions (the number of times someone sees a tweet in their feed or search results) was similar. However, the number of votes halved and what really surprised me was that the result had changed.

I had run my first quick-fire poll in mid-April 2017, over the Easter bank holiday weekend.

Pinned Tweet

Kathleen Wyatt @kathleenwyatt · Apr 14

Twitter! I'm writing a book about #lying. Have you told a #fib in last two days? If so, how many? No fibbing. DM any Qs. All anon #whitelies

37% No

48% 1 to 4

9% 5 to 10

6% More than 10

2,520 votes · Final results

10   32   15

Users could vote only once, click only on one option and once they had voted they could neither change nor delete their answer. The poll was anonymous and active for seven days.

The results showed a win for low-level lying, with the majority saying they had told one to four lies in the past two days. The non-liars came second, although some contacted me to say that they simply had not had the opportunity. Of those who commented and made themselves public, Sam said: 'I'm a teacher, I have to lie all the time (both to children and parents).' Noddy said: 'Parenting a toddler is all about bending the truth. Constantly.' And Jan wrote: 'Congenitally incapable. It's a real pain!'

I am particularly grateful to the 151 people who admitted telling more than ten fibs.

That was 2017. Was it a more innocent time? Were people simply more ready to open up about how they behaved or did lying behaviour actually change? Was it because the threat of imminent death felt further away than in a pandemic? By the weekend of 4 July 2021, the drawbridge seemed to go up, the gates were locked and the consensus was: no fibs were told. It was most confusing.

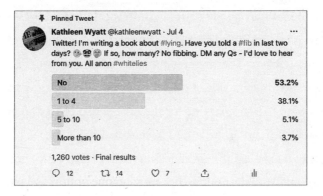

I crunched the numbers (remembering that Twitter statistics do not always tally in different parts of their analytics and that my sample was limited to people who were in my thinly stretched web of digital connections).

	April 2017	July 2021
Impressions	59,810	62,831
Engagements[12]	3,201	1,126
Votes	2,520	1,260

---

12 Total number of times a user engaged with a tweet. This is defined by Twitter as clicks anywhere on the tweet, including retweets, replies, follows and likes: https://help.twitter.com/en/managing-your-account/using-the-tweet-activity-dashboard

A whopping 53.2 per cent of people said that they had not fibbed in the past two days. (My thanks again to the forty-seven people who admitted to fibbing more than ten times. Unless they were lying about that, as one of them wrote in a comment.) Perhaps it was because after sixteen months of lockdowns and restrictions on social interaction, people simply had less opportunity to lie?

Alexander said: 'No but haven't seen many people due to pandemic so that may be the reason.' Andrew said he had been in hospital so it was in his interests to be honest, but it might have been different 'outside'. The theme continued. Shalom wrote: 'I haven't spoken to anyone outside of twitter for over two weeks, so the worst i can fess up to is simplifying for the sake of 280 chars and possibly lying to myself, but if the latter i haven't realised it yet.'

Rachel picked up the toddler theme that came up in 2017: 'I've got two small children. Probably get to 10+ before breakfast.'

And in one that would fit perfectly in DePaulo's diary studies, Asimah wrote: 'My husband just asked if I had ordered the socks he'd asked for and I said yes. I'm ordering them now.'

Things certainly got more deceptive when people did venture outside. Will said: 'I went on a date… so more than 10.'

One anonymous tweeter said: 'Definitely more than 10! I have a good reason though, early pregnancy and no one knows, so I'm having to make up all sorts of excuses.'

From my sample of more than 2,000 people,[13] the key to fibbing and recognising the fib is recognising the opportunity. It seemed that the threat of the pandemic did not exacerbate or stifle fibbing

---

13 I would like to say 3,780 people, but I have no way of knowing whether the same people took part in the polls in both 2017 and 2021.

behaviour, it was the lockdowns and the loss of social interaction that did. As we suddenly socialised less, we fibbed less. This was just one more indication that our small, hidden, daily deceits play a vital role in our interaction with others. And if I needed more proof that they help us to build and maintain our relationships, then two private messages I received on Twitter left me in no doubt at all.

The first was from a mother of two whose husband was in his early forties when he died suddenly and exposed a devastating lie. Not long after his death, she found out that he had been having an affair with a colleague for many years.

'I have seen all their messages, texts, emails and photos shared,' she wrote. 'He had lived a parallel existence.' He lied to both women, as well as 'to his family, to his work colleagues, to our children'.

She finished her message with the worst part of all: 'I have no doubt that the psychological stress of the deception contributed to his death ... Who was this man I shared my life with?'

I asked her if this experience had made her think differently about white lies.

'I'm much more aware of lies of any kind, including the things you let pass within the family.' Once she had been confronted with this enormous lie, all bets were off. There would be no more 'smoothing over' or 'avoiding'. The betrayal came from someone she had 'shared twenty years of my life with and trusted implicitly'. This is what broke the lie balance for her.

'Now I'm more likely to challenge things and call out those little established "lies" or things everyone chooses to ignore/pretend they don't notice.'

This is what it takes to shock someone out of the niceties and truth-avoidance that help to strengthen so many of our social connections. Her story will stay with me as I keep writing about lies, because when it comes to lies, I was discovering that there is only one moment worse than being caught out as a liar, and that is when you have been caught up in someone else's lies. It is the moment when the music stops, the chair is pulled away and some cherished and deep part of your life turns into a cheap 'gotcha'.

The second message was a counterpoint to this one – and it was no less powerful. It was also an echo of what Foxtrot had told me many chapters ago.

'As a police officer who spent much of his career in covert policing, lying was an integral part of my work undercover or on surveillance. Without lying I couldn't do my job, which was to protect society from bad people.'

It was the next part of his message that really got me. It took the world of covert measures to a new level, and it did so by being about love.

'Also in my private life, I lie dozens of times a day to protect my wife. She has dementia and the world she lives in in her mind is at variance with reality. But confronting her with reality causes real psychological pain.'

In a later message, he said he only left the service because his family was put in danger.

'Ironically during that time my wife was my rock to sanity. Now I'm hers.' His description of his career and his excruciating account of his wife's condition speak of the powerful good that lies can do.

I thought again about what it takes to maintain a successful illusion, no matter how small. A person needs to believe in their own story; to hold several different propositions in their head at one time; to read minds (almost); to conjure up only the emotions they want to show; to keep calm under pressure and, at all costs, they must remember to forget the purple dinosaur.

It is like being a good storyteller. If I do not believe in the Big Bad Wolf or the Never-Ending Love, then I lose interest and we have stopped connecting. Tell me a good story and I do not just suspend my disbelief, I give you my mind and let you pick freely from a vast library of emotion. Whether your story entertains me, improves me or harms me is another matter.

In almost every different instance of deception, human beings do the same incredible thing: they project their own take on reality into someone else's mind. They could be talking about Santa or Satan, but their brain is performing the same astounding feat: 'meta-representation'. It is such a simple act but magnificent in its complexity – and to see just how powerful it is, I will finish with the ending of two secrets.

CHAPTER 11

FREEDOM | *LORD BROWNE*

The sheer horror of being exposed as a deceiver, a fake, a fraud is a feeling that is hard to forget. I can easily imagine it happening again. It could be a careless lie that has grown too big, a shared secret exposed, or a petty act of villainy held up to the daylight. The cold hand on my shoulder that tells me: 'Wait a moment, we have a few more questions for you.'

I suspect that this moment of dread is another reason we tell little lies about our little lies. This fear is what helps to keep the balance between the manageable, beneficial, pro-social lies and the destabilising ones that undermine our social connections. It is the moment the curtain creaks apart slowly to show just one person on stage. Naked, revealed and revolting: the liar.

I was that person once and I never want to go back there. This is what makes me catch my breath every time I see someone else exposed in a lie. Again, it is that dreaded 'gotcha!' But it is this moment too when the power of lies is at its clearest.

I thought of the anonymous mother and how she believed her husband's lies played a part in his early death. I thought about Rose, my elusive female spy, and the lasting positive effect of her subterfuge. In both cases, a sustained deception was exposed only after their deaths. As DePaulo found, we tell lies not because we do not care but because we do, so very much. But most of all, I thought that if a lie can be powerful enough to destroy a person, the end of a lie is powerful enough to free them too.

There was one person in particular I had in mind. This was the story of a professional giant brought down by a single personal deception.

It was May 2007. He had a choice to make. Take a side exit, slip out and dodge the media or walk straight out of the lifts and, as he puts it, follow the green line 'into the scrum'. He chose the scrum. But this is no rugby player, injured at the hands of incautious team-mates. This was a captain of industry, the head of a global company, and the green line he followed was the one built into the floor of its headquarters in St James's Square, central London. After so many years of hiding a powerful secret, he stepped into the daylight and faced the photographers.

'The press of the world,' he says to me, the rich bass of his voice making it sound like a wildlife documentary, a description of thirsty beasts gathered around a rare pool of water. 'It was quite… full on.'

In his book *The Glass Closet* Lord Browne of Madingley describes the moment: 'One shutter click became a thousand. I paused on the pavement and smiled. What else can you do? Cameramen pushed and shoved, and some attempted to get a rise out of me, which surely would have made for better photographs. Someone shouted the epithet "gay scum".'[1]

His secret was out, and he was out of the closet and out of a job

---

1 *The Glass Closet: Why Coming Out Is Good for Business*, John Browne (2014).

– he had announced his resignation as chief executive officer of BP that afternoon.

Lord Browne of Madingley leaving the BP offices after his resignation on 1 May 2007.
© Peter Macdiarmid/Getty Images

Less than ten minutes' walk but a lifetime away, there is a discreet entrance to another office. It is hidden by the lively bustle of Cecconi's, an Italian restaurant, and hard to find even with directions. It is here that I meet Lord Browne, seven years after he followed that green line all the way out.

I buzz in, take the lift to the top floor and enter the elegant offices of Riverstone Holdings, a private equity firm specialising in the energy sector. The tinted windows look out onto the Royal Academy in Mayfair, central London. I am early for our meeting and beginning to fret that our interview might not work out as planned. I had read his book and found it so open and engaging that I pictured us chatting in a relaxed setting. Refined china cups, leaf tea, careful questions about his lie and what it was like to have his secret savaged in public. Instead, our meeting is supremely formal. The corporate hush is alien and disconcerting, especially as back then I was still working at *The Times*. I am shown quietly into an empty boardroom. Browne worked for BP for forty-one years, twelve of them as CEO, so, of course, this was still his natural terrain.

When Browne appears, the man so often cited as a charming, charismatic interviewee hobbles in, impatiently eschewing help, his leg strapped up in a fearsome knee support over his crisp suit.

His assistant sits in on the interview. Browne assesses me. I sense he is not impressed. It is a cold day outside, but I am beginning to feel rather hot and almost certain that our meeting will be brief – and painful. I introduce myself and babble on about the book. I expand on truth and lies, the ending of secrets.

He is completely still.

I carry on speaking. Thankfully, out of nowhere, his face suddenly lights up.

'If I may, it's interesting that Joel Grey – he was in *Cabaret*, do you remember the musical *Cabaret*?' I think of that brightly painted face above a pink bow tie in the 1972 film, singing: 'Willkomen, bienvenue, welco-o-o-ome'. I am not sure by what magic the *Cabaret* star appeared and saved me, but it seems he has. My interviewee smiles.

'He came out today. He's eighty-two. I think it's rather wonderful.'

'And sad too…' I venture, still cautious.

'It's sad, it's happy, it's so strange.'

I forge ahead and ask him how hard has it been, breaking the habit of his own lifelong lie?

'My big lie, obviously, was being in the closet, and I didn't come out, I was outed. Slightly different.' These occasional, slightly stern interjections keep me alert throughout the interview when his deep voice risks hypnotising me:

> I was also outed *incredibly* publicly. I mean, it really was a big piece of news. And I think it's best summarised by a young guy who worked here who was gay. He said, it's all right for you John, coming out, you never have to come out again, everyone knows you're gay! So, no. I don't revert. I never revert now to the lie.

Later, when I go through my notes, I notice that in his full answer he used formulations of 'I'm gay' five times in the space of a couple of minutes. This man who lived and breathed an industry, quintupled the market value of a business, negotiated deals across the world and worked with leaders as challenging as Vladimir Putin and Muammar Gaddafi was terrified of only one thing. It is summed up in those three simple words: 'I am gay'. It is remarkable how easily and fluently he now uses this term, considering what that truth cost him in 2007.

The events that would end with him in the middle of a media scrum were set in motion by a personal tragedy: the death of his mother. She was very much at the heart of his life and he refers to her as 'my dear late mother'. Paula was a force of nature who greatly influenced him and lived with him for the last fourteen years of her life, becoming 'a surrogate partner' and a fixture at BP events. As one profile in early 2007 put it: 'Browne created a flat for her at the top of his Notting Hill house, marking the beginning of what would become the most famous house-share of the oil world.'[2]

---

2 'Sun King of the oil industry', *Financial Times* (January 2007), ft.com/content/2a42aa08-a261-11db-a187-0000779e2340

After her death in 2000, Browne writes that he was 'desperately lonely'. It took at least a year, but he began looking for a partner. Browne met Jeff Chevalier on the escort site suitedandbooted.com in 2003. He would become his first boyfriend. When Chevalier moved in nine months later, their agreed cover story was that they met while running in Battersea Park. How else could an unconnected 23-year-old have bumped into a 55-year-old lodged so firmly in the upper echelons of society? It seemed simple and safe enough, but this was the white lie that would fell a CEO.

According to the accounts in the media at the time, their relationship became an open secret as Chevalier accompanied the head of BP to functions across the world, and in their home in Chelsea sat across the table from guests including the then Prime Minister Tony Blair. This would make tabloid fodder. The relationship crumbled in 2006, and when Browne eventually ended his financial support, Chevalier started to send him more and more messages. Among them was an apparent threat ('I do not want to embarrass you, but…'), which Browne, so new to the iniquities of break-ups, thought was best ignored. He had spent too long hiding this part of himself to know how to manage it with the same deftness he applied to business.

On 5 January 2007, Browne received the chilling news that no one with a secret ever wants to hear. Chevalier had sold his story, their story, to a newspaper – the *Mail on Sunday*. As he recounts it in his book, Browne was on a beach in Barbados 'in a state of anxiety and stress'. He was out of the office and out of sorts. He panicked. From having spoken about it to only those closest to him, he suddenly found himself having to outline the intimate details of his 'second life' on a mobile phone: 'To a stranger. Complete strangers... complete strangers.' He is referring to his new legal team. He says that perhaps this is why he decided 'not to tell the whole truth'. They asked him how he had met Jeff. His answer was Battersea Park.

Thereafter followed an ill-advised injunction, claims and counterclaims, and a witness statement that would prove to be a small but deadly timebomb. Browne corrected his statement two weeks later, but it was too late. The corporate gods fell foul of the legal gods. Mr Justice Eady said in his ruling: 'I am not prepared to make allowances for a "white lie" told to the court in circumstances such as these.' It was Browne's story that made me think so much about the context of a lie. And as I would see the more I talked to him, it was not just the context of his outing but the context of society that made such a difference to his story. He grew up in a time when it was expected that gay men would hide their sexuality and fell foul of a time when almost everyone but him did talk about it.

After a set of appeals, the injunction was quashed, the story published and Browne resigned immediately then faced the paparazzi firing squad outside the BP offices in London.[3] He had wanted to go in January, but his own gagging order meant that he could not explain his reasons for leaving and had to wait until May. The rules he had played by his whole career were the very ones that ended with him, as he puts it in his disarmingly matter-of-fact way, 'being undressed in public'.

What happened once he had made it through 'the scrum'?

'They followed me around for three days,' he tells me lightly. 'I

---

3   'The Sun King who lost his shine', *Daily Mail* (1 May 2007); 'The TRUE story about Lord Browne – by ex-rent boy lover', *Mail on Sunday* (6 May 2007).

253

think I was a "sought-after" photograph, you know. Through my apartment window... and all sorts of stuff like that. But, very quickly, you become yesterday's news. And it's amazing how quickly it goes away, overnight. After three days... they'd gone!'

The initial impact was high-speed and ferocious. In his book, he quotes the *Daily Mail*'s description of him: 'How close he came to being remembered and revered as one of the greats. How much he yearned for it. But the truth reared up yesterday to expose the top-to-toe impeccability of Lord Browne of Madingley, group chief executive of BP, as a hubristic sham.' The knock-on effects lasted for years. He writes: 'Driving away from the corporation that I helped to build felt like dying ... On that day, almost inevitably, my two worlds collided. In the fallout, I lost the job that had structured my entire life.' He retreated. He had therapy. He rebuilt.

Today, his demeanour remains supremely calm as he remembers the events.

'I think... when I was outed, I just avoided the subject for a long time,' he tells me. 'It's only recently I've got there.'

So how did someone who rose through the ranks, from his first posting in the macho wilds of Alaska ('it was BP's way of knocking the stuffing out of you') to the C-suite where he would be dubbed the Sun King by the *Financial Times*,[4] have such a blind spot when it came to managing his personal life?

It was his mother's tough life lessons that schooled him.

'She told me very clearly never tell anyone a secret because they'll always let you down. In her experience, exactly right. And actually,

---

4 'Sun King of the oil industry'.

not a bad description of a lot of life.' It was not just his early years but his mother's early years that had such a bearing on how he chose to lead his life. The social context of his lie spanned generations.

His mother's earliest lesson had come when she was a child, living in Romania. She and her family could have escaped the Nazis but they were betrayed and ended up in Auschwitz. She survived, but others in her family did not.

'She said don't be a minority, because the majority hurt the minority whenever the going gets tough.' For her, the perils of being different were to be avoided at all costs. 'While she loved life, she thought that some risks were not worth taking.'

Did she share the burden of his lie and know his secret?

'I tried to tell my mother, but she absolutely wouldn't listen. She wasn't stupid. She must have known.' These last three statements come out in rapid fire. He looks impeccably tranquil, but it would not be too wild an assumption to say that this subject still hurts. She protected him and, in turn, he protected her.

'She's a woman of the world from a milieu before the war that was clearly quite semi-tolerant of gay people. But she wouldn't have a word of it. Her view was "this is too dangerous".' He pauses, 'I think.'

I ask him about his upbringing and the influences that shaped him. From the lies shared with me – and from my own lies – I knew that currents from long ago can quite suddenly turn into a storm surge.

He went to an all-male boarding school in the 1960s, and it was there that the rule he would follow for fifty years was first drummed in. He remembers neither homophobic bullying nor whispering campaigns; instead, 'students who had a sexual encounter were quietly expelled'. There was no explanation, only a clear message that 'being gay was wrong'.

Homosexuality was still illegal. He tells me firmly that staying in the closet when he was at the University of Cambridge was a 'no-brainer'. The pattern continued as he entered business:

Everyone used pejorative, homophobic language the whole time. This was the oil industry. So, no one in their right mind would think of coming out in – this is in 1970, '71, '72. It was only when I went to the States that I discovered a sort of gay subculture, which really was a subculture. It was very, deeply dark.

His voice goes quiet as he says the words.

'And so that simply reinforced it.' He switches with disconcerting speed to being his younger self, justifying the lie to himself. 'There you are, you see! All these people running two lives. So why shouldn't I?' He pauses. 'And one thing led to another.'

And what would he say now to his younger self?

'Be careful, just be careful of the long-term consequences… and just think… just watch how things are changing. And that's true about everything.'

And if he could, would he intervene, helping his younger self to make a different choice?

'No. I would have said just watch, watch how the world is changing. Because I… I kind of didn't notice how the world was changing. Literally.'

In fact, it changed so much in the decades he was at BP, that what brought him down was not being gay but lying about being gay.

Similar dynamics would play out in the story of David Laws, former MP and Cabinet minister, and another high-profile figure who was exposed at a high point in his career. In 2010, he was publicly outed at the tail end of the expenses scandal that had swept through Parliament. He had been Chief Secretary to the Treasury for just seventeen days when he decided to stand down because of his own financial arrangements. He had long hidden the fact he was gay, and in order to keep his living arrangements with his male partner secret, he submitted misleading expenses. Contrary to what he had feared throughout his life, in the end it was dishonesty not homosexuality that was his undoing. What was once a necessary and understood concealment in a different time became the unacceptable motive for a lie.

I ask Browne if he thought he should have stayed at BP, helping others to come out and helping to make changes at all levels of the industry?

'Well, I can't reconstruct the past... I resigned because', he lingers on the word, 'I felt guilty. I was guilty of big and small lies in relationship to being gay. And I felt *genuinely* guilty about it, and that guilt carried on for a period of time. Until I realised that actually, there was no point in it.' He is looking forward, just as his mother would have told him to.

'I talk about my dear late mother who... who did just that. I mean, I can't imagine... She was always a forward-looking person. Had she dwelt in the past, the resentment about the Holocaust would have eaten her up alive.'

Looking ahead too, I was itching to ask him about life on the other side – the after-lie. But first I had to know if he regretted not ending the lie himself and coming out.

I do. I do... I mean, I regret it but I'm not sure, you know... so people ask what would have happened if you'd come out – and these questions are increasingly hypothetical because all other things are not equal when you change one thing. So the answer is I don't know. I wish I'd been a more active role model. I've hoped I can make up for lost time.

He cannot go back, so he does not. Besides, the aftermath of his outing was very different from what he had feared. I remembered watching his story unfold at the time and wondering if this man could ever go from the horror of exposure to the freedom of telling. The answer is yes.

'[After resigning] I was sitting in my apartment saying: right, I've got no friends, no one will come and talk to me, no one will like me,' his voice lowers again as he continues his bleak list. 'They'll all think I'm demeaned and you know, weak, and no business, nothing. And it was quite the reverse,' he says smiling. 'I made *more* friends!'

Far from destroying him, the brutal exposés gave him a new lease of life.

'People stopped me in the street. And it was very embarrassing because I'm, you know ... It was touching. I mean, strangers would come up and shake my hand. A lot of people, I think... I guess did not approve of the coverage. Generally.'

The untouchable king of the energy sector was suddenly fallible and human. His lie had revealed a truth that few corporate press releases could have conveyed. Before, when ostensibly he had everything, he was incomplete. Now he could be, as he says, his 'full self'. Nearly ten years on, he says he smiles more, he is more open – and he is in love.

Among the many letters of support he received in 2007, one was hand-delivered to his home. It was from a Vietnamese banker. They met for a drink a month after Browne resigned and have been together ever since.

And what of his business contemporaries, did they too welcome the new him with open arms? Had his fears about big business been in any way justified? The vast majority did, he says, but the 'limelight' of a public company was too much for him and he had little desire to return to it.

And now, how does he deal with other people's lies? He gets 'very impatient' with spin ('you should be absolutely blunt') and the corporate double-speak that tries to avoid the truth.

'I listen to half the chief executives saying why the profit isn't really the profit they've announced. And that's nonsense. It is what it is, seems to me.'

Even in daily life, he is much more aware of the little fibs and 'exaggerations' and tries to 'aim off' instead of resorting to even the smallest deceit. Ask him 'how do I look?' and he will answer with a 'pretty good' or a 'not bad'. I make a mental note never to ask him this.

And how has doing business across the world changed since he was outed?

'I've not been to Saudi Arabia since I've been out.' In Saudi Arabia, being gay can be punishable by execution.

But in Abu Dhabi I'm very happy to say to people, you know,

I am who I am – and, obviously, you don't immediately say to people 'I'm gay', but if they ask '...and what about your wife', I say 'I'm gay, I have a partner'. You know. And sometimes it shuts the conversation down immediately, other times people are quite intrigued and they ask questions.

When I begin to ask if the bravado of the boardroom has changed, he rattles off the mysterious words 'super lean in' before I can finish.

'Yes, that's it. It really is,' he says. It takes me a moment to catch up with him. It is a reference to the book *Lean In*[5] by Sheryl Sandberg, chief operating officer of Facebook, as the company was known then. In *Lean In*, she encourages women to do just that when they are around a table in a meeting: take part, assert themselves – there, and in every other part of their lives. The point is, of course, that this is what men do, and do so successfully.

And will that culture ever change?

'I hope boardrooms are changing – although I think they're changing very, very slowly.' He says that during his time on boards 'it was pretty male', that the analogy of a fight came up often, and a plea for reason would instead be met with 'let's go to war'. His calm voice registers the greatest displeasure in his final example. 'People would actually try and do deals while you were standing at the urinal. And that's just not on.'

Toilet politics aside, if there is progress, there is still one fact about the world's biggest businesses that stuns Browne.

'Of both former and present CEOs of gigantic companies, there's

---

5   *Lean In: Women, Work, and the Will to Lead*, Sheryl Sandberg (2013).

only me and Tim Cook [who are out of the closet]. You know. So it's not that many really… in fact, it's statistically *remarkable*.'

He wants to change that, but even someone with his energy and influence has a challenge on his hands. We spoke in January 2015. By 2020, there were still only four openly gay CEOs in the Fortune 500, the annual ranking of America's largest companies.[6] It seems that wider society can change quickly but its institutions take a lot longer. Cook, the CEO of Apple, was the first to come out in 2014.

> I don't believe Tim Cook ever lied about his sexuality, but he never admitted it. There's a fine difference there. And I think that when you're a leader, in today's society anyway, you have actually signed a statement to yourself to say: 'I have no privacy while I am a leader.'

The private Browne left the world of public companies. He was at Riverstone until summer 2015 and that year became executive chairman of L1 Energy, an investment company controlled by Mikhail Fridman, a Russian billionaire.

In July 2021, he launched BeyondNetZero – or BnZ, a partnership with General Atlantic, a growth fund which manages more than $53 billion. BnZ will invest in companies working on ways to reduce carbon emissions and tackle climate change.

As well as his charitable foundation, which supports 'causes associated with his life as an engineer, businessman, patron of the arts and son of a Holocaust survivor', he actively promotes gay rights in

---

6 'Fortune 500 CEOs praise landmark LGBTQ antidiscrimination ruling', Maria Aspan, Fortune (16 June 2020), https://fortune.com/2020/06/16/fortune-500-ceos-supreme-court-lgbtq-ruling/

the business world and beyond. He has also found the time to write five books. *The Glass Closet* not only recounts Browne's rise, fall and rise, it doubles as a manifesto for anyone who is hiding themselves at work. As the opening of the book says: 'It's better for you and it's better for business when you bring your authentic self to work.'

The very public nature of Browne's fall from grace and his subsequent redemption make for a strong parable. His story has also encouraged others to engage with him differently.

'People really began to communicate with me, and I realised I had to really communicate with them, and since I was undressed in public, you know... it makes you feel better.' He tells me a story of a director putting on a West End show that featured several naked scenes.

'So, his first-day opening line was: "I think if we all get undressed, we'd feel better about it now." And they all became much better actors, because they had absolutely... nothing... to hide. And he said it was remarkable.'

Browne found that people were suddenly prepared to show him their vulnerabilities. One executive even came out to him when they were alone in the very boardroom in which I am sitting. Perhaps it is not such a forbidding corporate den after all.

'It took him probably 1,000 per cent of his energy to get to the point where he could do it,' says Browne. 'He went back to the bank and told everybody. And that's very good. I think he's doing very well now.'

Browne's truth may have been terrifying for him, but from 2007 onwards, it not only began to enable him, it enabled those who encountered him too. I had the urge to tell him all my stories, but luckily for him, I only had forty-five minutes with him (and his assistant). I wonder if personally, he could ever have come this far if he had not been catapulted from the safety of his lie. It certainly seems to have been a liberation so strong that it shines in his eyes when he talks about it.

The biggest, warmest laugh I get from him is when I mention his partner. I know I am risking sycophancy, but the romance is too much for me to resist.

'And I love the story about your partner,' I say, in an embarrassed rush. 'It's beautiful.'

He laughs. 'Yes! It's a great… it's an amazing story.'

From the moment he walked the green line, to the present day when he is still advocating for personal and professional truth, Browne's story shows the power of a little lie – and its deep effect on social connections. His lie became so commanding that not only did it manage to hold back a man who is a force for change, it silenced a confident speaker and blinded a perceptive business leader to the point where he could not see what was plain to others.

When Browne was promoting *The Glass Closet* at a literature festival, an audience member rose to his feet. He was from the energy industry. He said: 'You know, the thing is, John, that we all knew you were gay, but none of us were brave enough to tell you.' And Browne's first thought? 'Yup, that explains it all.'[7]

---

7   'Lord Browne interview: I'll talk about being gay, but Huawei's off limits', Bryan Appleyard, *Sunday Times* (26 May 2019), www.thetimes.co.uk/article/lord-browne-interview-ill-talk-about-being-gay-but-huaweis-off-limits-xggmtmq6c

CHAPTER 12

THE SECOND LIE
| *CLOSET CASE*

I too had a little lie, that simply grew and grew. It came from a doubt, an acorn of shame, and it rose tall and mighty inside my being. Eventually, it too silenced, blinded and trapped me. And even if I did begin to sense the truth in my late teens and early adulthood, I could never call it by its name. Now, more than two decades after I first told the truth, the dread that made me hide for so many years makes me stutter still. I live in London in the twenty-first century, I worked in media and now in communications, I have been in a civil partnership – and out of one – and still I hesitate to say: I am gay.

My second big lie is ultimately about love, yet it had a greater impact on my identity than my cardiac arrest. It was mighty and sneaky, this one. This is what shame can do.

My near-death had made me see things differently. At first, as I had started to get my memory back, different versions of 'me' kept trying to surface, then disappearing again. Who was I? Why was I there in that strange room? My identity was made of loose constructions, like origami that unfolded before it ever took shape.

As I lay there in hospital, I would tell my visitors repeatedly about 'the parties' on the other wards; the drugs I had to keep taking; the music I could hear. What caused these hallucinations? The hourly cycles of tablets brought by the nurses? The tubes plugged into my arms? Or was it guilt, a coiled memory waiting to spring? Amid my fervid ramblings, I made my younger brother swear never to take drugs, but I was an evangelist without religion because I could not remember why I was telling him this.

I survived and my stories survived too. Time allowed them to separate and they began to make sense. I was awestruck to glimpse how a mind translates information. Patterns seemed to form, then become clear images, feelings and memories. They had not ceased to exist; I had just lost the ability to find them.

My life was sliced in two, before and after. I could now say truthfully – and with a certain degree of scientific accuracy – something that was very strange indeed: I was twenty when I died.

I survived by a fluke and as the memories and stories came tumbling back awkwardly, my other lie, my sneaky second lie, reasserted itself. Had it always been there?

I had grown up fulfilling the comfortable contemporary checklist of life stages: from a childhood in different countries to schools in leafy towns, gap-year jobs and university. I did work experience, I did life experience; I picked up scars, I was bruised by some things but I was lucky, I was happy. So why the deceit? Why could I not talk openly about who it was I loved? I look back now and see that it was simple: I was ashamed.

My lie, I told myself with gentle thoughts. (Of course it's not that... Don't be silly... It's perfectly normal to...) But fear turned those thoughts into a muscled squad of enforcers. (Lesbian? No. Not here. Go away.)

I compartmentalised my mind and as a result, there were small parts of me that simply did not grow. I quietly and delicately suffocated anything that felt inappropriate, uncomfortable or wrong. My lie was nothing compared to a sadist's or an arch manipulator's, I was not the victim of a crime nor did I carry anyone else's dark burden, but still, it owned me. I began to notice it over the years and grew to resent it, but how on earth could I dismantle something so deeply embedded in my personality? It was one lie, but it was made up of so many little lies. If this had become a habit, part of my psychological muscles, how could I stop myself?

It took me ten years and three relationships to summon enough courage to try to end the deceit.

In those years, I worked at *The Times*, I learnt London's secrets, I met more and more people who were different and challenging and engaged. They stood for something and I could not even speak the light words of love. I used words to hide: they were cloaks, shields, spikes – anything I could use to ward off questions. There was only one thing I could do: find a better way to use words, write my way out of the closet.

It was early 2010, I was newly single, sore of heart and had just had major surgery to replace my defibrillator for the third time. I had had enough. It was time to reclaim at least one part of my life.

I asked Emma Tucker, who was the *Times* features editor and now edits the *Sunday Times*, if we could meet for coffee just outside the office. And this was how everything started in the yellowing interior of Pumblechooks café. I remember, my stomach tight with fear, how I told her that I wanted to write about coming out of the closet. Even those words were terrifying. Would she be angry that I was wasting her time with such a dull story or would she walk away in moral disgust? Logic had left me.

'Sounds… interesting,' she said, a little underwhelmed, looking at me quizzically. Had she misheard? The lie was making me stupid.

Then she got it.

She laughed loudly.

'Oh! You mean about YOU?'

Yes, I said, bamboozled.

'Great!' She laughed again, then machine-gunned me with questions. Why had I been so afraid? Over the weeks she encouraged me, and what started as an anonymous feature in print, with an illustration of a woman cowering in a closet, became an online column that, if I did not chicken out, would end with me revealing my identity.

'Closet Case' illustration by Nathalie Lees. *The Times*, Body & Soul, 25 May 2010.
Published with kind permission of *The Times*

'Closet Case' was born. It would be about all those times I had pretended, the people I told, the ones I did not, the girlfriends, the boyfriends before them, the scandal. Week by week, I would write my way out of the closet, finishing with a 'coming-out' feature under my own name. It would be about life and love, family, friends and the mysterious 'X+X', the formula for sexual attraction.

According to my photograph albums and a few shoeboxes full of old diaries, I calculated that I had been in the closet for fifteen years. At least that was when I had my first 'encounter' with a woman and tried to hide it. That was when I started building my closet. If there ever had been a sapphic switch, a mini-epiphany, it happened a few years earlier. I was in my mid-teens when a girl pretended to kiss me. It was just a joke, I laughed it off, but it felt like a lightning strike. I may have found ways to forget it and carried on chasing boys, but suddenly there was electricity in the air.

However, as I braced myself to write about it, finding the words to capture my lie was another matter.

The empty page taunted me, the keyboard glowed, untapped. After a long and painful wait, a short phrase came back to me. Distorted, echoing loudly. After all the years of ducking and diving, one gentle question had rattled me more than all the others. Its innocence made it all the more potent. It was the pointed tip of the iceberg that pierced my hull.

'Will you be bringing your man?'

It was a colleague's sweet attempt to get to know me better. I had set things in motion over the months by acknowledging the presence of a boyfriend. It was, of course, a lie. Just a little white one. I had not seen her for a while, and we were chatting nervously. When the subject of a colleague's wedding came up, she fired her question.

I remember the look on her face when I reacted with fright. She backtracked. 'Or will you be coming alone?' I think she wanted to let me know that it was OK. Inside my head, a voice was screaming at me to tell her. Why couldn't I just say it?

My road had forked. I could have said that I most certainly did not have a man. We could have laughed together, acknowledging how silly the whole thing was. I had fibbed before! So sorry! The truth was that I adored my girlfriend, but no, I would not be bringing her to the wedding because I was ashamed of being gay. My colleague understood, didn't she? I intended to go and celebrate one relationship while perfunctorily dismissing my own.

Instead, I lied. Another small but toxic lie. I said 'we' had argued and I would be going alone. It was like lead poisoning. Years and years of little lies were floating around my bloodstream, and this one would just prove too much for my system. Would my colleague remember that moment? Doubtful. But she might recall that there was something odd and untrustworthy about me. I had lost my way, I was in a quagmire. Shame's lies kept me so busy trying to hide things that I was not paying attention to the most important detail: I had become stuck.

Those lies made me abbreviate relationships – especially work ones, where I ended up excluding myself from the conversations that bind colleagues together. What did I do at the weekend? How was my life outside the office? Where were my photos?

Like a malevolent nurse, the lie taught me many tricks. I had become a mistress of pronouns. 'We' was my favourite one – after all, why bother people with the intricacies of 'he' or 'she'? But the mental gymnastics were exhausting, and 'we' created invisible conversational barriers. You tell someone a little, but actually, you tell them nothing. Worse still, you wear away at something precious: your own relationship. 'He' or 'she' marked a border for me, a Checkpoint Charlie that I simply could not cross.

'Did you go away with someone special?'

'Yes, we had a great time.'

It was dire. I wonder how much energy I spent hiding those parts of my life. Gigawatts of shame. Where did all this madness begin? Was I born a lesbian? Did my parents grow me in such a way that I became one? Was my heart broken by a badly behaved boy, or a terrible adult? Was I bent out of shape? Or was I a happy child allowed to make my own mistakes, allowed to change? Could it be that I just did not know and, growing up the '80s, society did not help me much. Unlike Lord Browne, I do wish I could beam myself back and have long chats with my younger self. Or at least, it would have been wonderful to have had a gay aunt or uncle who could suggest to me that there were other ways of being – that in order to widen my social circles and make new connections, I did not just have to conform. So maybe yes, I was born gay and the unease I felt was very much of my own making. I do know that my sexuality never flipped back and forth, it simply grew stronger. Like a compass needle, it took time to find north. And in the meantime, to make those social connections, I fibbed about the things I could not understand.

My radar did begin to pick up powerful, attractive women, but surely that was just because I wanted to be like them? I remember being haunted by Emmanuelle Seigner after she starred opposite Harrison Ford in the thriller *Frantic*. It was set in Paris and, as her character might have said, I was '*bouleversée*'. I duly hoovered up the theme tune (a cover of 'Libertango' by Grace Jones). I rewatched and relistened but could not catch that elusive feeling that seemed just inches away. Theirs was a forbidden, doomed love, ignited when they first danced together. I would have been mortified if you had suggested I would rather be Harrison in that scene than Emmanuelle. I feel embarrassed writing about it now.

I had boyfriends I loved and was with for years, but the truth was that something was missing. No matter how many reasons I gave myself, those relationships did not last.

It is tempting to wonder what would have happened if everything had gone 'according to plan', my heart had not stopped and my student life had carried on, uninterrupted. Would I have married a man, had children, hid my regrets?

I am extremely grateful for 9 January 1995, for all the obvious reasons but for another one too. There were downsides. The scarring from the operation, along with the heart device that was visible under my skin (those older models were the size of a bar of soap) and the unsettling mental reboot meant that I stayed away from intimate relationships. But all that also gave me a chance to reset. I had time to reconsider submerged moments from long ago. Why were they under water? Still, it took me a year and a half to start stumbling in the right direction.

I first saw her at a drinks party. It was my second summer at Oxford. I could drink again, and I certainly was. Without a word, nor even a name, she took centre-stage in my thoughts. By the third sighting, and again with the help of alcohol, we talked, danced and eventually, kissed. In a marquee. In front of a party full of people.

It may have been a small rebellion against convention (and good taste), but it was a huge, two-fingered gesture to my carefully managed lie. I could not unkiss her. The photos that people had taken with the disposable cameras on every table could not be untaken. It was a small mercy that social media had yet to take hold. (Mark Zuckerberg would have been twelve back then.) Still, my own technology platform of plastic cameras did the job. After so many years of subterfuge and shadows, my secret was out.

Except it was not.

My lie ruled me like a Tudor tyrant and as soon as my new paramour began to hesitate, the secret was back. After that very public beginning, we kept the relationship quiet. So quiet that eventually it made no sound at all. When I left in September to begin a year out studying in France, she finished it. My courage was gone. I retreated, and rejection made the lie even stronger. This was my first glimpse of how much work I would have to do if I really wanted to come out.

I started my year out working as an *assistante* in a secondary school in France, in the southern city of Nîmes. The old Roman town was splendid in the late autumn when I arrived, bright with possibilities. I made a close set of friends, my dearest being a gay man also on a year out, who patiently listened to me circumnavigate the topic of lesbianism for months.

I was based near Maison Carrée, a Roman temple dating back to AD 2. Opposite it sat the bold contemporary lines of a glass library and arts centre designed by Norman Foster. For me, though, those stunning buildings were dwarfed in significance by a sweaty gay club that was round the corner. It was called Lulu and you could only enter it through a battered metal door. I remember tiny, dark rooms under archways, with a tinny sound system and groups of men disappearing into '*le backroom*' for hours. We would dance all night to terrible techno-disco and we loved it. None of it fazed me because that was the place where I forgot my lie. It was the home of secrets, and in there, mine felt very mild. Outside and in the day-light of daily routine, the lie was beginning to hurt.

I had to start talking. I began to tell my friends, one at a time, pain-fully, awkwardly. Were they shocked and disgusted? No. There were a few surprises, but I learnt quickly that fear and deceit made extraor-dinary allies. How had it taken me years to say such a simple thing?

Telling my parents was another matter.

First thing one morning, I blurted out that I had 'something' to tell them. It took me all day to follow through on this rather men-acing promise and then all I managed were three words. It sounded as if I were speaking in tongues.

'Itzzzawoomin.'

That was all that came out after their full day of nervous guessing about my most recent relationship.

'It's a woman?'

My father shook his head in disbelief, my mother seemed frozen, limbs tightly locked. The lie about the drugs had haunted me; I could not carry on lying about my first gay relationship. It was not an easy switch for any of us, I had grown too good at applying my boyfriend-themed camouflage. They thought they knew me, so did I.

However, those moments of honesty revealed a lie that was so powerful and so old that it revealed me at the same time. And every time I told a close friend, it strengthened the friendship even further. If I could have looked more than a decade into the future, I would have been astounded to see my father wearing his favourite suit and giving his best speech in front of all those friends at my civil ceremony.

I realise that I am making it sound as if I told the whole truth. (Is that embroidery – or fibbing?) Back then, I told them about one relationship, and one relationship only. In no way was I ready to accept or utter the terrifying fricative of doom: 'lezzzzzzbian'. I carried on inefficiently, telling what I could tell.

In some cases, the lie proved a knot I could not untie. Not everyone believed me, which was magnificently confusing. Back at university, a confession at a party led to a tipsy row in the street with the man who would be my last boyfriend. I finally whispered that I thought I might be gay. He was not listening. I repeated it, a little louder. Suddenly, in full soap-opera mode, he shouted: 'YOU... ARE... *NOT*... A... LESBIAN!' There was that word again. But if my cover was blown, so was my confession.

I got to the point where I was out in private but had no stamina left to make it part of my public identity, my work persona. I had hit a roundabout. When I moved to London in 2000 and started at *The Times*, I did as Browne had done: I lived two lives. In work, in the closet; outside work, at relative liberty. Over the next few years, these half-lies combined with rumours to create a boyfriend and I never quite got round to contradicting them. Gossip, one of society's most irresistible of lies, glued together a male being from almost nothing and made it bafflingly easy for me to keep up the deception.

Not that I was particularly gifted at this mendacity of mine. Reluctant about my lie, I had not even prepared myself properly. Asked 'his' name, I panicked, and the best I could come up with was the name of my Brazilian girlfriend's friend: Nataniel. Unfortunately, it sounded a lot like Natalie. My seams were coming undone. This coincided with a gay journalist telling me merrily that he 'knew' about me'. There was no green line and no paparazzi, but it was time to tell the whole truth. Soon, I would be meeting Emma, the features editor, in the yellow café.

'Closet Case'[1] ran in weekly instalments not long after the paper had started charging for its online content. Before that, *Times* articles had been free to read online and available to all. As one senior wag put it, coming out behind the digital 'paywall' was tantamount to cheating. Still, I took a deep breath, started typing and week in, week out, I set about dismantling my lie.

Those stories I had squashed out of view started to take shape – it was intimate and on a personal level, it was terrifying. The anonymity helped me to grow franker, and without a name to put on the story, it seemed to make other people think about themselves more too. The comments on the column grew each week, good and bad. I was telling the truth in small steps, and people were listening and responding. It felt like vertigo.

At the time, I fought two contradictory horrors in my head: making a fuss about such a little thing and the idea of being a degenerate, causing shame, outrage. I wrote about my relationships,

---

1 'Out of the Closet', *The Times* (14 September 2010), www.thetimes.co.uk/article/the-closet-case-columnist-reveals-her-identity-799pxdbpt3w

the fear, the inspirations, the bullies and even that first almost-kiss: a moment deeply buried and wretchedly powerful.

Writing online proved a strange alchemy between writer and reader. I told strangers, those I loved – and me – the full story I had never dared tell before. The comments would terrify me each week. Some of them were the voices I dreaded most: polite society, passers-by, mini-judges who suddenly had the power to issue a verdict on my life. Lie be damned, I wrote about it all anyway: the drunken highs, the lying lows, the embarrassments and absurdity, the tears. Then I would cower behind the sofa and wait.

At first, there was a supportive set of comments, but these began to attract hecklers. These were subscribers who could only post comments under their own names, so the wilder fringes of homophobia, prurience and hatred did not have an outlet. Nonetheless, one particular week, the commenters ganged up. The online editor had given the column a provocative 'Lesbian Secrets' headline, but unfortunately, I had not written about X-rated hotties nor desperate lustings.

'But God. You are boring,' wrote Sharon-the-commenter, which really got them going.

Ian wrote: 'Why don't you just admit who you are without all this hand-wringing? Then again I suppose *The Times* pays you to write this self-indulgent drivel.'

One summed up the perfect British put-down. Why was I making such a spectacle of it? But why were they reading, those online bullies? Why go to the trouble of belittling it, if it was so boring? Did my gradual exposure of small lies make them feel uncomfortable? Or was it that lies are such an inevitable part of our lives that they knew the story all too well?

The 'spectacle' comment went to the core of my motivation. I did not want a fuss made about me, so I lied. But it turned out that the only way I could come out meaningfully was to make the biggest fuss I could. That is how I would beat my lie. From the moment the bullies joined in, I knew I would no longer chicken out.

One woman, a stranger, kept supporting me throughout. Jessica gradually explained that she was, as she put it, transsexual, and that through her own story of self-doubt then self-acceptance, she found resonance in mine. I was stunned. I had only had to change my own mindset to come out. Here was someone who had to face up to society, fight prejudice at every stage, possibly face painful and prolonged medical procedures – and she identified with me?

She introduced herself in the second week of the column:

> To most people online who encounter me, I am just a name, I'm Jessica. 'So what?' you may ask. Well, time for truths – I'm a 45-year-old, transsexual woman, who came out to herself, much to my own surprise initially, a little over a year ago. Came out as both a woman and a lesbian. The lesbian bit is easy – everyone knew I liked women. But everyone, me included, assumed I was a man. Turns out that we were all wrong.[2]

My little lie was turning out to be powerfully cohesive the more it was exposed. That Frankenstein's monster of self-delusion, active and passive lying was ringing true, no matter the scale of the personal and social challenge.

---

2 'Closet Case, Week 2 – Comments', *The Times* (8 June 2010).

Jessica wrote that she lived in America, was an expat and had come out when she was forty-four. She talked little about her own suffering, but every time I took more barbs from the commenters, she fended them off, stood by me. I was humbled. She touched on far more potent subjects than I did. When I wrote about my fear of the circus of coming out and the imagined disgust and rejection that would come, the commenters reacted with disdain asking what was 'the big deal'? Jessica was not having any of it.

'When I came out I was warned time and time again that the transsexual woman, in my case, must be prepared to lose everything – home, job, family, marriage (if one is married), visitation rights (if one is not but has kids).'[3]

She wrote that one of 'the biggest killers of gays, lesbians and certainly transsexuals' was suicide and that this was caused by the fear of 'judgment and condemnation of those around'. In my column, I had shied away from addressing the extremes that others might feel. I did not want to undermine their suffering by linking them to my story. I could only imagine how it must be to have no relief from the shame in your head, the self-denial, the scorn, the cruelty and violence of others. Where society nurtures, it kills too. When something is so repressed that it cannot come out, that there is no escape and no succour, the only way to change the story must seem to end it. Shame on bullies: in some cases their small voices have terrible power. The statistics are sobering. Facing up to a lie about identity is not a trifle.

The Youth Chances survey is the largest of its kind in England,

---

3   'Closet Case, Week 5 – Comments', *The Times* (29 June 2010).

was conducted over five years and focused on the experiences of 7,126 people aged sixteen to twenty-five who identified as LGBTQ. (As the spectrum of recognised labels broadened, so did the acronym. At the time, this stood for lesbian, gay, bisexual, transgender and questioning. Some now add 'I' for intersex, 'A' for asexual or '+' to be even more inclusive.) The results they came up with were stark. They found that 44 per cent of the LGBTQ respondents reported ever thinking about suicide. This compared to 26 per cent of heterosexual cisgender respondents.[4]

In America, the Trevor Project is a leading national charity that works to provide crisis intervention and suicide prevention services for LGBTQ youth under twenty-five. Its 2021 survey provides the most recent sense of the scale of suicidal thoughts in the young: '42 per cent of LGBTQ youth seriously considered attempting suicide in the past year, including more than half of transgender and nonbinary youth.'[5]

I use these statistics loosely to show how the pressure of living a lie about sexual or gender identity is such that it can almost double suicidal thoughts in young people. The wrong kind of little lies about who we are can be profoundly damaging.

Jessica has never contacted me directly – we only ever spoke through the comments under my articles. I liked our unspoken agreement that we engaged only in a forum in which we did not know each other. No face to look at, no distracting superficial information. I did search for her online after I came out, and found her,

---

4 'Youth Chances: Integrated Report 2016', https://metrocharity.org.uk/sites/default/files/2017-04/National%20Youth%20Chances%20Intergrated%20Report%202016.pdf
5 'National Survey on LGBTQ Youth Mental Health 2021', The Trevor Project, www.thetrevorproject.org/survey-2021/?section=Introduction

but I was led by her discretion and did not make contact. We stood side by side briefly, and our connection came from somewhere far deeper than upbringing, career, social status, face, gender. Two strangers in different parts of the world, united only by the same lie. A lie about identity.

Soon, all that was left to reveal was my name. I was so close to coming out. I had written everything I could about my lie, except the most important thing: to whom it belonged. As the day drew closer, so did the fear. I googled my name and found hundreds of other Kathleen Wyatts popping up like mushrooms. That string of thirteen letters summoned us all. It occurred to me that I might be able to hide behind them. The urge to disappear in a mass of people was very strong at that point.

Before I knew it, it was Monday. The final article, the big reveal, would be published in print and online the next day and it became a topic in the morning editorial meeting. Sixteen people sitting around a table, and unfortunately, one of them was me. At the time, it was my job to plan the pages in the main news section. Emma, who had kept my secret for so long, ended up sitting next to me. I was so focused on everything that was due to happen the next day that I forgot 'Closet Case' could well be discussed in this meeting. I saw it on her news list and froze.

Each editor took their turn to read out their lists. I was on a rack being stretched and each minute was another turn of the handle. Suddenly, it was Emma's turn.

'At last, we're unveiling the identity of Closet Case after fifteen weeks.'

My face turned scarlet. I stared down at the table, studying my page plan furiously. It was happening. I was about to be naked on a stage.

Keith Blackmore, the deputy editor, was in a playful mood.

'Has it been running that long? God. Will you finally tell us who this bloody woman is?'

No, she said, earning my eternal loyalty.

I looked up to see one of the female executives staring at me with what could very well have been disdain. Had I been identified without realising it? I was not ready.

I went into a catatonic state for the rest of the meeting, but nothing more was said.

Afterwards, on jelly legs, I went in to tell Keith that it was me. He was flabbergasted, not an expression I had seen often on his face. For a moment I thought I was going to be sacked. The paranoia of the lie was still there – and it had the distorting power of a funfair mirror. His face broke into a smile.

Later that day, before it went to press, Keith asked the team to show me how the article would be promoted on the front page. He said he wanted to make sure I was happy with it. I was astonished. What was shameful in my head was now being given a proud display on the front – and they were checking it with me. The puff showed only my eyes sitting below the *Times* masthead with the words: 'Out of the closet'. It was not in print yet, but it was close.

I could not eat, I could not sleep, I could barely drink. This was definitely a sign that things were getting tense. The stage curtains were about to creak open – and it was me who had set all this in motion. I cursed my stubborn, stupid, misguided self. Thankfully,

I was kept calm by a squadron of people who were helping me to cross the line. My partner, my close friends and family were all majestically supportive. In just a few hours, I would be out.

The Times, page 1, 14 September 2010,
featuring Rose (Eileen Nearne) as the main image
Published with kind permission of *The Times*

Would anyone even notice? Why had I been so worried? That morning I left home feeling utterly ridiculous. I remember seeing commuters rushing past vertical racks filled with that day's copy of *The Times*. Life carried on. But when I realised the image they were rushing past, the dread returned. The papers were folded so that all I could see was a column of my eyes, staring right back at me. Talk about coming face to face with yourself. I squirmed. What on earth would it be like in the office? What had I done?

The reaction was incredible. I remembered Browne's face when he said: 'I made *more* friends!' This was how he must have felt. I had just wanted to get rid of my lie, stop being a coward and perhaps help a few people who had also been hiding themselves. Instead, I was met with a positivity that was overwhelming. I had been honest and it released an honesty in others that came in intense waves. It resonated for a few weeks and during that time, I saw a different side to my colleagues. The day itself was immense with change, but what struck me was not the relief of being free but how surprising people were in their reactions.

It was not 'news', yet so many journalists came to talk to or even confide in me. Not all were kind, some were indifferent, but I was talking to them in a way I never had before and they were doing the same in return.

I saw then why the psychological effort of living in the moment, being true to yourself, is unsustainable. If we tried to be absolutely ourselves all the time it would be too disruptive, too unpredictable. Stories and expectations set the scene and spare us from having to renew ourselves constantly. But for that brief time, I was explained. I could simply be. I was not floating along on assumptions, I was not weaving this way and that as my social muscles had taught me to, I just was. And exposing not just the truth but the lies behind it allowed other people to do the same. I thought again of Browne and the people who suddenly started walking up to him on the street and taking his hand. This is what happens when a social pretence falls away: this is the power of lies.

The moment of profound shame that I had dreaded for so long never came. Instead, I was repeatedly enlightened. Family members got back in touch after years of silence, people told me about their gay siblings, parents or children, and I even felt bold enough to begin seriously considering a civil partnership myself.

Strangers too were surprising. One, who said only that he was in the British Army, wrote to me asking whether he should come out.

'As you can imagine, the average soldier still uses the word gay as a derogatory term and some see homosexuality as a weakness,' he said. 'The question is do I continue to live the way I do or make a change in my life?' I answered that if he was already asking those questions, he was making progress but only he could decide when was the right time for him. I wish I had had a more practical answer for him but coming out is so personal that I dared only speak for myself. He had contacted me on Facebook and his anonymous profile was quickly deleted. I regretted not being able to speak to him for longer, but I was not surprised. I too used to spend hours deleting message trails and the smallest specks of evidence.

The female executive who had stared at me in that Monday's morning meeting showed me that not all paranoia was misplaced. She came up to me in the office, drew close to my face and, sarcastic and sibilant, she whispered: 'I alwaysss knnneew.'

She swept away in displeasure before I could answer. So, that is what the 'don't-make-such-a-fuss' brigade looks like. A friend of my parents left them an answerphone message to say that she was disgusted we had all lied to her. Suddenly, I could see her more clearly too. I got more heckling online, but that was it. Those tiny smatterings of rejection and humiliation were worth it – in fact, they made the freedom feel even better. They could say their worst, because I had finally said mine.

I needed my lies to get this far, but this was the point when I started to make a conscious decision to leave them behind. Today, I feel dread if I sense that I am getting drawn into someone else's lies. Pro-social lies? No problem. Big lies? No way. (Not if I can help it.)

In the course of writing this book, living in these times – and having the inordinate fortune to live twice as long as I should have – I have seen repeatedly the vital role that lies play in our lives. Whatever disinformation pandemic comes next, whatever kind of Trumpism or fakery suddenly erupts in modern life, I want to remember this: for every boy who cries wolf, there is a Rose whose hidden tale is saving lives.

My mercurial spies frightened and intrigued me, one of them had evaded me and everyone she came across, but all three nudged and shaped history in ways no one realised at the time. They also certainly helped me to test the boundaries of what counts as a good lie and to see how big lies – and even black lies – can be put in service of truth.

It then took a troupe of toddlers and a purple dinosaur to demonstrate how early lies are a sign of advanced development, and it took an empty teacup to unlock the secrets of meta-representation and the incredible effort it takes to tell a fib. I knew from my own lies how powerfully cohesive they could be, both in the telling and the ending of them. What worried me throughout though, was that if every type of lie came from such a powerful 'toolkit' (my thanks to Alan Leslie), what happens when our digital social tools tip the balance and make even the lightest white lie toxic?

Thankfully, just as it seemed that too many of us had been led astray, I realised that the fightback had begun in earnest. Maria Ressa's campaign for the truth amid a mirror maze of digital disinformation is now justly recognised across the world, not least by the 2021 Nobel Peace Prize. It is the tools that are the issue and the tools that need tackling. We do not tell more lies now than we ever have done, we are simply living in a time when it is easier to track all the different lies told. And for me, this is a cause for (careful) celebration.

From the toddler tests of Toronto to the offices in Mayfair and the digital hideouts in Manila, I kept finding the same explanation for lies: we are storytellers, fabulists, dreamers; the magnificent narrators of our own lives; myth machines, making sense of ourselves every minute of every day. And we do it because we are social creatures, we tell stories to define ourselves and others, to form bonds, perhaps even to answer the universe's profound silence. And within us, we each have a lie scale, running from the untruths that do good to the deceptions that do us down. What matters is what we choose to tell each other.

And of all the lies, there is one class of lie that is most remarkable. The little lies. Story after story told me that we would not be successful social creatures if we could not transform painful, unexpected or unexplained events; take away the sting of truth; perform daily transactions with reality and lie to ourselves when we love most.

Little lies are an extraordinary mental feat that often we do not even notice, yet they are indispensable. They hold us together, they push us apart and they come cloaked in invisibility. If we were to rip open our shirts and reveal what really makes us so good at connecting with others, it would be our power to fib – our social superpower.

On this at least, you can trust me.

ACKNOWLEDGEMENTS

To Tony Collings, for your professionalism, heroism and incredible timing; to all my interviewees, named and unnamed; to Simon for the introduction and Olivia and James at Biteback Publishing for the belief, enthusiasm and excellent edits; to Sophie Hicks, for first taking on the book; going back in time, to the Blue Boar Breakfast Club, for our long friendship, the laughter, love and support; to the BNC brigade in five very different years, from Stamford House, to Cooper's rooms and Frewin (bhaji!); to Paul and Laurent, my partners in crime in Nîmes; to Emma Tucker, Keith Blackmore and James Harding who set this particular 'Closet Case' free and Corinne Abrams and Margaret Clark for helping me over the finish line; to every other supportive member of my beloved *Times* family, including Potty, Knighty, Tim, Paul, Simon (mentor and flatplan tormentor) – and Louise Newman and Sarah Vine who gave me my first shots at writing in public; to Rob Hands, a ninja among proofreaders, who lent me his time and talent, even in a very Covid Christmas; to Felicity and Jonathan for the kindness that refeathered my wings; to Kerry for the introductions; to Sally and Trolly for the encouragement; to Caroline Mylon, editor extraordinaire; to the crew of the Dolce Vita for the escape; to the four Ls and that tricky L-word; to my family far and wide, starting with a special mention for our gorgeous nieces, cousins and god children; to the Risbys, for the love, inspiration and marvellous mischief; to my mother, who never once gave up on 'la jument' and whose talent, creativity, conviction, kindness and meticulous reading helped smooth these pages into life; to my beautiful partner – M, my love, I could not have done this without you; to all of you, two words that barely cover the sentiment: thank you!

.